Something Old,
Something Bold

Something Old, Something Bold

Bridal Showers and Bachelorette Parties

Beth Montemurro

Rutgers University Press
New Brunswick, New Jersey, and London

Library of Congress Cataloging-in-Publication Data

Montemurro, Beth, 1972–
Something old, something bold : bridal showers and bachelorette parties as traditions of transition / Beth Montemurro.
p. cm.
Includes bibliographical references and index.
ISBN-13: 978-0-8135-3810-5 (hardcover : alk. paper)
ISBN-13: 978-0-8135-3811-2 (pbk. : alk. paper)
1. Showers (Parties)—United States—History. 2. Bachelorette parties—United States—History. 3. Marriage customs and rites. I. Title.
GV1472.S5M66 2006
793.2—dc22
2005028197

A British Cataloging-in-Publication record for this book is available from the British Library

Manufactured in the United States of America

For my bridesmaids: Christy, Traci, Candy, Diane, Jen, and Jennifer

Contents

Illustrations

Acknowledgments

Many people have supported the production of this book; thus, many thanks are owed. First, I thank the women who shared their experiences with me. Without the candid conversations and openness that they wholeheartedly gave, this book would not exist. I thank these women for welcoming me into their homes for interviews as well as including me at their bridal showers and bachelorette parties. I have much respect and admiration for all of those who participated and wish them the best in their marriages and in their lives.

I owe a great deal of thanks to my undergraduate mentor, Dr. Maryann Groves, who was and is such an inspiration to me. She is an excellent teacher and role model who helped me develop my passion for sociology.

I began this research while in graduate school at the University of Georgia; it was the support of Barry Schwartz, Paul Roman, and Linda Grant that helped me to undertake and complete this research. Paul Roman encouraged my independence, challenged, and supported me, helping me to meet my goals. I appreciated his vast knowledge, his suggestions, and encouragement. Linda Grant, my methodological mentor, offered continuous guidance and suggestions for theoretical development and was always available to me, and I am grateful for that. Barry Schwartz motivated me to rethink, revise, and re-theorize, introduced me to the works of great sociologists, and helped me to take this project further than I thought possible. He has been a driving force, in the form of an encouraging voice in the back of my head, in the process of transforming my dissertation into a book. Additionally, I am grateful to the Institute for Behavioral Research at the University of Georgia, which supported me during the course of this research. Also, I wish to acknowledge the support of grant T32-AA-07473 from the National Institute on Alcohol Abuse and Alcoholism. With this training grant, I learned the skills necessary to be a professional and skillful sociologist and was able to travel to collect data for this research, allowing me to expand my sample and observe parties and showers in different regions of the United States. I also thank my great colleagues at University of Georgia, especially Aaron Johnson, Marina Karides, Hannah Knudsen, Marybeth Stalp, and Diana Cannan, for their willingness to read drafts, listen to presentations, offer helpful advice, and be on the lookout for potential interviewees. Finally, I thank my mentor, cheerleader, and friend, Joya Misra, who even when she was no longer at University of Georgia provided as much encouragement and guidance as if she were. I greatly appreciated the quick, detailed, and invaluable feedback on all matters sociological.

With the topic of bachelorette parties and bridal showers, I was fortunate to be aided in my academic pursuits by friends and family, a few of whom acted as participants and most of whom provided me with contacts. I especially thank my mother, Susan, for scouring the halls of her office for brides-to-be; my sister, Christy, for encouraging her friends and coworkers, and their friends and coworkers, to participate; my sister-in-law, Traci, for recruiting her frequent bachelorette-party-attending friends and helping me to maintain contacts; and my cousin Tara, who also eagerly enlisted participants. Additionally, I thank my friends who have been faithful supporters, sounding boards, sources of information, and sympathetic ears, especially the exceptionally loyal Kim Maialetti, Jen Bruder, Diane Saccone, and Candy Mazze. I have appreciated hearing all of the bachelorette party and bridal shower stories over the years, reading the articles that have been sent my way, and receiving the endless support. I also thank everyone who offered title suggestions. And I am very grateful to all who were willing to share photographs from their bridal showers and bachelorette parties. I am also thankful to my cousin Cari, for her artistic vision and time in working on cover images.

Additionally, I want to thank Gary Fine for the "matchmaking," for introducing me to Kristi Long, and for helping with that first step on the road to publication. I thank Kristi Long for believing in, encouraging, and seeing the potential in this project and Adi Hovav for seeing it to completion. I also am grateful to the staff of Rutgers University Press for their assistance in the publication process as well as to Elizabeth Pleck, who provided me with many excellent suggestions to improve this book. I also acknowledge Kathy Charmaz, who as editor of *Symbolic Interaction* helped me to develop and revise one of the most important parts of this study. I appreciate the contagious enthusiasm in my research, feedback, and all of the articles provided by Richard Bradford. My colleagues at Penn State University, Abington, also deserve recognition. I thank Karen Halnon for her collegiality, Jim Smith for encouragement and support along the way; and David Jwainer for taking interest in and promoting my research and for giving me the opportunity to share my findings with people across the country and around the world. I also thank the students who shared their stories and those who assisted me, particularly Bridget McClure, during the analysis and writing of this book.

The support of my family has been tremendous and I appreciate my parents and siblings for their encouragement and pride. Finally, I thank my husband, Fernando Charvet, for his support and love, his quiet faith in me, his patience with my writing schedule and strip-club trips, and his partnership.

Something Old,
Something Bold

Chapter 1

Introduction

Joining the Party

I cannot pinpoint exactly when I learned what a bachelorette party was; however, I do remember quite clearly when I heard about the first one for someone I knew. Years ago, I was a bridesmaid in a wedding and thus involved in planning the bridal shower. On the day of the shower, I arrived early at the restaurant where the shower was to be held in order to help decorate and set up for the event. Like every shower to which I had been invited or attended, this one was a surprise. The bride was unaware when it was happening, or even (as future conversations would reveal) if it was happening. As we set up there was a nervous, excited energy in the room, as this group of women, bridesmaids and the bride's mother, talked and laughed, wondering if the bride would be surprised or not. While innocently tying balloons to chairs and hanging up streamers, I heard the maid of honor and a friend of the bride discussing the bachelorette party. One bridesmaid was talking about the types of shots they would make the bride do; the words "sex on the beach" and "orgasm" floating freely out of her mouth with the bride's mother only feet away. "We're going to get her *so* drunk," one of them said. "What can we make her do? We have to think of things to make her do," another insisted. I listened with great interest and, as testament to my naiveté, shock as they talked about making her acquire men's underwear, wear a shirt adorned with lifesavers that men would pay her a dollar to remove with their mouths, and other equally embarrassing things. I was struck by how freely they talked about this, how normal they made it seem, to get their friend—one of their best friends—drunk and embarrass her as much as possible. In retrospect, I realize I was also a little startled that this conversation was occurring in this context. We were all dressed up and at a nice restaurant. The bride's mother, though obviously distracted, was well within earshot. We were at her *shower* after all! A ritual that was the very definition of femininity seemed like an odd site for such discussion.

I did not go to this bachelorette party. Though geographic distance provided a convenient and legitimate excuse, quite honestly, I was intimidated by the idea of attending this event—it sounded absolutely horrible to me. Not understanding why the goal of the bachelorette party was intoxication and embarrassment, I decided that bachelorette parties were not for me. Talking to the bride after the fact, however, I learned what the experience had been like for her. She described how much fun she had, how nice it was to go out and be "wild" with her friends because it was rare that they were able to do so anymore. It was more fun than her shower, she said, because she could just "let go." She was able to truly be herself and not feel pressured to conform to rules of etiquette as she did at her bridal shower. To this day she relishes the memory of the night as a truly enjoyable bonding experience that she was able to share with her close friends.

Both the idea of the party and the bride's reaction to it stayed with me. Being in my mid-twenties and thinking that I would be getting married sometime during the next couple of years, I thought about how I would deal with this ritual when the time came. I could not stop thinking about that party and the conversation at the shower, and I began to wonder what other women did for bachelorette parties. I had heard stories of going to male strip clubs or dressing the bride up in a veil and parading her through bars. I wondered how common this type of activity was and what women really did during bachelorette parties. Were there certain types of women who had bachelorette parties and certain types of women who did not? Were there varieties of degree and deviance at bachelorette parties? And what did this ritual mean? Why was it infused with sexual imagery and props?

I first turned to the academic literature for answers but found very few. Not only could I not find a single study on American bachelorette parties, I was also unable to locate any research on bachelor parties—which, evidence suggests, date back to ancient Roman times—or even much information on weddings. However, in the past decade several scholars have turned their attention to this central cultural event, and in-depth studies of weddings are now readily available (Boden 2003;

Corrado 2002; Freeman 2002; Geller 2001; Ingraham 1999; Otnes and Pleck 2003; Wallace 2004). The authors of these studies have offered interesting analyses of weddings and wedding planning. The dominant message of this research has been that American society is in love with a certain kind of wedding and works diligently to uphold it as ideal. This research also posited explanations as to why weddings have been neglected in the academic literature. Because weddings represent "magic," legitimate indulgence (Otnes and Pleck 2003), heterosexuality (Ingraham 1999; Geller 2001), and class identification (Ingraham 1999; Otnes and Pleck 2003), and because they are seen as sacred events, these scholars have suggested that perhaps others have been reluctant to explore the ways in which weddings maintain and celebrate inequality and discrimination. Cele C. Otnes and Elizabeth Pleck (2003) and Chrys Ingraham (1999) pointed to the fact that the American wedding industry is a multibillion-dollar enterprise that has continued to thrive in times of economic distress and that expenditures on weddings have reached extreme heights in recent decades. The current norm is to have a "lavish wedding" that demonstrates not only the bride's, groom's, and their families' class positions, but also their ability to put on a successful performance and create a unique and memorable event (Otnes and Pleck 2003). And this trend is not limited to the United States. The lavish wedding has become prominent throughout the Western world and in parts of Asia as well (Boden 2003; Otnes and Pleck 2003).

Weddings can be seen as a process of which bachelorette parties and bridal showers are critical parts. In the context of the wedding they function as pep rallies, as a means of increasing excitement and anticipation and of keeping up the wedding momentum. Since the contemporary wedding is the culmination of months of planning and preparation, the bridal shower and the bachelorette party are rehearsals of sorts for the bride-to-be, where she has the opportunity to "try on" her new role and bid farewell to her old one. Essentially, these rituals are wedded not only to one another but to weddings as well. And any analysis of these events must thus be placed within the context of the contemporary wedding. The way weddings are planned and produced by modern brides is certainly related to the spectrum of activities and events that precede them. In an age where traditional conceptions of marriage are threatened by the possibility of alternate arrangements such as cohabitation, civil unions, single parenthood, intentional singlehood, and same-sex marriage, it seems clear that weddings reinforce and celebrate heterosexuality and traditional conceptions of gender roles. At the wedding, the bride and groom are treated as royalty. Their status is revered and they receive both social and material rewards for legally committing to a heterosexual union. Additionally, the traditional elements of the ceremony and wedding as rituals reinforce different gendered roles for men and for women. For example, when the bride is "given away" either symbolically by being escorted by her father or parents or more concretely in ceremonies where an officiant asks, "Who gives this woman to be married?" her status as property or dependent is reinforced. Brides and grooms are expected to play their parts as hyper-feminine and masculine, respectively. Thus, bridal showers and bachelorette parties, as elements of the wedding process, must also be looked at as acts in this gendered show. Yet these events have not been studied in depth in the existing research on weddings. Bridal showers were discussed in several of these studies, but bachelorette parties were given passing mention at most. They are important components of the wedding process and deserve exploration.

However, bridal showers and bachelorette parties are not merely a part of the wedding process. Rather, each is a ritual with its own norms, role expectations, and significance—particularly since these events occur prior to the wedding itself. They are both means to ends and ends in themselves. Their meaning should not be reduced to smaller steps in a long process. Particularly when taken together and because of their relatively gender homogeneous characteristic, bachelorette parties and bridal showers also have much to tell about the ways in which gender is "done," about women's friendships and relationships with other women, and about constructions of masculinity and femininity. Through these rituals, invented and orchestrated primarily by women, we can see how traditional and modern gender norms and role expectations are negotiated, resisted, transformed, and reinforced. Bridal showers and bachelorette parties are events during which friends, who present elaborate and exaggerated scenarios that demonstrate both what the bride is sacrificing and gaining, initiate the bride-to-be into the role of wife. She is transitioning from the status of single to that of married and engages in various rites of passage along the way. Because her status is elevating, she is made to endure various embarrassing or uncomfortable tasks and to show that she is fully cognizant of her impending commitment. Through the ritual action at these parties, women expressly recognize what they are abandoning and what they are becoming. This affords both them and their community the opportunity to express the mixed emotions that often accompany status transitions (Wuthnow 1989). What bridal showers and bachelorette parties illuminate then is the ambivalent position in which contemporary women—brides, bridesmaids, family, and friends—find themselves. Somewhere between independence and dependence, between femininity and masculinity, between virgin and vixen, modern women are expected to locate themselves. With the proliferation of conflicting messages ranging from unrestrained sexual freedom on shows like *Sex and the City* to marriage as ideal and motherhood as an ultimate and natural calling in magazines like *Ladies Home Journal*, this is not an easy task. The bridal shower and bachelorette party represent these two extremes and thus function as space where women can ritually enact the divergent role expectations they face as they transition from single to married. Bachelorette parties and bridal showers are not just women's parties. They are rituals of status, consumption, and materialism, of transition and ambivalence, of friendship and reinforcement of relationships among women, and of transformation. They are both part of the wedding process and independent of it as well. The study of these events can tell us much about the lives of marrying middle-class women at the turn of the twenty-first century.

Love and Marriage

Americans love weddings and thus love love. Elizabeth Freeman (2002), Jaclyn Geller (2001), Ingraham (1999), and Otnes and Pleck (2003) all provided compelling evidence of the ways in which weddings have been embraced and revered in popular culture. These studies documented the prevalence of wedding imagery in American literature, film, and television. In addition to media, other agents of socialization also participate in fostering the relationship between Americans and love. Ingraham described the ways in which industries not directly involved in the supply of wedding merchandise use the American infatuation with weddings as a means of attracting consumers. For example, Mattell has produced more than thirty different bridal gowns for its still unmarried Barbie doll, in addition to creating a "My Size Bride Barbie" in the late 1990s (Ingraham

1999, 62–63). When girls are given Bridal Barbie or any bride doll, when they dress up in white dresses and veils for Halloween, the bride becomes an envied role and the women who play it are seen as having achieved something important. Women are "educated in romance" such that some prioritized finding a future spouse over education during college years (Holland and Eisenhart 1990). Toys, peers, and families teach girls and women the value of relationships, and the wedding is the penultimate celebration of and reward for achieving in this domain, and "men are taught by the absence of these socializing mechanisms that their work is 'other' than that" (Ingraham 1999, 81). Love and romance become the responsibility of women, who are encouraged to spend a disproportionate amount of time pursuing and trying to maintain relationships, with marriage as the final goal.

The dominant form of relationship in American society, and throughout most of the Western world, is that of the monogamous, heterosexual couple, with clearly differentiated roles and genders. This image as "right" and normative has been vigorously defended and revered, particularly of late as threats to it have emerged. As other nations like Canada and Spain move toward more progressive definitions of marriage and legal partnership, conservatives aim to prevent such actions in the United States. More than five years prior to this most recent wave of heterosexist activity, Ingraham (1999) suggested that such attitudes might explain why weddings had been neglected by academics. Labeling weddings as events that work to maintain heterosexuality and emphasize it as "natural" and "right," she noted that "efforts to critically examine many sacred or valued practices and institutions are frequently resisted and suppressed" (Ingraham 1999, 9). Since heterosexuality is so well institutionalized and defended, it is certainly logical that weddings, as the ultimate celebrations of heterosexuality, would be institutionalized as well. Yet, the relationship valued in these institutions is not just based on a union between two people of opposite sexes; rather, specific images of man and woman are expected and enacted here. The contemporary lavish wedding is "based on expressing exaggerated forms of masculinity and femininity" (Otnes and Pleck 2003, 111), as are the events that precede it. Brides-to-be who might not identify fully (or even partly) with traditional conceptions of femininity may, in fact, find themselves playing the feminine role at bridal showers. And since masculinity and femininity are defined as binaries and as opposite of one another, this conception of femininity is dependent on the image of a groom who performs (or strives to perform) hegemonic masculinity. As Connell (1995) defined it, the critical component of contemporary hegemonic masculinity is heterosexuality and dominance over femininity, thus dominance over women. Throughout our history there have been cultural images that typify grooms as reluctant or uninvolved in weddings, underscoring the idea that weddings are feminine and that men must be lured into marriage (Howard 2000). Even present-day advice manuals for grooms address them as hesitant and assure them that they will not lose their independence or masculinity by committing to marriage (Geller 2001, 79). Furthermore, Connell argued that hegemonic masculinity is a performance, a display, something that is done publicly in order to demonstrate power and status. Working from the stereotypical conception of the bachelor party, fueled by media images that support and construct it as reality, the groom-to-be is expected to have had many sexual experiences, to value his sexual freedom, and to view monogamy as a compromise or something to commit to reluctantly. As such, a stripper often entertains him on his "last night of freedom." The performance expected in this scenario is for the groom to show his "manliness" by viewing the dancer as a sexual object, by acting turned on, and by making some attempts to engage her. The man asserts his status as the sexual pursuer, the subject—the person with the power in the interaction to be the watcher rather than the watched (E. Wood 2000). The groom-to-be is also supposed to drink excessively, to show that he can hold his liquor or at least that he is able to drink large quantities. Understanding this image of masculinity is critical because this is what women have responded to, adopted, and mocked at the bachelorette party. Yet, it is also the image that is tacitly upheld at the bridal shower when women subscribe to and support traditional gender roles. The bridal shower and bachelorette party must also be interpreted then as having much to do with masculinity and femininity and traditional conceptions of love and romance. Particularly, these events ritualize ideas about gender and marriage.

"Tea Time for Ladies" and "The Final Fling"

So what exactly is a bridal shower? A bachelorette party? While most people are likely to have a fairly accurate idea about the former, a description is important. Bridal showers date back to the sixteenth century,

1.1. A bride displays a gift for guests at her bridal shower

when, legend suggests, a woman wanted to marry a poor Dutch miller who her father feared would not be able to support her. Thus he would not provide a dowry or approve the union. Sympathetic to the love between the two, the would-be bride's friends gathered gifts so that she was able to wed (B. Clark 2000, 7; Jenkins 2000, xi–xii). However, it was not until the early twentieth century that bridal showers became popular in the United States (Bentley 1947). Bridal showers have been modified from the original purpose, and most modern brides have them, regardless of their financial or residential status. Yet, the traditional bridal shower follows a fairly ritualized order. Women gather, eat, socialize, and watch the bride-to-be open presents.

Little has changed in the format or tone of the bridal shower thrown for women marrying in the late twentieth or early twenty-first century as compared to those given for their mothers or grandmothers. In fact, like the traditional wedding, the shower is a ritual that implicitly and explicitly socializes women into the hyper-feminized traditional wife role. In most cases, and particularly among white middle-class women, it calls for an enactment or at least tacit support of "emphasized femininity," which R. W. Connell (1995, 33) described as "defined as around compliance and subordination to men and . . . accommodating the interests and desires of men." Women give and brides receive gifts that are to be used in cooking (for the husband), cleaning (in the homemaker/housewife role), and enticing (in the bedroom). That these gifts are given to the bride alone is significant because this reinforces gender differentiation and reminds the bride-to-be of her future role and place in marriage. Women's conversation and activities at showers—games and general behavior—are also suggestive in terms of constructing gendered expectations and norms for all of the women present (Casparis 1979). Even if as individuals the women who participate in bridal showers see themselves as independent or their relationships with significant others as egalitarian, the fact that they take part in and only sometimes passively resist a ritual that suggests otherwise merits investigation. Wedding showers demonstrate respect for tradition and pay homage to the weddings and marriages of mothers and grandmothers and the institution of marriage itself. Thus, part of the performance of femininity expected at bridal showers involves showing appreciation for the wife role as it has been performed by different generations. Women not only reproduce femininity in their behavior as they "do gender," they also reinforce tradition and traditional gender roles. It may be that the format of bridal showers has only moderately changed because tradition, and the ideas surrounding the importance of replicating tradition, limits possibilities or alternative practices.

The bachelorette party is a modern ritual that seems to have become a normative part of the wedding process for many women only during the last decade of the twentieth century. While there is evidence that something like the bachelorette party has been around since the 1960s, there is nothing to suggest that it was formally labeled as such or identified as a ritual and expected part of the engagement period until the mid-1980s or early 1990s. Even during the middle to late 1990s, when I began this research, it seems that the bachelorette party was something toward which the wedding industry was ambivalent. Although guides for planning bridal showers are abundant and date back to at least the mid-twentieth century, it seems that the first bachelorette party planning guide was an inexpensively produced, desktop-published guide put together in 1998 by two enterprising women who had hosted several bachelorette parties (Liveris and Johnson 1998). In *Bride's* magazine's 1997 wedding planner, the bachelorette party was given only passing mention,

1.2. A bride adorned with a bridal headband and veil that she wears during her bachelorette party

and friends of the bride were advised not to feel it necessary to do anything outlandish. The most popular wedding magazines, *Modern Bride* and *Bride's*, rarely addressed the bachelorette party during the 1990s. However, by the turn of the twenty-first century, attitudes and practices had changed. The publishers of *Bride's* and *Modern Bride* recently reported that 94 percent of brides-to-be whom they surveyed planned to have bachelorette parties (Barker 2003); and, with so many women engaging in this practice, it seems economically beneficial to these periodicals to include information about this growing trend. An indulgent wedding is one that includes all of the extras, not only for the big day, but also throughout the process. The bigger the wedding, perhaps, the bigger the "warm-up" (Otnes and Pleck 2003). The increasing popularity and prevalence of bachelorette parties is certainly complemented by the increasing emphasis on weddings as occasions of excess.

Despite its apparent newness, it is clear that the bachelorette party was modeled after a centuries-old ritual, the bachelor party. In fact, many parties have a similar structure to the stereotypical men's event. Bridesmaids and other close women friends of the bride-to-be gather to celebrate her last days of singlehood. Most parties start at someone's home and then move out to a bar or club. Women drink excessively, hire men exotic dancers, and talk about sex; and the bachelorette is instructed to complete tasks such as asking a random man for his phone number or boxer shorts. Not simply a night out, the bachelorette party represents a critical change in women's sexuality and norms for public sexual expression. At the bachelorette party, women claim the right to be sexually expressive, to approach men, to have men undress for them. This is not inconsequential. Prior to its invention, the formalized rituals of bridal shower and bachelor party clearly differentiated men and women and their places in marriage. During bachelor parties men grieved over the end of their single days and the loss of their sexual freedom while women were expected to gush over new pots and pans and express elation about leaving the ranks of the unmarried. Somewhere along the way, women began to publicly acknowledge that they too made sacrifices when they married and were leaving behind some parts of their lives that they enjoyed and would miss. While some women have felt ambivalent about marriage throughout history, fearing the costs of marriage, lives of servitude, leaving family, or the dangers of childbirth (Rothman 1984), marriage was still a status elevation for women and viewed as something to which women should aspire. Thus, the dominant belief was that women should not publicly express doubts about marrying as it may affect their chances in it. Before romantic love became the dominant motivation for marriage, marriage was an economic transaction, "a discussion among men" (Geller 2001), in which girls and women were expected to willfully participate. Reluctance or the expression of doubt may have hurt a girl or woman's chance for marriage, which may have lead to ill treatment from her family, who considered her a financial burden. With the bachelorette party, there is a forum to publicly express anxieties or ambivalence, to ritually and symbolically face one's past and future.

The bachelorette party is also important because the very idea of it is predicated on the fact that contemporary women are not virgins when they marry. Like men, they have sexual pasts and relationships that they symbolically acknowledge, lament, and bid farewell to at the bachelorette party. Research suggests that approximately 70 percent of never-married women and 78 percent of never-married men aged eighteen to twenty-four have engaged in sexual intercourse (Laumann et al. 1994). And age at first marriage has increased as well. For women in the United

States, the average age is twenty-five years old, and for men about twenty-eight years old (Otnes and Pleck 2003, 14). Thus, women marrying now are more likely than their mothers to have lived independently or to have gone away to college, thus having more time to pursue relationships and to engage in sexual experimentation. In sharp contrast to the bridal shower, the bachelorette party relies not on traditional conceptions of femininity, but on the image of a modern bride who can drink "like a man," who is sexually experienced, and who is in a somewhat egalitarian relationship where both partners acknowledge that they sacrifice as well as benefit when they say "we do."

RITUAL

Thus far I have used the word *ritual* liberally, and some might wonder how this concept is defined and how precisely bachelorette parties and bridal showers fit within this definition. I conceive of ritual as an event or activity that is repeated over time and has a unique cultural and symbolic meaning, not only to those who are directly involved, but also to the members of the culture in which it takes place. This definition springs from the work of several ritual theorists. Tom Driver (1991) asserted that ritual has three "gifts" or utilities: it maintains social order, unites people emotionally as members of communities, and facilitates change. Thus, in this book I analyze bridal showers and bachelorette parties on these three levels, arguing that they do serve all of these functions.

My definition is also influenced by Victor Turner, who, in *The Forest of Symbols*, described ritual as a "prescribed form of behavior for occasions not given over to technological routine" (1967, 19). Turner's definition is a bit more concrete and specified that there are norms or conventions for behavior in ritual activities. In several works (1967, 1969, 1974), Turner detailed the properties and characteristics of rituals and symbols, and he spent much time identifying different ritual forms. Building on van Gennep's (1908) work on rites of passage, in *Forest of Symbols* (1967) Turner discussed two types of ritual—rituals of affliction and life-crisis rituals. The latter can be seen as relevant in analyzing both bachelorette parties and bridal showers. Turner suggested that a life crisis is a turning point between one phase and another, usually marked by formal ceremony. These ceremonies often take ritual forms, as status transformation is celebrated. He stated, "'Crisis' ceremonies not only concern the individuals on whom they are centered, but also mark changes in the relationships of all the people connected with them by ties of blood, marriage. . . . Whatever society we live in, we are all related to one another, our big moments are big moments for others as well" (1967, 7). In other words, life-crisis rituals mark transition from one stage in life to another and involve and have meaning for not only the initiate, but also those connected to her. As members of a community, be it a small community of women or citizens of a nation, the significance of an individual's actions comes to light only with the interactions, reactions, and responses of others. As social creatures, changes in the lives of women and men affect and alter their relationships with family members, friends, and even strangers. This is a useful lens with which to look at pre-wedding rituals. When a woman is married, her relationship with her parents, her siblings, and her friends is likely to change. For parents, a daughter's wedding is likely to be a day that was anticipated for many years and that represents a formalization of adulthood and the alteration of the parent-child relationship. In this sense, rituals help to clarify roles and expectations attached to those roles and to call attention to how roles change during periods of status transition. As Robert Wuthnow noted, "Through ritual the actor's roles and obligations in each setting are dramatized to their confederates. . . . In ritual, a bond is established between the person and the moral community on which he or she depends. It is in this sense that ritual reinforces the moral order" (1989, 123). Those close to the initiate witness and participate in this dramatization of the new role and help to reinforce the moral boundaries associated with it. In the case of the transition from single to married, at the shower and the bachelorette party the bride-to-be is pushed to demonstrate the limits of her new role, the wife. In her ritual expression of what she should and should not do as a married woman, she demonstrates her understanding of the moral order associated with new her status.

Turner further contributed to the study of ritual by detailing rituals of status transformation. He distinguished between two major types: rituals of status elevation and rituals of status reversal. In rituals of status elevation the initiate passes from a lower to a higher status (Turner 1969, 167). Weddings can be seen as rituals of this type. In the United States, married people have more status than do single people as evidenced by, for example, tax benefits, legal benefits, and social recognition (Cott

2000, 224; Geller 2001). Thus, the bridal shower and the bachelorette party are conceptualized as rituals of status elevation as they are stages in the process of the transition to marriage and treat the bride-to-be as someone who is deserving of attention and respect.

Rituals can be seen as traditions. Inherent in the definition of ritual is the fact that it is an event, ceremony, or activity that is repeated over extended periods of time. As rituals become institutionalized they are performed for the sake of themselves. Thus, it is important to integrate the concept of tradition into any study or ritual in order to distinguish between tradition and ritual, and because each concept reinforces the other. Edward Shils discussed the power of tradition, saying, "A fully traditional belief is one which is accepted without being assessed by any criterion other than its having been believed [or performed] before" (1975, 187). Traditions, then, have an element of reverence that seems to come from the very properties of institutionalization and repetition that characterize traditions. It is not necessarily the specifics of a given tradition, but more that there is a respect for something that has stood the test of time.

Further, Shils argued that a key feature of traditions is that they allow for the past to be seen in the present such that engaging in a traditional activity is a way of recognizing and affirming the value and significance of the past, and thus the culture and society to which it belongs. To say that traditions are a "consensus through time" (Shils 1975, 186) suggests that because of their durability they imply cultural and societal acceptance of them and what they represent. Traditions are often protected and cherished for this very reason. Even when traditions are discovered to have less history than originally perceived or that the invention of a tradition was influenced by commercial or social forces rather than having a deeper meaning, people still embrace and support the idea of participating in or performing tradition (Hobsbawm and Ranger 1983). Wedding norms such as elaborate receptions, white wedding gowns as representations of virginity, or an on-the-scene wedding photographer are often misinterpreted as centuries-old customs, rather than "invented traditions" that have relatively recent origins (Otnes and Pleck 2003; Wallace 2004). The wedding industry often whitewashes and romanticizes traditions that are rooted in patriarchy, so that their practice is continued often without concrete knowledge of why or how such traditions originated (Geller 2001). Though many women have less manifest need for the bridal shower in 2006 than they did in 1966 or 1936, it is likely that showers are socially important as they connect generations of members of families, communities, or cultures. Women may have bridal showers because their mothers or grandmothers did or because that is simply what has been done in their family or in society more generally. Women may appreciate this opportunity to participate in an event that links them with their ancestors and friends who have been married before them. The role of the bride-to-be exists independent of weddings; thus, young girls may look forward to a bridal shower or wedding because they have seen and probably participated in this tradition throughout their lives and may have envisioned a time when they would take on this role themselves.

However, the concept of the bachelorette party and bridal shower as traditions must be used conservatively, as it can be misleading with respect to the power and meaning of the ritual act itself. And, as argued by David Kertzer (1988), rituals themselves can be forces of social change and thus may alter tradition. As opposed to merely recreating and reflecting the past, the performance of and participation in ritual allows participants to express beliefs about social institutions (such as marriage) and social roles (such as wife, husband, woman, or man) in a way that can be revolutionary. Kertzer developed this claim in his discussion of political symbols and rituals. He stated, "Though symbols give people a new way of understanding the world, it is people who produce new symbols and transform the old. . . . Symbols instigate social action and define individuals' sense of self. They also furnish the means by which people make sense of (the political) process, which largely presents itself to people in symbolic form" (1988, 5–6).[1] In other words, it is important to stress that there are conscious actors involved in ritual, not simply people who are blindly following tradition. These participants in ritual may have a vested interest in modifying existing rituals or traditions. Rituals can be used to transform existing social institutions, such as marriage or heterosexuality, or normative structures, such as gender roles. Kertzer made this point by saying, "People . . . are not just slaves of ritual, they are also molders and creators of ritual. It is because people create and alter rituals that they are such powerful tools of (political) action" (1988, 19). For example, when women hold bachelorette parties at male strip clubs, their decision may be based on the idea that it is what men do or have done. However, rather than just copying what men supposedly do, such action expresses something deliberate about women's rights and equality, women's sexuality, and gender norms in contemporary society. As more women do this for bachelorette parties, the norms regarding women's roles and appropriate behavior for women are transformed. Whereas, prior to the existence of bachelorette parties, women had few appropriate or socially legitimate occasions for patronizing male strip clubs or acting sexually aggressive, these parties have contributed to condoning women's right to express their sexuality, at least within this particular context. As Kertzer articulated, "Through ritual, beliefs about the universe come to be acquired, reinforced, and eventually changed. . . . Ritual action not only gives meaning to the universe, it becomes part of the universe" (1988, 9).

Given these definitions and components of rituals, it is important to conceive of bachelorette parties and bridal showers as rituals because doing so enables us to interpret the meaning in their enactment. We can see the ways in which women express their feelings about gender relations and marriage and both resist and reinforce traditional role expectations. It is valuable to interpret bachelorette parties and bridal showers as American rituals because our cultural rituals have much to tell us about what is significant and meaningful in our society. The way that bachelorette parties and bridal showers are organized informs us about gender, social roles, relationships among women, and women's perception of their status. These events allow us to see the structure of social relations in marriage and in society at large. Rituals also involve collective action. Multiple participants are necessary for rituals to be successful and thus affect not only the central actors but also the community at large. When we examine bridal showers and bachelorette parties as social rituals, we see the strength and importance of community and social solidarity in an increasingly individualistic society. As modern society is characterized more by rationality and less by emotion, rituals become important because they allow for dramatic emotional expression that is not common during everyday life. This emotion often functions as a means of unification as it is expressed collectively and people become aware of their common feelings and interests and connections with one another. As Driver (1991) noted, rituals solidify bonds among members of a community, and it is evident that this is a primary function of both bachelorette parties and bridal showers.

In the chapters that follow, I describe the ways in which these rituals call for both feminine performance and resistance to traditional conceptions of womanhood by first looking at, in chapter 2, the history of these events and the changes in society that influenced their development. In chapter 3, I focus on the bridal shower and forces of etiquette, tradition, and femininity that often create an uncomfortable experience for participants. Then, in chapter 4, I describe the counter-ritual, the bachelorette party, as one in which women's sexuality is flaunted, though also subjected to feminine constraints. Next, in chapter 5, I examine both rituals within the context of gendered consumerism, looking specifically at the shower as a gift-giving event and the development of the bachelorette party industry. As there are variations in the ways weddings are celebrated around the world, it is logical that there would be differences in pre-wedding rituals as well. In chapter 6, I discuss cultural variations and the practice of rituals like the bridal shower and bachelorette party within and outside of the United States. Finally, in chapter 7, I explore the meanings of these rituals for women participants, arguing that when taken together they reflect societal ambivalence toward modern women's place and roles. Throughout, I use empirical detail, based on ethnographic research. Before proceeding, I offer a brief summary of the methods used to gather the evidence for this study.

Ethnographic Methods

This book is based on qualitative research conducted during the late 1990s through 2001. I began studying bachelorette parties and bridal showers by interviewing several of the women who participated in the party and shower described at the beginning of this chapter, including the bride. I then asked those women if they knew other people who had similar experiences and thus began building a snowball sample. During the next two years I conducted in-depth, qualitative interviews with fifty-one women who had recently participated in bridal showers and bachelorette parties. Thirty of the women were either recent brides (married within the previous eighteen months) or engaged during the time of the interview. The remaining twenty-one women had been bridesmaids or participants in bridal showers and bachelorette parties.

Because showers and parties involve different participants with different perspectives, I thought it important to interview women who filled these variant roles, rather than only interviewing brides. Each woman had many stories to tell about her experiences with both rituals and provided valuable in-depth descriptions of the things they had seen and done. Most of these women were white and self-identified as middle or upper-middle class and almost all were under the age of thirty (the median age was twenty-six). These women were also well educated; 78 percent had at least a college degree. Thus, the results of this study cannot be generalized beyond this particular race and class group. It may be that other women have similar experiences, but, due to the homogeneity of this sample, such conclusions cannot be drawn.

Because many bachelorette parties take place in public, I also interviewed several people working in the industry that caters to these events. I conducted in-depth interviews with a bartender and managers of two different male strip clubs as well as one informal interview with a dancer at one of these clubs. These individuals provided important insights into the bachelorette party industry as well as information regarding the behavior and activities of bachelorette party participants in strip clubs.

In addition to interviews, I conducted participant observation at four bachelorette parties and five bridal showers at which I was a guest. I also observed at five different nightclubs, in four different geographical locations (major cities and suburban areas in Pennsylvania and Georgia), that were known as common places for bachelorette parties. Three of these were strip clubs, two of which catered specifically to bachelorette parties. Both offered special packages including free admission for the bride-to-be and special VIP seating. One of these clubs sold merchandise on site, like a "bachelorette survival pack" which included a veil, a phallic-shaped drinking container, and other novelty items. Both strip clubs were located in large cities, one in the Northeast and one in the Southeast. The other clubs were large nightclubs that also offered bachelorette party packages and consisted of different theme (e.g., piano bar, beach volleyball, 1980s music) rooms that allowed party participants to barhop within one location. Research was conducted with women in two regions of the United States: the Northeast, comprising Pennsylvania, New Jersey, New York, and Washington, D.C., and the Southeast, comprising Alabama, Georgia, Kentucky, Louisiana, North Carolina, and Tennessee.

The world of weddings is elaborate and complex, and this book takes its reader through two events that illustrate the degree to which American society is married to tradition and traditional conceptions of masculinity and femininity. Yet, women's status has changed and is considerably different than that of the mothers or grandmothers of women who married in the late 1990s and early years of the twenty-first century. In the next chapter, I provide an in-depth background of past and present performances of the bridal shower and the development of the bachelorette party.

Chapter 2

Origins of Bridal Showers and Bachelorette Parties

A kitchen shower is popular, because there is such a variety of things to choose from, and so many things are needed to establish a working kitchen. . . . Unless the bride plans to employ a cook, she's going to spend many hours bending over that well-known hot stove. In one fell swoop, guests at your shower can do a great deal to make those hours happy ones. Why not have a kitchen gadget shower? . . . Why not have a pots and pans shower? . . . Don't overlook the sewing shower. Every home has to be supplied with sewing materials, even though its mistress isn't exactly a whiz with a needle. There are always repairs to be made. . . . A small but useful article that can be made of terry cloth is a dust mitt. You can give the bride something to protect her manicure if you cut out roomy mitts of terry cloth. . . . A gay and amusing shower is the Rag Mop Round-Up. Only cleaning aids are allowed. Every guest is required to attach about four lines of verse to her gift, describing the horrible life of a scrub lady.

Germaine Haney, *Showers for All Occasions*

Okay, you've all gone out together and talked over old times and discussed the wedding theme ad nausea . . . [and] now it's time to party. . . . Candy shirts are made up in advance with Life Savers or other candies sewn on a T-shirt. Guys get to lick or bite them off for a dollar. . . . Hiring a stripper to perform in a semi-public place like a secluded beach or office or park can be a scream, especially if some of your group doesn't expect it. In a public area, especially in a conservative town, have someone on the lookout for the police. . . . One fun activity is to see who will do the most daring act

> with the stripper. This can be sitting on his lap or having him sit on yours, or helping him strip, or joining in the stripping, or signing his rear, or dancing or kissing him. Use your imagination.
>
> Herbert Kavet, *The Bachelorette Party*

Two pre-wedding party-planning guides written more than forty years apart offer very different suggestions for how to host a successful event. In *Showers for All Occasions*, Germaine Haney (1954) offered themes and games for bridal showers, most of which assumed the bride-to-be would take on a traditional wife role. Herbert Kavet's (1999) guide to bachelorette parties, published at the turn of the twenty-first century, instructed friends of brides-to-be how to find an exotic dancer and adorn the bride-to-be with items like plastic penises and condoms. This bachelorette party-planning guide, like others (e.g., Liveris and Johnson 1998; Long 2000), was written for a non-virgin bride and makes little mention of the tasks of a traditional wife—or of the wife role at all, for that matter. How did these different parties originate? And how did we move from conservative congregations to erotic events? To answer these questions, it is necessary to describe the history of bridal showers and bachelorette parties as well as the factors that led to the development and inclusion of the latter ritual in the pre-wedding process. And to trace these transformations, I discuss variations in the wife role in different eras and how they impacted women's ritual expression of attitudes toward marriage.

Dowries and Domesticity: The History of Bridal Showers

Most evidence traces the bridal shower to sixteenth- or seventeenth-century Holland. Legend suggests that love was not enough to win the approval of the father of a would-be bride. Because the man she wished to marry was poor, the woman's father would not provide a dowry. As Arlene Hamilton Stewart noted in *A Bride's Book of Wedding Traditions*:

> Wedding lore has it that the bridal shower dates back over 300 years, when a young Dutch maiden fell in love with a poor miller, a man with a small fortune but a large heart. Because he often gave his flour to hungry families, he had no money to marry. The young lady's

> father refused to allow the marriage to take place without having his daughter properly set up. Seeing the girl's misery and knowing the miller's goodness, neighbors and friends figured out a way to provide her with enough household goods and furnishings to make a home. How? They gathered together and walked toward the girl's house, each bringing a gift, and it seemed as though she were "showered" with gifts from heaven. This act of love so impressed the maiden's father that he gave his consent to the marriage. (1995, 19)

In this recurrent tale—included in most of the shower-planning guides I reviewed (B. Clark 2000; Jenkins 2000; Rogers 1992; Stein and Talbot 1997; Warner 1998)—the shower functioned as a means of providing a dowry so that romantic love could be realized in marriage. Necessity drove the bridal shower. Worried that his daughter's household would lack essential supplies, the father hesitated to allow her to marry a man with negligible income. Like the plot of many modern stories, "true love" won out as the community came together when they realized that they had the ability to help the would-be bride and groom marry.

Several practices can be viewed as precursors to bridal showers. As early as the late nineteenth century, women had sewing or quilting parties (Howard 2000). At these gatherings, women helped the bride-to-be by spending an afternoon embroidering her monogram onto sheets and towels, quilting, or sewing items like dishcloths or clothing. Women rarely lived on their own prior to marriage and instead were dependent on their families for support. In Colonial America and continuing through the Victorian era, some girls had "hope chests" filled with items that they had made or been given and saved for their future marriage. In rural areas, young women often spent time in the evenings sewing and embroidering linens and clothing items. They put these goods away into the hope chest so that they would have a valuable and attractive trousseau, a "collection of all the possessions a young woman would carefully assemble to take with her into marriage, including useful household objects and family keepsakes of great sentimental value" (Stewart 1995). The trousseau often included clothing items such as lingerie and traveling outfits suitable for the honeymoon, if the couple was wealthy enough to afford to travel, and household items like silver and bed linens. The trousseau was a part of the bride's dowry, as it was expected to become the shared property (legally, the husband's property) of the couple once married. Prior to the practice of the shower, it was the bride's task to assemble her own trousseau, and doing so was in her best interest as unmarried women's value was largely determined by their potential as future wives. As Carol Wallace noted, the trousseau was "part of the bargain of matrimony" as the groom was expected to establish the couple's place of residence, and the bride to furnish it with "soft goods" (2004, 45). Although women on the frontier usually had modest trousseaux consisting of essential household linens, this was still an asset in the marriage market, "enough to attract suitors [as] some men married to acquire a level of comfort they couldn't achieve on their own" (Wallace 2004, 45).

The earliest documented bridal showers in the United States occurred among the upper classes in the late nineteenth century during the height of the Industrial Revolution (Bentley 1947; Pleck 2000). While there is evidence that wedding gifts have been bestowed on American brides and grooms for centuries (Rothman 1984), it seems that showers were introduced during the late 1800s (Casparis 1979). When the bridal shower was introduced in American society, its purpose was to help women assemble their trousseaux and to provide a formal time and place for bestowing bridal gifts. There were two types of showers, the gift shower and the "trousseau tea" (Baker 1977). During the trousseau tea, women had the opportunity to show gifts that they had received since their engagement, essentially displaying their trousseaux. At the gift shower, the bride-to-be received and opened gifts in the presence of the givers. Initially, showers were confined to the upper classes, given and attended by women with high incomes who lived in urban areas and had easy access to ready-made household gifts and clothing items (Baker 1977; Howard 2000). For the American urbanites among which this tradition was first documented, the shower was time for the display of social status and an opportunity for the increasingly important practice of conspicuous consumption (Litwicki 1998; Veblen 1899). The shower provided an opportunity for wealthy women to act as consumers, a relatively new role in modern society, as the economy changed from manual to industrial production (Litwicki 1998). Evidence suggests that showers were a regular activity on the social calendars of elite debutante women, who were given many parties and showers prior to their weddings in the early twentieth century (Howard 2000).

The shower also gave the hostess a chance to entertain guests in her home. Given its emergence during the height of the Industrial Revolution, it is likely that these showers were given by wealthy capitalists' wives who were expected, in the course of their wifely duties, to display their husband's status. This was the era in which the "cult of domesticity" was normative, with wives being seen as micro-managers of their households, responsible for creating a haven for their husbands (Padavic and Reskin 2002). Thus, the shower provided an opportunity to give gifts that could be used in such pursuits. A bride-to-be received goods that allowed her to "feather the nest," to create a home that displayed her husband's hard work and the family's class status. The middle and upper classes who were expected to present gifts to the bride gave not necessities but luxuries such as silver or decorative items like paintings or books (Rothman 1984, 167). These gifts were offered to the bride rather than the couple because they had an association with luxury and leisure—silver tea services, rich linens—as the future middle-class wife was viewed as someone whose husband-to-be would afford her a lifestyle of "conspicuous leisure" (Veblen 1899). As gifts impute identity on their recipients (B. Schwartz 1967), brides-to-be who received decorative rather than useful gifts were perceived as coming from or marrying into positions of high social status.

Vicki Jo Howard (2000), in her historical research on weddings, noted that the shower was practiced by women working in white-collar jobs during the early twentieth century as well. Likely, in addition to showers given by family and friends, coworkers hosted work showers so brides-to-be could celebrate with their fellow employees. At companies like Strawbridge and Clothier, newsletters covered important events in the lives of employees, and weddings were frequently mentioned. During the period of 1906–1919, 120 weddings and twenty-five showers were covered in the newsletters. Sometimes these were grand affairs held at restaurants, clubs, or rented halls with more than one hundred guests, and other times the showers were small gatherings held at work during the lunch break. Though the variation was likely related to social class and work environment, Howard (2000, 223) noted that work showers in the first half of the twentieth century always included cake, decorations, and gifts.

This was an era in which the wedding was achieving heightened popularity and attention. During the majority of the nineteenth century lavish weddings were restricted primarily to the very elite members of society. Yet, with the turn of the century and the development of retail stores that sold wedding clothing and ceremonial items, those who could afford to do so began to plan more elaborate weddings. Stores like John Wannamaker's and Macy's displayed wedding gowns in store windows, drawing attention to the bride and encouraging consumption of extravagant accessories for the big day (Otnes and Pleck 2003, 32–35). Rather than having small private ceremonies, weddings became grand affairs (Otnes and Pleck 2003; Rothman 1984). As weddings became more popular, the bride achieved a celebrated status, one deserving of social recognition and one that advertisers used as a symbol of luxury (Otnes and Pleck 2003, 37). It is likely that the bridal shower increased in fashionableness in the United States partly due to growing societal interest in weddings.

The attention given by popular media during this time period to weddings, generally, and to bridal showers, specifically, is also indicative of their appeal to the women of higher social classes that could afford to purchase magazines and books that discussed showers. A 1902 wedding guide provided one of the first printed mentions of the shower, identifying it as a celebration designed to help those brides-to-be who had few material items and who truly needed the support of the community to establish a household (Kingsland 1902). Yet, by 1904, *Ladies Home Journal*, which included information about weddings and wedding planning, published a column on the bridal shower, labeling it a new ritual in which guests could demonstrate their affection for the bride-to-be by providing her with a nice gift (Litwicki 1998). The shower was quickly transformed from a practice for the needy to a social event. The readers of magazines like *Ladies Home Journal* were primarily white women from upper- and upper-middle-class backgrounds who were or would become stay-at-home wives and mothers. And the magazine's editorial staff directed their columns, advice, and advertisements toward such women (Otnes and Pleck 2003). The staff of these publications advised readers to plan bridal showers with themes that emphasized the middle-class wife as a lady of leisure, such as "plant showers, recipe showers, sachet showers," and they encouraged potential shower guests to present gifts like pillow cases, handkerchiefs, china, and silver (Litwicki 1998). These magazines correctly assumed that brides-to-be would need such domestic accoutrements for their new status.

In addition to bolstering the traditional wife role, suggested shower activities underscored the importance of marriage generally for all women who attended. Advice columnists in women's magazines encouraged shower hostesses to include games that would provide hope for unmarried women in attendance (Litwicki 1998). Unmarried women were viewed as future brides who eagerly waited their turn in the spotlight. For example, one magazine article instructed hostesses to make cakes in which they hid trinkets indicative of the professions of the imagined future husbands of these women. Each woman would be served a piece of cake and would discover the little symbol inside, which gave her a clue as to what the man she might marry would be like.

The presentation of gifts and the format of the shower were different in early years. An etiquette book written in 1920 advised potential hostesses that showers should be "purely spontaneous and informal," whereby women surprised the bride-to-be by arriving at her home laden with presents (Ordway 1920). However, in time, the popularity of the shower and the etiquette that governed showers caused the replacement of spontaneity with structure (Casparis 1979). In the Victorian era, when parasols were in fashion, women friends placed small gifts in Japanese crepe-paper parasols that, when opened, literally showered the bride with presents (Casparis 1979; Stewart 1995). Wishing wells were also traditional during this time period. In these days when a bride-to-be had few essentials for her future household, hostesses would craft a well out of tissue paper and ask guests to bring small gifts such as dishtowels or cooking utensils to put in it. And though bridal showers were most often women only, in some cases men were included or given showers by their friends, where they received gifts suitable to men's household tasks (Pleck 2000).

Eventually, around the 1930s, the shower became customary in more areas of the country and among women of varied economic backgrounds (Baker 1977). Howard (2000, 2001) noted that factory workers from women-dominated companies like Maidenform and Jantzen frequently held bridal showers for their engaged friends during the 1930s, 1940s, and 1950s. Such events were an important part of work culture as they provided an opportunity for women to socialize and affirm their bonds with one another. As there was significant turnover among young employed women during this time period due to marriage, discrimination, and childbirth, weddings and showers allowed women a chance to reconnect with former coworkers who sometimes reunited to celebrate these joyous events (Howard 2001). Although women's roles and laborforce participation changed significantly during the first half of the twentieth century, showers remained the same. Even brides who would continue to work after they married had showers that emphasized their socialization into the traditional wife role (Howard 2000). Occasionally, women's employment status was acknowledged, such as at the 1946 shower for a woman who worked in the knitting department for an apparel company. At her shower, coworkers provided her with their favorite recipes, many of which were made from packaged or canned goods and involved minimal preparation (Howard 2000, 224).

It was not only in the workplace where showers were garnering attention during the middle of the twentieth century. Manufactures and advertisers recognized showers as events for gendered consumption and marketed a wide range of wares to gift givers. In the 1940s popular magazines like *Look* and *Life* advertised household items as potential shower gifts. In a 1946 issue of *Life*, for instance, Pyrex was billed as a shower gift that would "thrill her now and help her later." In the ad, readers were told that they could view the bride romantically or realistically and that, in either case, cookware was an indispensable and desirable gift. As the text noted, "You can take the practical view and remember she'll have a hungry husband to feed. Even if she's a natural born cook you can't give her a more inspiring present that Pyrex ware." The sentiment during the mid-twentieth century was similar to that of earlier years. Weddings in the mid-twentieth century were based on the traditional breadwinner husband and stay-at-home wife, and so household items, particularly those for cooking and cleaning, were marketed as perfect, practical gifts. And even less practical or customary items were marketed to women shower attendees. The United States Steel industry, for example, offered in-store display kits for retailers, suggesting that guests "shower the brides with gifts of steel"; and Velon film also attempted to profit in the successful wedding market by encouraging retailers to advertise its products as suitable shower gifts (Howard 2000, 82).

Wedding-planning guides published in the 1950s and 1960s emphasized the importance and practicality of bridal showers, offering suggestions for themes and types of gifts to be given. However, these variations still assumed and celebrated the traditional wife role. As noted above, working women were expected to perform wifely duties such as cooking and cleaning in addition to their full-time jobs, and so for most women marriage meant domestication. For example, in *Showers for All Occasions* (1954), Germaine Haney encouraged hostesses to plan showers that assumed that the bride-to-be would be the cook, child-care giver, and housekeeper in the family, as noted in the quote at the beginning of this chapter. Haney suggested that women should have kitchen showers or sewing showers because the middle-class wife was expected to be proficient in these areas. *Showers for All Occasions* also included suggestions for entertainment in the form of skits and readings about marriage as well as games that could be played during the shower. For example, Haney recounted and recommended this game: "One hostess who had a fairly large kitchen solemnly led all her guests into it, gave the guest of honor an apron and told her to whip up some biscuits. No recipe was provided. Guests heckled and gave suggestions. The biscuits were baked, wrapped up, and presented to the groom-to-be when he called for his girl" (1954, 66). In this game, the bride-to-be was assumed to be (or learned that she should be) knowledgeable about baking because she would need to do so for her husband. Similar to the women of the Victorian era, the wife role in the 1950s was an enviable one, and games like this called for brides-to-be to prove their worthiness of it. Other games reinforced women's dependence on men or traditional relationships in marriage. A game called "Trousseau" (59–60) had guests match potential outfits or patterns that a wife would wear (e.g., if he was a banker, "checks," or a fireman, "hose") or what her name would be (lawyer-Sue, gas station attendant–Ethel), depending on her husband's occupation. Though humorous in nature, these games supported the breadwinner-husband, homemaker-wife ideal. After all, there was still considerable stigma against married women's employment (Cott 2000, 167) as well as against remaining single. Married women were enlisted to work only in times of need, such as during the First and Second World Wars. The strong belief in the "family wage" meant that when men returned from war the right thing for women to do was to go back to their places at home and let their husbands support them (see Padavic and Reskin 2002; Cott 2000, for more detailed discussions on women's marital status and work during the twentieth century). Thus, marriage was perceived as a career for women in the way that paid work was for men, and games at bridal showers as well as marital advice guides reinforced these sentiments. LeMasters, for example, suggested that "marriage means more to women. . . . [I]t represents the center of their universe, the core of their existence, whereas for the man it is a peripheral interest, secondary to his work or career. . . . In the case of the man, the banquet celebrating his winning a letter in football or his initiation into a fraternity is usually much more impressive than any affair resulting from his engagement" (1957, 156). Consistent with the rhetoric of the time and media images like Donna Reed and June Cleaver, married women were depicted as, and in large part understood to be, "happy homemakers" who relished the wife role and were content to not be employed outside the home.

It is likely that men were generally excluded from showers during this era because women were seen as responsible for entertaining, for utilizing the goods they would receive at such events, and because marriage was not seen as a dramatic or significant status transition for men. Arguably, it was also not seen as a status elevation, as it was for women. Thus, it was expected that women be thrilled when they made the first official step toward assuming this role. As LeMasters wrote, "It is a very big day for the average American girl when she can show off her new diamond ring to the girls in the dorm or down at the office" (1957, 155). In the post–World War II years, women were marrying at young ages and thus thinking about and preparing for marriage as teenagers. Girls as young as thirteen or fourteen began accumulating household goods like china or glassware, indicating their anticipation of and desire for marriage, which for many came only six or seven years later (Howard 2003). The types of gifts given at showers during the 1940s, 1950s, and even into the 1960s might have been "humorous such as the traditional rolling pin with which to discipline her husband, but most [were] eminently practical: sheets, pillowcases, towels, cooking utensils, and the like" (LeMasters 1957, 155). Though some advice manuals or studies of courtship rejected the idea that men would participate in the shower (LeMasters 1957), others recognized that men might help with the care of the home. However, this recognition was coupled with reinforcement of gendered tasks and responsibilities. For example, Haney (1954) suggested that men not be neglected when planning a bridal shower:

> Why not give a few kind thoughts to that almost forgotten man, the groom? At an all woman-party you could surprise the bride with an array of presents for the man in her life. . . . Or you could invite couples, with everyone bringing a present not for the bride, but for the groom. Certain departments of home-keeping belong strictly to the man. Why not give him a hand in setting one of them up in style? For instance, what is a home without a tool box? . . . Here are some suggestions: hammer, paint scraper, pliers, saw. . . . You can imagine the hilarity that ensues when the bride unwraps articles like the above at a strictly feminine party. But you can also imagine how pleased and surprised the groom will be when he has the honor of unwrapping them at a couple party (29–30).

This author's suggestion that it would be "hilarious" to present tools to women, as it would be to present pots and pan to men, communicates the rigidity and normalcy of traditional roles.

Bridal showers in the 1970s changed little from those of previous decades (Casparis 1979). Hostesses planned parties that upheld feminine ideals. Johan Casparis (1979) and his students studied bridal showers among college-aged women in the 1970s and found that they were a customary practice, strictly regulated by formal etiquette. Although about half of the interviewed women knew women who did not have bridal showers, most expected to have them before they married. Like their predecessors, women brought household gifts for the guest of honor and watched as she opened them. A decidedly feminine atmosphere was typical, with the hostess displaying "her best china, linens and crystal" and setting the table with "a centerpiece with a bridal theme and in bridal colors" (Casparis 1979, 15). Unlike the showers of previous generations,[1] women made direct or indirect reference to sex or the wedding night in the form of conversation or gifts. Casparis noted, "Although contrary to etiquette someone often slips in gag gifts such as risqué panties, sexy lingerie, contraceptives, and baby rattles. These not only revive interest of the guests but shift the focus away from the celebration of housewifely virtues towards the more explicitly sexual connotations of this status transition" (1979, 16). The introduction of sexual elements at these showers indicates changing attitudes about sexuality. Because fewer women who married were virgins than in previous generations, perhaps it became more acceptable to discuss sex more openly and to recognize marriage as a time for socially sanctioned sex. Some women reported receiving advice from older women about child care and homemaking, while their married peers "recapture[d] the flush or romanticism that [might] be wearing thin. They assure[d] the bride how wonderful being a wife [would] be" (Casparis 1979, 17). In this sense, marriage and weddings were romanticized at these showers while initiates were socialized into the wife role. The realities of troubled relationships or the bride-to-be's former flames were glossed over or ignored, focusing only on the positive aspects of marriage. It is also noteworthy that some of the women who attended showers of the 1970s did not enjoy themselves. About one-fourth of the interviewed women viewed the shower as a mandatory social event that bored them with its formality and emphasis on traditional roles. Evidence of the changing times and changing attitudes toward women's place in society and the division of labor between husband and wife probably made some women resistant to this ritual that so firmly and narrowly defined the bride-to-be as future homemaker. Single college students were the group who most frequently reported being dissatisfied with showers, labeling them as "trite" or "stupid" (Casparis 1979, 18). These women were probably being exposed to new ideas about gender roles, given the flurry of feminist activity on college campuses at that time, and may have disliked the shower because they saw themselves as more career oriented than their non-college-bound peers. Such women would be more likely to be critical of the traditional wife role than would those who had never had reasons to question it.

Though women's work experience, societal attitudes, and the actual wife role changed significantly throughout the twentieth century, the bride role, as enacted at the shower, has not changed very much. Wedding shower–planning guides published in the late 1990s and early 2000s (e.g., B. Clark 2000; Jenkins 2000; Rogers 1992; Stein and Talbot 1997; Warner 1998) suggested similar themes and assumed that the bride-to-be would have at least one shower that underscored the importance of the traditional wife role and imposed a domestic identity. These wedding advisors also still suggested that different gifts need be purchased for brides and grooms, bolstering ideas about gender differentiation (Montemurro 2005), as will be covered in the next chapter. This stereotypical and seemingly outdated view of the wife is still supported in the bridal showers of the twenty-first century.

Origins of the Bachelorette Party

The history of the bachelorette party is less established than that of the bridal shower. In contrast to the legend of the bridal shower, which appeared in most of the bridal shower advice books that I reviewed, there was no information in planning guides regarding how the bachelorette party started. While American bachelorette parties are modeled after bachelor parties, which have been dated back to ancient Roman times (Fletcher 2002; LaPeter 2003; Stewart 1995), it was not until centuries later that women developed a complementary ritual. Because the bridal shower was viewed as the counterpart to the bachelor party and because women were not seen as needing a "final fling," the bachelorette party was not culturally relevant until attitudes about sexuality and marital roles changed. Specifically, the virgin bride-to-be had to be viewed as a rarity, and the woman with sexual experiences the norm. And general societal attitudes toward public sexual expressiveness had to change as well, as did sentiments regarding the subordinate status of women in marriage.

Until now, academic literature offered little insight on the origin of bachelorette parties as they remained unstudied until the late 1990s, when Diane Tye and Ann Marie Powers (1998) published research findings from their observations of "stagette" parties in Nova Scotia, Canada. Prior to that, women's parties had been given only passing mention in research on male exotic dancers. Paula L. Dressel and David Petersen (1982) studied male strippers and the male strip show during the late 1970s and early 1980s. They suggested that some women went to the strip club in celebration of friends' upcoming marriages. However, the term bachelorette party was not used in their research. Dressel confirmed that this term was not common at that time, although the activities were similar to what is currently labeled a bachelorette party (personal communication). Rebecca Clark (1985), who also conducted observational research at a male strip show, was the first researcher to use the term "bachelorette party" in describing what motivated some women's attendance at a particular club. Clark noted that audience members "come to celebrate a birthday party, divorce, or an upcoming wedding (the bachelorette party)" (53). However, there is no discussion in either of these articles about the activities of the women who were at strip clubs as part of pre-wedding festivities. It is not known whether they dressed up in costumes or carried phallic symbols, or if the bride-to-be was made to complete varied tasks, as is normative in the contemporary enactment of the ritual.

The only reference that I found to the origin of these parties was in an article on the popular wedding-planning Web site Wedding Channel.com. In it Mary-Beth Brophy (2000) wrote, "Bachelorette parties were relatively unheard of when our parents were getting married. That one last night of wild singles fun was strictly the province of the groom and his buddies. In 1965, the year of my parents wedding, the closest thing to a bachelor's party was the 'personal shower.' . . . The bridesmaids would organize a separate personal shower attended only by close female friends. In this second shower, the bride got her lingerie and anything else she wouldn't want to open in front of her extended family." It seems that that bachelorette parties may have grown out of these "personal" or "boudoir" showers, progressing from women having suggestive theme showers with peers to going out for drinks afterwards with friends. Before premarital sexual activity was socially accepted or expected, the bridal shower functioned as a time for sexual socialization. Women received gifts of lingerie and were teased about what would happen on the wedding night. These showers seem to have been precursors to bachelorette parties, where a different type of sexual expression occurs. Rather than hinting at future sexual activity, the bachelorette party is based and dependent on a non-virgin bride who symbolically celebrates her "last days" of sexual freedom. Thus, it is unlikely that they would have been practiced prior to the 1960s, as the previous decades and centuries were characterized by public sexual conservatism. Virginity for girls continued to be valued during the 1940s and 1950s. While girls were presumably engaging in premarital sex, as suggested by the Kinsey reports published in the 1940s and 1950s, they were strongly discouraged from admitting that they did so. A girl's reputation was in large part based on her ability to control sexual advances and temptations (Giddens 1992, 9). Following the end of World War II, the rise in conservative family values affected norms and attitudes regarding women's sexuality. The 1960s, however, marked a turning point in attitudes toward sexuality generally and women's sexuality in particular. During this time sex became disassociated with procreation as a result of the development and availability of female-centered birth control (Scanzoni et al. 1989). As people were able to have sex with a lesser likelihood that women would become pregnant, people were able to become sexually freer. The proliferation of sexual imagery in the media throughout the 1970s also allowed for greater sexual freedom for the country as a whole. Whereas in past generations married men and women characters were not allowed to be shown even sharing a bed on television, restrictions began to loosen in the 1970s (Douglas 1995). These factors, along with increasing affluence, rising social equality in the labor force, and the women's rights movement, contributed to a changing climate of sexual liberation for women (see Falk 1998; McLaren 1999). In the 1970s women were encouraged to not only seek, but demand sexual gratification from their partners. Barbara Ehrenreich (1986) suggested this was a means of taking control, of acquiring power and redefining sex as important to women as a class or group as much as it had been culturally associated as important to men. Bachelorette parties appear to have become a recognized option during the late 1970s and early 1980s, when attitudes about sexuality were changing. Though clearly not caused by the countercultural sexual revolution, transformations in ideas about sexuality were necessary for the bachelorette party to be socially acceptable.

In addition to changes in women's sexuality, women's increased labor-force participation also impacted the role of the wife and thus women's relationship with marriage. The bachelorette party is dependent on a bride-to-be who symbolically acknowledges that she has assets to bring to marriage and that marriage is a choice, not merely an economic exchange as it was for women in previous centuries. In the past, the resources she contributed to marriage may have primarily been related to her ability to care for her husband and provide a trousseau and her value as a mother-to-be. However, the bride-to-be whom the bachelorette party celebrates is a woman with options. Namely, she could choose to remain single and support herself or spend more time searching for a compatible mate. She, like most middle-class women in the latter decades of the twentieth century and at the beginning of the twenty-first century, works and earns her own money and potentially has her own savings that she brings to the marriage (Wallace 2004). While married women, particularly those with young children, are still somewhat stigmatized for working outside the home (Hoffnung 1998; Scanzoni et al. 1989, 16), their presence in the work force has greatly increased. Research suggests that approximately 70 percent of all mothers were employed in 2003 and 62.5 percent of married women with children under the age of six worked outside of the home in that year as well (Employment Policy Foundation 2004). As economic necessity propelled many married women into the workforce throughout the twentieth century (Israelson 1989), the stay-at-home housewife became less and less of the norm. While many men considered their wives' wages to be "helping out" or "supplemental," they were, in fact, making a middle-class lifestyle possible (Rubin 1994). Throughout this period the roles of husband and wife were again redefined. While married women retained (and retain) the bulk of the responsibility for housework and child care (Bruess and Pearson 1998; Hartmann 1995; Hochschild 1989; Padavic and Reskin 2002; Rubin 1994; P. Schwartz 1994), many became aware that they were making valuable economic contributions to the household (Scanzoni et al. 1989, 189). Furthermore, women were able to be economically self-sufficient so that if marriage did not work out they had options. Women did not need to marry, and the possibility of remaining unmarried, though still socially stigmatized (Geller 2001), was a reality. Additionally, age at first marriage was increasing, and thus women were more likely to be established in a job or to have attained education helpful in acquiring gainful employment prior to marriage. They were thus able to bring tangible assets to the marriage in a way that was not the case in earlier years. All of these factors influenced women's greater equality in marriage. When the wife role becomes perceived as one of partnership rather than one of dependence, it becomes socially acceptable for women to publicly express that they have made a choice in deciding both who to marry and whether or not to marry at all. Instead of only being perceived as "lucky" for moving out of the ranks of single women, grateful to have found a husband who could provide her with stability and bliss, the contemporary middle-class bride-to-be was one who brought assets to marriage and, like her husband-to-be, both gained and sacrificed after she said, "I do."

The Bachelorette Party in Popular Media

A more detailed record of the history of the bachelorette party can be pieced together by looking at popular media. Most of the coverage of these events was in newspapers in the late 1990s. Prior to this, a couple of films in the 1980s gave some attention to bachelorette-type activities but did not call the women's gatherings bachelorette parties. Such celebrations were identified as bridal showers or girls' weekends. In the popular 1984 Tom Hanks film, *Bachelor Party*, while the men engaged in a wild night, almost as a way of getting even the bride-to-be and her friends went out to see a Chippendales-type male revue, but their activities were not labeled as a bachelorette party. Instead, their visit to the strip club followed a bridal shower and was designed as a means of distracting the bride-to-be so she would not think about what her fiancé was doing. Like the personal showers described by Brophy (2000), it seems that early bachelorette parties, from the 1960s through the early 1980s, may have been like this one, where women decided to go out following a women-only shower. Such parties may have been spontaneous or planned, but did not seem to be concerned with mimicking the bachelor party. Instead, women seemed to be having their own version of a gender-segregated event, which involved less risqué though somewhat deviant behavior. This can be seen in the film *Shag* (1989), set in 1963, which depicts a final weekend of freedom as four friends traveled to Myrtle Beach to celebrate and create lasting memories before one of them married. Like the contemporary bachelorette party, the motivation for the weekend away was to spend quality time bonding as friends and reliving the old times of going out together. It is evident that the women were aware that their relationship with the bride-to-be would change after she was married. They seemed to be concerned with reaffirming their friendship and providing the bride with an unforgettable last weekend where she would be able to realize the magnitude of the transition from single to married. However, in neither the movie nor the publicity for it was the term "bachelorette party" used to describe these pre-wedding activities. This suggests that in the 1960s and even into the late 1980s bachelorette parties were not standard pre-wedding rites or that such festivities were perceived to be "girls' nights out" and not doing what the men do. In other words, women were celebrating in their own right by having dinner or drinks or going dancing, but not for the purpose of expressing the end of their sexual freedom. Thus, the term bachelorette party was not perceived as an appropriate label for such activities.

A few newspaper articles in the 1980s and dozens in the 1990s attempted to explain what happens at bachelorette parties and how they compared to men's pre-wedding festivities. In 1981 before society bride-to-be Evangeline Gouletas married New York governor Carey, women friends and family hosted a pre-wedding gathering at the legendary "21" (Duka 1981). The *New York Times* identified this event as a "bachelorette" party, placing the term in quotes, as if it was not an established moniker for the women-only festivities. The March 21, 1983, society page of the *Daily Oklahoman* described a cocktail party held two days before the wedding of a local couple as a "bachelorette" party as well (Gandy 1983). It seems that the journalists covering these events were using the phrase as a creative label for the event, rather than identifying an existing ritual celebration. Several years later, when the bachelorette party was next mentioned in a newspaper article, the quotation marks were gone and the event was listed, without explanation, along with other common celebrations. An article in the *Chicago Tribune* noted that among the patrons in attendance at a club featuring female impersonators were "women . . . using the Final Approach as the backdrop for special occasions such as birthday celebrations, wedding showers and bachelorette parties" (Cohen 1985). The first newspaper article that actually explained the bachelorette party as a social ritual appeared in the *Chicago Sun Times* in 1988: Richard Roeper's "Hey—bachelorettes can act sleazy, too" attempted to describe what happens at these parties. Directing his story at seemingly naïve readers, Roeper noted that the perception of bachelorette parties as subdued lingerie showers was inaccurate or maybe outdated and that in reality women drank excessively, talked about sex, and sometimes were entertained by strippers. He identified the "main ingredients" of bachelorette parties as if he was writing about a ritual for which information was lacking. At this time, he suggested that most bachelorette parties were confined to "private residences, so the participants [could] drop their inhibitions." Roeper's brief but detailed account of bachelorette parties, like other media coverage in the 1980s, was indicative of the newness and tenuous place of these events in the wedding process. However, Roeper's article also seems to date a shift from more subdued, spontaneous events or personal showers to pre-planned nights where women intentionally orchestrated parties that were like those of grooms-to-be. Unlike the dinners described in previous articles or the surprise visits to strip or drag clubs, it seems that the bachelorette party of the late 1980s and early 1990s began to take on a different tone, one that was more licentious, more deviant, and possibly more fun. It is likely that the growing affluence of the 1980s and early 1990s, as well as the increasing age at first marriage, influenced the changing tone of the bachelorette party, as did changing attitudes about women's sexuality and gendered norms for sexual expression. Research suggests that marital infidelity was on the rise for both men and women at this time. One study suggested that in the late 1980s anywhere from 50 to 75 percent of men and approximately 50 percent of women had extramarital sex by the age of fifty (Scanzoni et al 1989, 26). Increasing norms of self-interest and self-fulfillment and a growing culture of individualism provided the social climate that encouraged or at least permitted behaviors that sacrificed relationships for personal desires (Scanzoni et al. 1989; Bellah et al 1996).

More attention was given to the bachelorette parties in the 1990s, though primarily in the latter half of the decade. In 1990 a *New York Times* reporter researched bachelorette parties by attending a couple of parties and interviewing several brides-to-be. Though evidently these parties occurred for at least the previous decade, they were described as novel and it was noted that they should be seen as distinct from other women's pre-wedding rituals. "The new bachelorette party should not be confused with the traditional bridal shower. Nobody brings gifts of pots and pans to bachelorette parties. Nobody festoons the living room with paper wedding bells. Nobody invites aunts and mothers" (Dullea 1990). Instead, women partied like men did. For one bachelorette party, a stripper who showed up at the restaurant as post-dinner entertainment surprised the bride-to-be. Another bride went to Atlantic City with her sister and two friends, where they gambled and drank heavily and she was given "X-rated gifts." Two years later a similar piece was published in the North Carolina *News and Observer* (Moose 1992). The article, "A Tame Version of Sowing Wild Oats," read like a planning guide for bachelorette parties, providing information on who should be invited, what guests should wear, appropriate settings, entertainment, food and drink, and party duration. Unlike the bold bachelorettes in the *Times* article, southern brides were described as more subdued: "The goal is to feel wild without actually being wild." The brides described in this article did not hire strippers or take shots of liquor, instead they preferred champagne and "racy themes [turned] bridal shower[s] into . . .

bachelorette-like part[ies]"; this was attributed to the increasing age at first marriage and post-AIDS safe-sex sentiments. It seems as though wilder bachelorette parties, like those described in the earlier *Chicago Sun Times* and *New York Times* articles, had achieved some level of popularity in the mid to late 1980s, but greater societal changes regarding sexuality and the postponement of marriage stunted their growth. The only American film to date that explicitly featured a bachelorette party, *Live Nude Girls* (1995), contained a subdued event that seemed somewhere between shower and party. In this film, four friends arranged a sleepover party for a fifth, played by Kim Cattrall in a pre–*Sex and the City* Samantha Jones–esque role, in celebration of her wedding. Though this was the bride-to-be's third wedding, her friends decided to have a low-key in-home party during which the women drank margaritas, the bride expressed her doubts about marriage, and the women shared stories of sexual experiences and fantasies. Although the hostess identified the event as a bachelorette party, there was little in it that bore similarity to most contemporary rituals.

The first *Bride's* magazine article that I located that gave any advice on organizing a bachelorette party appeared in 1995. Consistent with the theme of articles that followed, the author noted that "while some bachelorette parties have the rowdy atmosphere of the stereotypical bachelor party, many brides have found that they prefer an approach that reflects what women do best: connect emotionally" (Martin 1995, 242). Cooking lessons, spa weekends, hiking, or having professionals style hair and makeup were proposed as alternatives to strip clubs and bar crawls. Other evidence from popular culture indicates that the bachelorette party was increasing in practice in the late 1990s and once again becoming more risqué. In the April 1998 issue, *Cosmopolitan* magazine's "Bridal Department" included a piece by Lori Etter titled "How to Throw a Bride-to-Be Blowout." In it, Etter offered suggestions for planning "an unforgettable bash" of "sanctioned debauchery," although she emphasized that the party should be tailored to the bride and should not be risqué if she would be likely to take offense. Bar-hopping, dressing in outrageous outfits, seeking out a stripper, and perusing pornography were all recommended activities. Etter suggested more risqué activities than did Martin, consistent with the variant images of *Cosmopolitan* and *Bride's* magazines; however, both noted that the bride-to-be might not want to engage in such behavior and that doing so was not necessary or even normative. Throughout the late 1990s and into first few years of the twenty-first century, there was a boom in print media coverage of bachelorette parties, reflecting the increase in the popularity of the parties themselves (e.g., Bader 1999; Barker 2003; Brace 1999; Cates Moore 1997; Depoali 2000; Etter 1998; Fox 2004; Kulish 2002; Lerche-Davis 2003; Levine 1996; McCutcheon 2003; Musante 1997; Navratil 1998; Oliviero 2003; Owens 2004; Palmer 2003; Saulny 1998). With headlines such as "Prenuptial Parties Aren't Just for the Guys Anymore" and "Blushing Bride? Try Bold Bachelorette," the bachelorette party began to be touted as a "feminist" activity, described as women of the millennium asserting equality and demonstrating the ability to flaunt their sexuality. The articles in the last few years of the 1990s offered descriptions of racy nights on the town, visits to strip clubs and dance clubs, and very intoxicated brides-to-be. There were several critical differences from the bachelorette parties described in earlier decades. First, women were having them in public places. No longer confined to private residences, women were letting loose in restaurants and bars. Second, women were often quoted as perceiving the bachelorette party as a chance to get even with men. Also, these bachelorette parties were becoming more elaborate and involved pre-parties at someone's home, gifts, and visits to multiple locations. Consequently, it seems these parties were also becoming more expensive, as an at-home party was decidedly less costly then an evening out where guests were expected to pay for transportation, cover charges, drinks, and sometimes hotel rooms. Finally, these articles also indicate that bachelorette parties of the 1990s and early 2000s were wilder, although this is certainly questionable. Because women were in public, it was easier to see their deviant behavior than in previous years; however, changing norms regarding sexual expression probably allowed for greater public sexualized behavior among women, particularly given the framework of the bachelorette party.

Throughout this era, as in earlier years, tales of ribald romps were usually qualified as one option for a pre-wedding party. Like the readers of *Cosmopolitan* and *Bride's*, women and society at large were reminded that a subdued spa day or a getaway weekend could be more fun than dancing on tables or being seduced by strippers. Furthermore, despite their apparent twenty-year history, bachelorette parties were still promoted as mysterious and novel events in the early twenty-first century. In 2002 bachelorette parties were featured in a front-page article in the *Wall Street Journal* (Kulish 2002). The author noted that women were "turning the tables" and participating in activities that had previously been restricted to men, including watching pornography and patronizing strip clubs. This fervor of attention and interest in the bachelorette party at this time implied that this was a ritual that inspired curiosity and about which public information was lacking, even though similar articles had appeared in major newspapers during the previous fifteen years. So, while informal parties or "girls' nights" may have been happening for decades, the bachelorette party was still certainly not an institutionalized part of the wedding routine.

The popular press seems to have a history of ambivalence toward the bachelorette party. There was simultaneous attraction to and rejection of salacious details of strippers and sin. While reporters told tales of wild women who were partying like men, they often identified them as exceptions, sure to emphasize that most brides behaved themselves. And the articles in the different years also communicated mixed messages about what was happening at bachelorette parties. Women were described as both wanting nights of reckless abandon and craving quality bonding time with friends that would have been hampered by too much alcohol or sexualized games and gifts. Probably, given the diversity of women, some had bachelorette parties that were more like bridal showers and some chose to celebrate with their own version of a bachelor party. What is most useful to glean from this print media coverage is that bachelorette parties were labeled in the 1980s and increased greatly in practice in the 1990s. It was not until the middle to late 1990s when a new breed of bachelorette party, that which I describe extensively in this book, was noted as common practice. Given the growing popularity of the lavish wedding in the 1990s, it is likely that women began to plan more extravagant and excessive pre-wedding parties as having more extravagant and excessive weddings became normalized. The cost of the average wedding increased dramatically between 1984 and 1994, from an average of four thousand dollars to sixteen thousand dollars in one short decade (Otnes and Pleck 2003). As people began to spend more on weddings and more ceremoniously celebrate this status transition, it probably became common practice to have pre-wedding events that were comparative in scale. The increasing coverage of bachelorette parties in the 1990s reflected more expensive and lengthy festivities of this era.

Yet, there is still concern among some contemporary women about the propriety of the bachelorette party and where it fits within the traditional bride role. Centuries of depicting women as subordinate to men and perceiving women's sexuality as private and tied primarily to childbearing have resulted in images that are difficult to re-envision. In other words, the bachelorette party, though increasingly practiced and accepted, is not yet institutionalized in the wedding process in the way that bridal showers have been. Perhaps because of the hyper-feminine image of the bride and romantic notions of love as the basis of marriage, some women seemed concerned about participating in a ritual that symbolically expresses ambivalence. Others challenged the idea of the bachelorette party, labeling it a pseudo-feminist activity, suggesting that it does not present an image of women or marriage that should be supported. Michelle Depoali, for example, expressed her doubts about the interpretation of the party as a ritual that indicates progress for women: "Along with female liberation came the bachelorette party—an excuse for women to act in the same degrading and unacceptable ways that men do at the bachelor party. It is the last night, supposedly, to assert oneself as a sexual being, which society seems to think that marriage kills. I'm not sure that a woman is naturally inclined toward wanting a bachelorette party, but it keeps the score even" (2000).

Others have argued that such parties are sexist and result in the perpetuation of sexual objectification and degradation of women that brides-to-be have objected to as a part of bachelor parties (e.g., Daum 1998). Furthermore, it seems that some women are still not sure about whether or not is okay to party "like men" or if it is even proper to address it in the same space where showers, gown choices, or bridal bouquets are discussed. On a popular wedding-planning Web site, one bride-to-be raised questions about bachelorette party "etiquette" tentatively, seemingly unsure of how the raucous image of the bachelorette meshed with that of the demure woman in white walking down the aisle. She wrote, "As I was pondering this question, I realized I don't recall ever seeing questions about bachelorette parties. Is there an unwritten rule about this topic?" In a different discussion, another bride-to-be asked whether or not it was okay to have a bachelorette party because she had been receiving mixed messages from family and friends. She wrote: "My mother says that nice girls do not have bachelorette parties because of what may happen on that particular night. Is it proper for women to celebrate the last night of singlehood by having a bachelorette party? Men do it and have far raunchier parties than we would." Both of these comments were posted on message boards in December of 2002. That women discussed the appropriateness of having or even mentioning the bachelorette party is indicative of the relative newness and tenuous status of the ritual. These comments imply that not all women are comfortable with or want to participate in a stereotypical bachelorette party. And though some women did converse on line about what they did at their parties, bachelorette parties were discussed far less often than bridal showers on message boards on Web sites like the Knot and Wedding Channel in 2002 and 2003. Most often, women sought suggestions for what to do, where to go, how to find entertainment, all of which also implied that this ritual was not standard practice with clear-cut norms. It has only been in the last decade that books containing party-planning advice have been available. Despite the seeming boom of these parties in the 1990s and in the first decade of the twentieth century, they seem in many ways to be a separate part of the wedding, compartmentalized from the feminine image and tasks that characterize the bride-to-be.

Chapter 3

Something Old

Etiquette, Tradition, and Femininity at Bridal Showers

The room is filled with hushed, anxious conversation. About twenty women sit at beautifully decorated tables. The women are dressed-up and made-up, wearing skirts or dresses—after all, this is a formal affair. It is one-thirty on a Saturday afternoon and we have all gathered to celebrate a wedding that will happen in just one month.

Some of the women are sipping mimosas from champagne flutes. There are several flower arrangements in glass vases tied with pastel blue ribbons in the center of each table. In the corner, next to the table with the fountain of champagne punch, sits a smaller table for gifts. At this point it is already overflowing with elaborately wrapped packages, most in white paper, trimmed with ribbons, bows, and flowers. On top of the gifts sits an opened lace umbrella, brought by a friend of the bride's mother. The guests talk as they wait for the bride-to-be to arrive, trading opinions on whether or not the supposed surprise will be successful. The bride's mother has taken on the task of luring the bride to the restaurant where the bridal shower is being held. There is talk of where the couple will go on their honeymoon, if the color of the ribbon on the flower arrangements is similar to that of the bridesmaids' dresses as well as of another bridal shower, given by bridesmaids and attended by friends, held for this bride a few days earlier. Most of the women present are friends of the bride's mother, and there is conversation about the engagements, weddings, and honeymoons of their own children.

The bride's father and the groom-to-be are here as well. They had the responsibility of bringing the flowers to the restaurant but will leave shortly after the bride arrives, as this is a traditional women-only bridal

3.1. As a bride opens her presents, her maid of honor keeps a record of gifts and givers

shower. The bride's father asks, "Are these things boring? I've heard they're boring." He looks around anxiously, wondering if perhaps he should have the waitress start serving food to give people something to do other than wait. But soon enough the bride-to-be arrives, quite surprised but seemingly pleased with the atmosphere and the array of her mother's friends, her friends, and family. Food is served, and soon the focal activity of the event begins—the opening of the gifts. The bride sits on a chair in the center of the room, a friend next to her collecting bows to make a "bouquet," and commences work opening the presents handed to her by one of her mother's friends. People watch intermittently, seeming to pay more attention when the bride is opening their gift, but take breaks to eat, go out of the room to have a cigarette, or simply spend their time talking to other women at their table. The bridal shower lasts approximately three hours, during which time the bride opens all of her gifts, guests write advice in a journal passed around by the hostess, and a four-course meal is consumed.

This shower, at which I was participant-observer and guest, was similar in format and atmosphere to others I participated in and to those described by interviewees. The formality and the predictable routine were typical elements that evoked conflicting emotions, ranging from anxiety to apathy, from participants.

In describing the feeling she had getting ready for a friend's bridal shower, Abby said she felt like she was being preparing to be interviewed for a sorority. "Well, it's just . . . I never went to rush but it would be just how I imagine rush to be, you know? The whole—you just feel like you've got to really watch your etiquette. I mean, I'll admit for that shower it was like I really thought about what I was going to wear." And Vicky, a former bride who married when she was twenty-two, summarized her feelings about showers this way: "It's kind of a pain in the butt to go to showers, isn't it? It ends up being—at least down [South], it ends up being like a rush party. The wedding and the reception is fine. And even the bachelorette party. But, like showers, you're just like, so what? . . . But you do it because of the bride." By likening showers to sorority rush, Abby and Vicky implied that they expected to be evaluated, to make sure they fit in and were following the rules for the day. Like other women who described the bridal shower as a time when they were really aware of themselves and sure to follow the proper etiquette, these women were conscious of the formality of the occasion and the performance they were expected to give. The shower is a space where women are called to do gender, and more specifically, femininity, in a structured and specific way. Unlike seemingly any other event in the pre-wedding process and even at the wedding itself (which allows somewhat more room for individuality), the bridal shower demands that women enact traditional roles or at the very least play along with outdated assumptions about men's and women's places in marriage.

How and why do twenty-first-century women follow this archaic cultural script? Why is it that a ritual that was created in the sixteenth or seventeenth century and adopted in the United States in the early 1890s has changed very little since its introduction in America? How did modern women, all of whom worked and many of whom were career-oriented, feel about participating in a ritual that called for them to act the part of happy homemaker-to-be? Why has the ritual not been transformed as women's status has changed? To answer these questions, it is necessary to look at the components of the ritual and the script that it presents for brides, hostesses, and guests.

The Rules of the Game: Bridal Shower Etiquette and the Performance of Femininity

The bridal shower became prevalent in the United States in the earlier part of the twentieth century with a specific focus on "domesticating" women and preparing them for their role as wife and homemaker (Bentley 1947; Otnes and Pleck 2003). During this time period most women transitioned directly from their parents' to their husband's household, and most had little experience in or material necessities for housekeeping. The shower became a practical way to both socialize women into their new role and provide them with supplies so that they could set up house. Thus, the bride for whom the shower was designed was an innocent who needed the guidance and material and emotional support of other women to successfully transition from daughter to wife and future mother. Given the origins and history of bridal showers, it is not surprising that there is a fairly rigid structure to these events. Women who participated in showers were well aware of what was expected of them. Regardless of whether women identified as feminine in their everyday lives, they were expected to display femininity at the shower, with what they wore, how they acted and interacted, and through the various symbols used during the event.

Learning the Ropes

When I began this study, I tried to recall my first bridal shower and when and how I learned about bridal showers. Although I am fairly sure that I was about nine or ten years old when I went to my first shower, I have no specific memory of how I learned what it was. I imagine that it was through this experience that my mother explained to me why we were gathering in a banquet room and bringing presents for my cousin. Most of the women in this study had equally hazy memories of their introductions to bridal showers, and many suggested it was just something that they always knew about or learned about when they were very young. Almost all remembered their mothers telling them about how to

3.2. Learning the ropes: a young girl assists the bride-to-be

behave at bridal showers, and many remembered attending bridal showers as children and being caught up in the excitement and the attention given to the bride. For example, Jamie's experience as a flower girl in a cousin's wedding when she was a child influenced her image of what she wanted for her wedding. When I interviewed her before her bridal shower, she knew exactly how she wanted it to go. She said, "I want it to be either at my mom's house or at [my fiancé's] grandmother's house. And, just, like, I can picture it, 'cause when I went to bridal showers it was like that. Like I picture my little sisters, you know; they make the little flowers that you carry for your rehearsal out of the ribbons. . . . I can see my little sisters doing that, and I always thought that was fun, and I want them to think that's fun. And then . . . I can picture all my friends and relatives, and good food, and that's how I want it." Girls learn from childhood experiences with bridal showers and weddings what women are supposed to do, and it was evident in Jamie's case that her family's weddings created a picture for her of how things should be done.

From a very early age, girls learn to value romance and to see that relationships are the work of women (Cancian 1986; Holland and Eisenhart 1990). Not only does family teach this, but the culture at large also communicates that "bride" is a high-status position for women. Little girls are encouraged to aspire to the bride role as they are given bride dolls as toys, when they wear bride costumes for Halloween, or as they are exposed to a culture that celebrates marriage through its media (Ingraham 1999). Popular fairy tales, such as "Cinderella," "Rapunzel," "Sleeping Beauty," and "Snow White and the Seven Dwarfs," create a romantic fantasy in which the title character is rescued and romanced by a handsome prince, with whom she falls in love and lives "happily ever after." Disney, Mattel, and other toy manufacturers produce dolls for girls to play with so that they may act out this fantasy and may even dress as a bride themselves. Chrys Ingraham noted in her study, *White Weddings*, "The marketing of wedding products does not begin with adult women. Toy manufacturers . . . have seized on the current wedding market and the opportunity to develop future consumers by producing a whole variety of wedding toys, featuring the 'classic' white wedding and sold during Saturday morning children television shows" (1999, 62). The wedding industry helps to lure girls and women into the world of love and romance by creating fantasies to be realized. Girls are viewed by the culture as future brides, and several of the women in this study noted that they fantasized about their weddings from a young age. The comments of a couple of women reflect this:

JOSEPHINE, BRIDE: I know as a girl I would daydream about my wedding.

BETH: When do you first remember learning about bridal showers?

LUANNE: Pretty early on. . . . I think there are some people that dream about their wedding and some people that just it's not an issue until it comes up. And I really did think about it a lot as a kid. . . . I imagined the whole wedding pageantry for myself—all the attention being on me. So I think that I just paid close attention to weddings at an early age.

These women indicated an awareness of weddings and aspirations to the bride role from the time they were children. When they experienced weddings, they were attracted to the images and looked forward to the day when they could live out their childhood daydreams.

Mothers as Mentors

When the time came to give a shower, most interviewees suggested that they turned to their mothers for assistance. Girls and young women learned from their mothers not only how to host a bridal shower, but also important lessons about how to cater to the needs of others and to put on a feminine display. When a childhood friend of Sloane's became engaged, she and her mother planned the shower together. Her mother told her who to invite, where to hold the shower, and what food to serve. Heather, a southern woman who had been a bridesmaid in several weddings, suggested that mothers are the ones who communicate the rules for the bridal shower by way of example, direct socialization, and the provision of cultural resources. She said, "[You learn] from the mother. Your mother always throws showers and she tells you pros and cons or what to do and what not to do. What's accepted . . . and you know you always learn more from etiquette books. We all have—god, I sound like Scarlett O'Hara—etiquette books. You start knowing [about bridal showers] when you're two or three because women bring their babies and you just grow up around them and you observe. You're told, ask questions: 'what's that?' And I mean by the time I was fifteen I could definitely give a shower myself." Heather's example implies that she grew up learning to be a hostess by her mother's specific instruction and by following the indirect advice of her mother by means of the etiquette book she received as a child. From the time she was a young child she was on the road to becoming a hostess and future wife and was being trained in gendered activities and emotions.

Colleen also believed that mothers were good mentors in shower planning. When I asked her how she knew what to do when it came time for her to give a shower, she said, "Actually my mom was a good source. She had done a couple of theme showers when she was growing up, so I asked her." Josephine asked the bride's mother for assistance when she, right out of college and inexperienced, planned her best friend's shower. "I actually asked her mom for help because I didn't know what to do. I took the bridal shower more seriously than the bachelorette party. I picked out like four different invitations and had her mom pick which one would go out. She helped plan the menu. . . .

She really helped. She got the cake; she decorated and let us use her house."

Since wedding etiquette dictates that mothers are not supposed to be hostesses for their daughters' showers, their assistance is usually behind the scenes. Showers were most often identified as being given by bridesmaids or friends of the bride, but in many cases mothers helped out by giving financial support and advice, so that they could have the shower the way that they wanted it to be or because they thought assistance was needed. For example, when the maid of honor initially failed to take the lead for one bridal shower that I observed as a participant, the bride's mother stepped in with suggestions about where the shower should be held, when, and who should be invited. She called the bridesmaids for a meeting, where she presented them with sample menus and locations and assigned tasks to complete for the shower. Although the mother of the bride paid for the majority of the shower, an expensive affair with a sit-down lunch at a restaurant for more than fifty guests, the invitations read "given by the bridesmaids."

When the mother teaches the daughter about bridal showers, several messages are transmitted. First, the novice hostess learns that it is women's task to entertain, to be sociable and polite, and to perform the role of the hostess in a specific and feminine way. When I asked Gretchen, thirty, a recent bride, why she thought women have showers, she suggested that it is about the acknowledgment of status transition from the community of adult women, who show her how her future role should be enacted. She commented, "It's the mother and the mother's friends' way of sort of initiating the daughter—you know, she's becoming a woman and a bride and all that stuff—and initiating her into that whole new circle, sort of introducing her to the mother's friends as peers. You're really raising up a social level. And it seems that showers given by the bride's friends—it's almost an attempt to sort of grow up a little bit. I don't want to say 'mimic' because that sounds patronizing, but to try their hand at the grown-up style entertaining."

The domestication of women is evident; and when mothers instruct their daughters to follow these cultural norms, they also teach them about their place in the world. Women are taught the importance of social relationships and women's role as maintainers of those relationships,

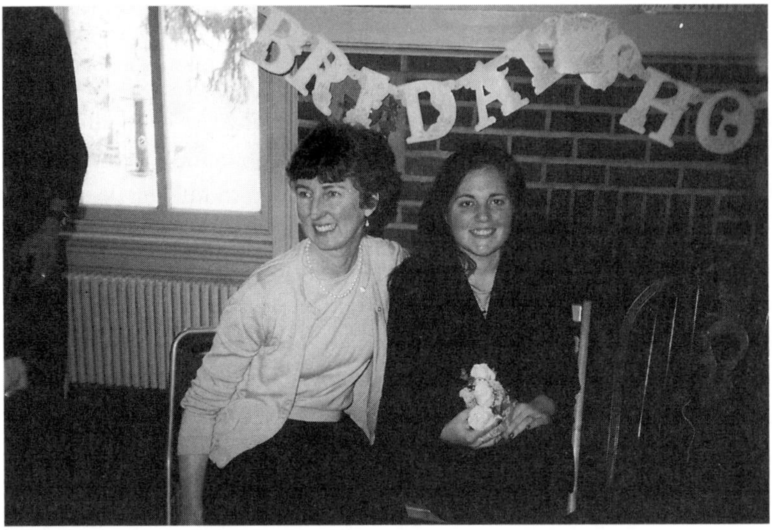

3.3. A bride and her mother pose for a photo

as friendships and bonds with family are particularly important during periods of status transition (Gilligan 1982; J. Wood 1994).

Beyond this feminizing, bridal showers also seem to be important times for mothers and daughters own relationships, as it allows mothers the opportunity to begin to see their daughters as adult women who will soon or someday have their own families for which to care. Shannon, who was a guest at several bridal showers, commented that she thought the bridal shower was meaningful for the mother or the bride because it signified "that [the bride is] growing up and becoming a woman and getting all of these things for her new house, her new life." Thus, women experience a connection to the women of their family, and the shower provides an opportunity to begin to relate to their mothers or other women family members as both wives and former brides. As Otnes and Pleck noted, "every traditional lavish wedding is . . . part of the great chain of marriage; tied to every one that preceded it and everyone that follows. Mothers and even grandmothers who enjoyed their own lavish wedding become key factors in transmitting the meaning and method of the ritual to the next generation" (2003, 16). Through the bridal shower, as hostesses or brides, women have the chance to see themselves as carrying on family traditions, and this connection to the past and the experiences of their ancestors may influence the reliance on and attraction to traditional methods of performing this ritual. By the nature of ritual itself, people come together. Tom Driver (1991) asserted that one of the gifts of ritual is the strengthening of bonds between members of the community as they experience special moments together, providing not only the physical bond of experiencing the same thing at the same time, but also the emotional unification of finding meaning and value in a status transition that affects the entire community.

The Experience of the Shower: Brides, Hostesses, and Guests

Weddings are about love and romance between women and men. Because of the traditional nature of weddings, the bride and groom roles most often reflect conventional conceptions of masculinity and femininity. During the ceremony, for example, the father or parents of the bride give her away or present her to the groom, indicating her status as subordinate or, consistent with the history of such customs, property. The bride wears virginal white and a veil, symbolizing her innocence and purity. Traditional readings in religious wedding ceremonies label the bride as the "helper" to the groom. Susan Brownmiller asserted that femininity is characterized by "vulnerability, the need for protection, the formalities of compliance and the avoidance of conflict—in short, an appeal of dependence and good will that gives the masculine principle its romantic validity and its admiring applause" (1984, 16). In other words, femininity is rooted in submitting to masculinity. Traditional definitions of marriage and the relationship between husband and wife, as enacted in the traditional wedding ritual, call for these exaggerated roles of hyper-masculine groom and hyper-feminine bride. When they participate in these rituals, couples reinforce the difference between man and woman and the "naturalness" of the heterosexual union between husband and wife, masculine and feminine.

There is a connection between femininity and romance, and brides-to-be seem to realize that this is the way the bride role should be played at the shower, at the wedding, and throughout the preparatory period. Even women who did not consider themselves feminine seemed to find it important to display themselves as such at the bridal shower. For example, Carol, a twenty-six-year-old bride, did not define herself as feminine.

Generally, Carol wore little makeup and rarely wore skirts, and almost never a dress. Yet, for her bridal shower, she found herself doing the things that brides-to-be are supposed to do, even though this did not coincide with her normal self-definition. Carol not only wore a skirt, but even went to a salon to have her hair styled on the morning of her shower. She described how she felt in the role of bride-to-be on that day: "It was really weird because I was very out of my element. I was all dressed up and feeling not like myself." As the bride-to-be, Carol felt distant from herself, as if she was in fact *playing* a role rather than experiencing it. She was "surface-acting" (Hochschild 1983), trying to feel what was expected but having difficulty as that expectation did not match her conception of self. For many women, acting out femininity comes much easier than it did for Carol. But what was particularly interesting about Carol's response to the shower and those of other less feminine women was that they felt compelled to conform to the bride-to-be role, rather than reforming it to suit their own personality or enactment of gender. This may be because refusing to "do gender" still results in doing gender, most often interpreted as doing gender poorly (Lucal 2004). Brides-to-be who were less feminine in general might have felt more pressure to demonstrate their femininity and their appropriateness for the bride role and their potential to successfully fulfill the wife role in front of a crowd of family members and, sometimes, future family members. In American culture the bride is the epitome of femininity; thus, it may be that it is hard to modify that conception for a woman who is not. Brides like Carol may find themselves playing the bride role in a feminine manner because that is the image of the bride they have been exposed to throughout their lives. Or, they may find themselves strangely attracted to this revered cultural role and enjoy the opportunity to play it. After all, the bride has star or celebrity status during her engagement and wedding, and this is certainly evident at the bridal shower.

The Star Performer: Emphasized Femininity on Display

Although several of the brides-to-be I interviewed truly enjoyed their showers, most were overwhelmed and found it difficult to be the center of attention, particularly as they sat, as if on display, and opened gifts. Since this is usually (in all of the bridal showers observed and all of the traditional bridal showers described by research participants) the focal activity of the shower and the manifest function of the event, it is easy to

3.4. Decorating the bride with a bow bouquet and hat constructed with the ribbons and bows from the gifts she received

imagine the heightened awareness of being watched. Julie, age twenty-eight, said, "I thought the whole thing was pretty bad, but uh, I don't know. I don't think there was any *bad*, bad part. I just—I'm not one of those kind of people who likes . . . those kinds of things." Similarly, Lori, age twenty-eight, commented, "It was very, very overwhelming. I just remember having a headache and being sweaty and hot and definitely feeling pressure. 'Cause, like, you know, you have to see everybody. . . . Like I remember coming home and being like a zombie." Goffman (1959) suggested that the "front region" is when we are in public, in the presence others. In the front region we must manage our behavior in order to convey an impression appropriate to the situation. We are aware that others are watching us or are at least aware of us, and we shape our behavior to the context of the interaction. Thus, one is obligated to express certain sentiments in order to express her solidarity to the group (Durkheim 1912).

Helen, a three-time bridesmaid and shower planner, sympathized with the bride's position, saying: "I think [showers are] kind of hard for the bride-to-be because everybody's watching you open your presents and, you know, you have to—there's a certain sense of expectation for the bride to be just thrilled with everything that she gets. . . . She's really the center of attention." In other words, there are certain "feeling rules" that accompany the role of the bride at the bridal shower (Hochschild 1983). Consistent with Durkheim's (1912) assertion that rituals are governed by moral, societal pressures to display certain emotions, Hochschild suggests that a social role, like the role of bride, carries with it expectations regarding proper feelings and emotions. These feelings or emotions are independent of individual or particularized sentiments. Rather, they are socially induced and considered mandatory by the society at large. The "bride at the shower" is a social role. She is responsible for appearing gracious and grateful to her guests and generally giddy about her impending nuptials. Such behavior is indicative of her feelings of attachment to and respect for the community. If she fails to perform properly, she conveys disregard for or disassociation with her gender community and with society more generally. Marriage is socially valued in Western society as a status elevation, and thus we expect those making the transition to be joyful about doing so. There is an expectation for the bride to present a certain self, one that satisfies the expectations of others as well as her interpretations of the role. And because she takes *center* stage, conformity to this role is important not only for her conception of self, but also because she is in a position where many others are focused on her enactment of it.

Nearly every bride interviewed expressed some type of discomfort with opening gifts, which seemed to be connected to their anxiety about playing the role of the bride at the shower properly. Several brides mentioned concern for guests being bored or belabored by having to watch this activity. Josephine, for example, commented, "I don't even remember much of it. It seemed like a blur. . . . It was so frantic for me because I was trying to get through the gifts 'cause I know people get bored sitting there for a long time." Joanna, another recent bride, expressed a similar sentiment: "I don't feel like anyone wants to watch you open gifts, so I tried to do it very quickly." Both brides seemed more concerned with the feelings of others than with their own. Bordo argued that women are taught to "develop an other-oriented emotional economy" (1993, 171), meaning they learn to nurture, to self-sacrifice, to care for others. Consistent with a feminine performance, these women thought about how others might be feeling, rather than opening the gifts at a pace that might have enabled them to feel less rushed and perhaps enjoy the shower more than they did. This seems related to the idea that women learn to be empathic and sensitive and also that they were uncomfortable being in the position where they were being showered with gifts and attention rather than caring or doing for others. If, as Chodorow (1978) argued, women see themselves as connected to others and learn from childhood to see the world as a web of relationships rather than as a hierarchy to be scaled, then they may experience difficulty or discomfort in a role that elevates their status above others. The preponderance of comments related to this from brides certainly suggests a pattern of a greater level of comfort being in a position of relative equivalence to others rather than being the star of the show.

Other brides were uncomfortable in front of their mother's friends or their fiancé's family. These brides were uncomfortable not only because they did not know these people well, but also because they felt they were being judged and evaluated by their future family or friends of that family. Tori, who had recently married for the second time, suggested that her performance at her shower for her first wedding was compromised by her uneasiness in front of people she did not really know. She said, "Everybody, as you're opening gifts, everybody's staring at you, and it's a little overwhelming. And they make you feel like—and not that you're not appreciative of what you're getting, but you have to make such a big fuss over everything . . . especially in front of my husband's family. I didn't really know them. I probably did better the second time around because I was older." Likewise, April described the way she felt at a shower thrown by her future mother-in-law. She said, "I felt a little bit uncomfortable sitting up there and opening these gifts and, you know, under scrutiny of a lot women I didn't know. And they were just staring at me. That was a little bit uncomfortable for me." The existence of feeling rules is evident here. As noted by Hochschild, "a social role . . . is partly a way of describing what feelings people think are owed and are owing. A role establishes a baseline for what feelings seem appropriate to a certain series of events" (1983, 74). April was aware that these women expected her to act in an appropriate way, to express certain emotions, which in turn made her fearful of violating the feeling rules consistent with the "bride at the shower" role. Further, the fact that her future family was evaluating April probably influenced her anxiety as she, to be sure, wanted to make a good impression on them. Thus, there was pressure for her to conform not only to the feeling rules of "the bride at the shower" role but also to the role of "future daughter-in-law," one in which the norms and emotions expected are certainly less clear. Bridal showers attended by family and friends of both the bride and the groom are unique opportunities to evaluate or "size up" future family members. Brides and other close family members are likely to be quite conscious of their behavior and the "face" presented in this interaction (Goffman 1967).

Even two brides who said they enjoyed being the center of attention in general felt very uncomfortable during the gift opening. Claire, for example, said, "I haven't liked opening presents. I don't know why—and I do enjoy attention. I just never like it. I don't know why it makes me kind of nervous. It's a weird feeling. I just, I tend to come home and . . . I do it and I can act—pull it off all right. . . . I've just—it's like I'm sweating, like a nervous sweat, but I don't feel nervous. It's weird." Claire's image of herself as outgoing, as someone who enjoys attention, made it difficult for her to accept the discomfort she felt while opening gifts at her bridal showers. Thus, Claire made every attempt to give a successful performance, such that she "pull[ed] it off," although her emotions and physiological reaction conveyed anxiety in the center-stage role. Claire may have felt discomfort because though she felt grateful for the gifts and the sentiments attached to them, the forum in which she was expected to express these feelings was uncomfortable. Sitting in the center of the room, with the rush of activity, makes it difficult for a bride to really thank anyone individually in any depth and may make her sense discord between what she truly feels and what she wants to feel. Claire may have wanted to feel happy and appreciative of the gifts but was unable to do so under the circumstances. In other words, she may have been surface acting, trying to call up the appropriate emotion but not able to truly feel what she felt was owed.

Lori, a recent bride, commented on the strain of feeling like she was not fully expressing her gratitude to people who had been very generous with her bridal shower gifts. She said, "I just remember . . . definitely feeling pressure . . . because you want people to realize how much you appreciate it, and it's hard to let people realize that." During her shower, at which I was a participant-observer, she had tears in her eyes when she opened certain gifts. Additionally, she made noises like "Aw!" or expressed surprise at the generosity of some of the givers by saying things like, "Oh my gosh, this is *so* nice! I can't believe you got me this!" In order to appear convincing, sincere, and grateful, then, the bride-to-be may alter the tone of her voice or make direct eye contact with the gift giver. At another shower I observed, the bride-to-be engaged each person whose gift she opened in a similar manner and after doing so made some type of comment to the friend helping her with the gifts about the meaning and significance of the present and the person whom it was from. Thus, these brides were legitimating their gratitude using "dramatic realization" (Goffman 1959, 30). This technique is used to substantiate or validate the self being presented in interaction. As Goffman stated, "While in the presence of others, the individual typically infuses his activity with signs which dramatically highlight and portray confirmatory facts that might otherwise remain unapparent or obscure. For if the individual's activity is to become significant to others, he must mobilize his activity so that it will express *during the interaction* what he wishes to convey" (Goffman 1959, 30). In other words, the bride-to-be must infuse her performance with the appropriate cues that make her gratitude seem sincere and legitimate. She must convey what she is expected and obligated to convey. Were the bride to simply open a gift with minimal or no reaction, she might appear ungrateful, insincere, and a failure in the expected social role of bride at the shower.

In fact, women who failed to express sincere appreciation for the gifts that they received were subject to negative judgment from those watching. This failure was on two interconnected levels, a violation of etiquette and a violation of gender norms for feminine performance. This is evidenced in the following quotes by two recent shower attendees: "I thought that [Rose] was not very enthusiastic or thankful to the people that gave her presents. She was like 'Oh this is nice' and never really—I mean, especially to her mother; we noticed that afterwards. We were talking about that. . . . It just seemed a little odd. I don't know if she was in a bad mood that day or what, but she didn't seem overly excited or thankful. I would think if someone threw me a shower I would be like thank you so much. I mean, it's nice for someone to do that for you." "[Kelly] was the most grateful bride I've ever seen. When she stood up and would thank everybody for their gifts, she meant it. And it made your heart feel good that what you did for her, she appreciated. I have never—in all of the showers that I went to—see[n] someone thank someone for a pillow to put [her] head on: 'Thank you for getting me this.' . . . She appreciated the smallest gift that was given to her."

In these two examples, the bride was either praised or criticized for her enactment of the role of the bride at the shower. Kelly displayed the proper emotions of gratitude expected of a bride-to-be. She conformed to the feeling rules of the situation. And while she probably truly appreciated the things that were done for her, it is likely that her expression of these emotions was partly induced by the obligation to show that she felt that way and by her internalization of the feminine role and the necessity of its display in these circumstances. Rose, in contrast, failed to communicate the appropriate emotions. Thus, she was judged as being less appreciative and, consequently, less committed or attached to the community. The interviewee who described Rose suggested that more gratitude, especially toward the bride's mother, was appropriate. Being grateful and thankful is particularly expected of women, as these are emotional qualities. Women who are not grateful enough, or who do not show it well enough, communicate disregard for the feelings of others and thus come across as not feminine. The shower, as the major pep rally for the wedding, demands exaggerated expressions of feminine emotions that the bride-to-be may or may not feel. The pressure to put on this act or to adequately convey the appropriate emotions is stressful for brides-to-be given the heightened level of scrutiny accompanying their star status at the shower. Furthermore, like adolescent girls who "try on" gender in the process of becoming women, "anticipating, experimenting, retreating, and resisting" (Williams 2002, 30), the bride-to-be at the shower, it seems, is trying on the roles of bride and wife. She may be uncomfortable because she is unsure of how or whether or not these fit with her self-image or if she is performing either role properly, particularly given the outdated notions of femininity and domestic relations she is expected to aspire to or at least tacitly support. Perhaps the experience of being formally recognized as the bride at the shower functions as a rehearsal for being the bride at the wedding. Having had the chance to anticipate and experiment, to practice, she is better prepared for the attention she receives when she weds. And though she may bask in the spotlight on her wedding day, when she is flanked by her masculine counterpart and appropriately adorned in the sacred gown that legitimates and transforms her (Otnes and Pleck 2003), the bride at the shower is still in the process of transitioning into this new status.

Hostesses

The hostess certainly plays an important role in the shower as she is expected to put the party together and keep it running smoothly. She is charged with the responsibility of coordinating details such as location, food, theme, and invitations. Popular bridal-shower etiquette guides suggest that she is also expected to fund the shower (B. Clark 2000; Jenkins 2000; Warner 1998). Interviews with women who hosted bridal showers revealed that the hostess role, like the bride role, produced anxiety in large part because women were expected to follow rules that they did not create and to give a feminine performance, in which they knew they would be judged.

Either bridesmaids or friends of the bride's family gave approximately 60 percent of bridal showers described by interviewees. Family (often the bride's aunt, sometimes the bride's mother or grandmother) threw nearly 30 percent of showers, and friends or coworkers not in the bridal party gave the rest. Most former bridesmaids that I interviewed felt fairly strongly that it was their responsibility to help orchestrate the shower. Several bridesmaids reported being hurt when they were not included in the planning or giving of a shower. Melissa, for example, described her feelings about being left out of a friend's shower. She said, "Her sister did everything. Like all of a sudden I got an invitation in the mail to go, and it was like—it wasn't anything that I would've done. It was very plain. And . . . I would have done something else for her. And I was never told." Similarly, Tori was annoyed when the bride's sisters planned a shower without even consulting with the other bridesmaids; she stated, "Her sisters took care of everything and didn't include us at all. Like just pretty much called us and said, this is when it is—didn't even see if we were available—this is when it is, this is where it is, and this is what we need for a gift. And it was a lot of money. And I was like really offended. *That* I didn't like at all." As bridesmaids, these women expected that they would and should be involved and perhaps were concerned about how their lack of involvement would be interpreted by the

3.5. The bridesmaid-shower hostesses with the bride

bride. They may also have been dismayed because what they viewed as tradition or proper procedure was violated. Because these women had the perception that it was the bridesmaids' job to plan and host the shower, they may have felt that others would interpret them as not being helpful or wanting to be involved, just as they judged the women who gave other showers. Also, Melissa and Tori seemed to have felt that the hostesses did not show the proper level of care or consideration for the brides-to-be by either not putting what they perceived as much effort into the shower itself or not consulting with the other bridesmaids about when the shower should be held, what the gift should be, or how much it should cost. This is an example of women's mixed feelings about bridal showers. Although most women I interviewed did not enjoy bridal showers, they took their roles as hostesses or guests seriously and felt that the bride-to-be, as a friend or family member, deserved a nice shower.

Another stressor for the hostess is her fear of the judgments and evaluations of others in putting on a successful show or performance. Interviewees went to great lengths to describe the effort involved in putting together a bridal shower. They seemed concerned with whether or not the showers they threw would measure up to other showers guests had attended or, in some cases, other showers that were thrown for the bride. As it is for the bride, there are expectations for what feelings or emotions the hostess is not only expected but also obligated to express. Interviewees suggested that the shower should symbolize that the hostess is happy for and cares about the bride-to-be. The hostesses' concerns for how the showers they threw would be evaluated, and how they would be evaluated as a result, were evident not only in the ways in which bridal showers were planned, but also in the way hostesses judged other showers they had attended. Hostesses described other showers as "bare bones" or "plain." Melissa, who hosted her sister's bridal shower, talked about another shower she had been to that she felt had not been well done. She said, "It was like a wishing well out of cardboard, which was fine, [but] even the decorations were [plain]. . . . I guess when my sister and her friends did it, which was the way I was used to, it's very—not that they have a lot of money, but they go and get really nice decorations, and they go really nice with the food and the table, and this was like totally down. . . . It wasn't like the big production like [she's] getting married; we're so happy for her; let's do all this stuff." Melissa's comments indicated that a proper expression of care was lacking at the shower she attended. She judged the hostess as not being happy enough for the bride, or at least not expressing the appropriate level of excitement about the upcoming wedding. Melissa's assertion that the shower should have been (and was not) a "big production" that suggested "we're so happy for her" implied that the hostess failed to communicate the sentiments that are obligatory in this ritual. Durkheim suggested that failure to express the right emotions in ritual is a way of betraying the community and denying one's commitment to it (1912, 403). In other words, if a family member or close friend as a hostess of a bridal shower fails to express the proper sentiments of joy, then that person communicates a lack of respect for the culturally valued ritual and thus a lack of unity or fidelity to the larger social network. Nearly all of the women who organized bridal showers had been to a shower before planning one, and thus they were aware of the evaluation process of not only the shower, but the hostess as well. Thus, it is likely that the internalization of that criticism and apprehensions about how they were being judged made the shower stressful.

Age may have impacted the stress felt by hostesses. As the majority of interviewees were in their mid-twenties, throwing a shower was often one of their first attempts at giving a "grown-up" party. Being less experienced in entertaining and hosting parties may have increased one's sense of insecurity. Perhaps for women who had thrown many bridal showers, hosting was less stressful. Similarly, women who have more money may feel less pressure when throwing a shower as they have the financial ability to purchase all of the appropriate props and symbols of a bridal shower, such as nice gifts, favors for guests, or gourmet or catered food. Additionally, women who are more financially comfortable may be less concerned with the evaluation of their wealth and social status since they are able to display it through the use of extravagant food displays and appropriate props.

Guests

The main etiquette expectations for guests are related to gift giving, which is discussed more fully in chapter 5. Gifts are required at bridal showers, and guests are expected to present certain types of gifts, corresponding with either the wedding registry or the theme of the shower. A few women interviewees hosted or attended theme showers. Themes were centered on the rooms of the house (bed and bath, kitchen and dining) or types of gifts (china or linen). Most interviewees stated that the majority of bridal shower gifts came from the bridal registry. Typically, one registers for household goods like pots and pans, linens, small appliances, and other items for decorating the home.[1] Selecting a gift that is not on the registry is sometimes considered a risk, as the bride-to-be might not want or need such a gift. Guests were expected to spend an adequate amount of money on a gift, and there was variation in the dollar amount that women deemed appropriate. The average amount spent on a gift seemed to be about forty dollars, with a range of twenty-five to more than one hundred dollars. Overall, women in the South reported spending less on shower gifts than women in the Northeast; however, women in the South had more showers per bride than did those in the North and thus generally spent more overall.

The nature of the registry and the types of gifts expected at the shower required a gendered performance where women gave other women gifts that communicated a specific gender role. Even when brides-to-be were known to be women who did not cook or clean, it was still considered appropriate to give gifts that suggested that they did. Brides-to-be were expected to play along with this idea and act like they knew how to use all of the items they received or, at the very least, like they were going to learn once they got married. In fact, in the case of one coed shower, when the groom, who was the cook in the relationship, was present, the idea that wives should be in charge of food preparation was reinforced. Hilary, a bridesmaid in this couple's wedding, described this: "They opened [gifts] together, which was funny because every time he would open up a set of pots he'd be like, look what someone got *you*. There were a lot of jokes about traditional male/female roles in marriage, which was kind of cute. But I just remember him doing that, which was funny, because she never, ever cooks." In this case, even though the bride lacked culinary skills and inclination, the groom still made gender-appropriate jokes, feminizing her by suggesting pots and pans were for her, consequently emphasizing his masculinity by clarifying that such items were not for him. Particularly relevant in the more common women-only showers, but also here, is that the guest is expected to play along with traditional roles by feminizing and domesticating the bride-to-be with wife-appropriate gifts. Although, presumably, the couple has selected many of these gifts themselves, they are often directed by sales people in the stores as to what they should register for and what they need (Geller 2001; Otnes and Pleck 2003). Consequently, people sometimes register for gifts that they do not want or need because they feel pressured to follow etiquette guides and the advice of wedding professionals so that they avoid making any mistakes on the road to planning a "perfect" wedding (Currie 1993; Otnes and Pleck 2003). Furthermore, when couples register for professional-quality cooking ware or turbo vacuums, it may be that they themselves know or expect the groom will use such items more than the bride; however, it is more likely that the bride will receive these at a bridal shower as gifts that are really more for her.

3.6. Domestic gifts at a bridal shower

Occasionally, women resist this domestic classification. At some bridal showers, guests were asked to bring along a copy of their favorite recipe to give to the bride so that she would have a collection of meal ideas to accompany her new pots and pans. The assumption that women have a favorite recipe is consistent with traditional gender roles that identify women as keepers of the kitchen. When I asked Abby, the only bride in the sample who defied convention and eloped, if she had been to a shower where there was a request for recipe cards, she replied, "Yeah, we've done that before. In fact one time I remember I just wrote Domino's number down on mine. I don't cook, so I was like, 'Yeah, you can look up Domino's.' "

Many of the women interviewed considered bridal showers to be mundane, "mind-numbing," and "redundant" and stated that they "dreaded" them when they received an invitation in the mail. Disguising boredom at bridal showers required "dramaturgical discipline" or the repression of one's true feelings (Goffman 1959, 216–217). Hiding true feelings also made the bridal shower uncomfortable for guests as they may have had to engage in emotion work in the form of surface acting to convey an impression that was different from what they were actually feeling (Hochschild 1983). Tom Driver noted that, as part of the maintenance of social order, "one of the functions of ritual is to release and direct aggressive impulses in such a way that aggressive hostility is kept under control, while aggressive love (moving toward) is enhanced within the group" (1991, 155). Any discomfort or disdain for the shower as an event or for its traditional format was channeled elsewhere, as the ritual required positive, pro-marriage sentiments. As a member of the audience at the bridal shower, the guest was obligated to appear excited for the bride and interested in her opening of gifts. Like the bride and the hostess, the guest, too, had a responsibility to the community to demonstrate her commitment to it by expressing the proper emotions in ritual. Individual emotions and feelings, like boredom, were irrelevant. When I asked the women if they looked forward to bridal showers, one woman said that if it was a close friend she did; but otherwise, she said, "I dread them. It's nice to look at the gifts if you're happy for the person, but, typically, that's not on my top list of things to do on a Saturday." Another woman, Alicia, considered whether or not she liked attending them for a close friend, but decided she did not really like them under any circumstances. In her words, "If it's for a really, really . . . no, I don't enjoy them. And I don't think I ever will. I don't like them at all. It just seems like . . . I don't know—just because it is so predictable and you have your kitchen things. . . . I don't know. It's nice and everything. They just don't really vary that much or anything."

Exceptions

There were some women who reported that they did enjoy attending bridal showers. All of these women were recently married, which is likely to have influenced their perception of this ritual. Most of these brides had several showers, at least one of which they described as a lot of fun. While two of the four women still found being the center of attention stressful, they were able to appreciate the effort and meaning of the event. April, for example, described a shower thrown by her mother and her sister. "It was nice. It was just like very civilized, women getting together and having a nice time. . . . I really enjoyed, just 'cause it's me and I can appreciate this, the beauty of it. I enjoyed all the little pieces that went together. I enjoyed that the room was so nice. I enjoyed the flowers, and the classical music in the background. I enjoyed just the whole package of the atmosphere they created and how pretty it was."

Reva, who had more than ten bridal showers, seemed to really enjoy the experience and expressed gratitude for all of the effort made by her friends and family. Kate, who had half a dozen showers and felt somewhat self-conscious during the gift opening at a couple of them, said that she thinks bridal showers are a wonderful tradition. Finally, Jamie, also a recent bride, enjoyed her shower for the most part and said she liked attending other women's bridal showers as well. She said, "I like to see friends and family and I enjoy it. I like to see what people get and give. I like food. It has all of the elements that I enjoy. I don't know why people don't like going to them. I think it's fun. . . . You catch up with old friends. You're happy for the person getting married, you know?"

While these four women were in the minority, it is important to acknowledge that bridal showers were not unpleasant for all of the women in this study. However, the marital status of all of these women is relevant.[2] Having had showers in their honor, receiving many, many gifts, and being able to appreciate the trouble people went to for them is likely to have influenced their opinions about bridal showers. Perhaps when a woman feels like she is always the bridesmaid and never the bride, or when she sees herself as career oriented, it is more difficult to sit through a bridal shower. Women are "educated in romance" or socialized and encouraged to seek romantic relationships with marriage as an ultimate goal (Holland and Eisenhart 1990). Marriage remains a symbol of status for women in Western society, and the bridal shower heightens the emphasis that the bride is moving up in status (and, perhaps, that others are not). Thus, these recently married women who enjoyed bridal showers may have felt so because they had already successfully completed this status transition.

A Bride Should Be Innocent, Know Her Way around the Kitchen, and Be Ready for Babies: Customs and Games

In addition to the norms for participant behavior, there were several rites or traditions that further emphasized the idea that women's place was in the home, caring for husbands and eager for children. While games were not popular at bridal showers and most women saw them as silly and outdated, many played games during at least one shower they had attended, and the nature of these games is fascinating and certainly worth atten-

3.7. Bridesmaids lead traditional shower games

tion. Furthermore, most wedding-shower-planning books featured sections on suggested shower games, implying that this activity was conventional. Several hostesses selected games from such wedding-planning books. Games can be separated into several categories:[3] romance related games, domestic games, and sexuality games. Romance related games were those that emphasized love and marriage, such as wedding trivia or word scrambles with words like "bride" or "groom" or "ceremony." These games seemed to have the purpose of creating a feminine atmosphere and reinforcing the idea that the bride-to-be is perpetually thinking about romance from the time she becomes engaged through her wedding day.

Domestic games were those that either reinforced or tested a woman's cooking or homemaking skills. For example, April described a game designed for a bride who would be spending a lot of time in the kitchen. "I think it was for my sister's shower. I don't know if it was my mom or one of her friends [who] had this game where they take one woman at a time and they blindfold them and they have you feel different things, like cooking things, like flour, sugar. And you have to say what's what from the texture. So I guess that's some kind of idea like you're getting married, you should be a good housewife and you should be able to feel sugar and flour and know which is which." The identification of baking or cooking supplies by texture clearly directs action for women, allowing the potential novice an opportunity to be socialized by older women who have been cooking longer and have the opportunity to show off in this game. One could speculate that this game may have been more popular when more women were stay-at-home wives. Such women were expected to spend more time cooking, and thus it may have been more important or likely that they would have a familiarity with the texture of flour or baking powder. Similar games were offered as examples by Germaine Haney in her 1954 planning guide, such as the one described in the previous chapter, where the bride-to-be was expected to be able to make biscuits without a recipe. April was the only one who mentioned this game, although similar games were listed in contemporary bridal shower-planning guides (e.g., Warner 1998, 80). While women still receive gifts that reinforce their role as homemaker and cook, explicit games that train women to bake from scratch or other related tasks are rare if not anomalous.

Otnes and Pleck wrote that the contemporary wedding is "based on expressing exaggerated forms of masculinity and femininity along with religious views of marriage as a monogamous and lifelong institution that encourages men and women to bear children" (2003, 111). As such, there were games that called attention to women's sexuality, specifically, as a virgin bride and as a future mother. One popular custom at bridal showers was to encourage brides to be careful in opening their gifts, suggesting that every time a bride broke or cut a ribbon on a gift that would indicate the number of babies she would have. Helen, a bridesmaid and shower hostess, said that at a shower she attended they "all teased [the bride] about breaking the ribbons—you know, how many ribbons you break, that's how many kids you're going to have." Many women mentioned this tradition, and I recall at my shower being teased about this as well. This joking about babies charts the path for brides-to-be; women should want to have children, so marriage is the first step toward motherhood.

Another bridal shower custom involved writing down what the bride said as she opened her gifts. A bridesmaid would record each remark the bride made in response to each gift and would compile a list of these phrases to be read back after all of the gifts were opened. In her book on planning wedding showers, Diane Warner described this game, called "The Wedding Night," as follows: "Someone discreetly writes down the exact words of the bride . . . as [she] opens [her] gifts. . . . After all the gifts have been opened, these words and phrases are read out loud as the supposed 'dialogue' of the bride and groom on their wedding night. This brings lots of laughs because most of the comments can be taken with a double meaning. For example, 'I can't wait to unwrap this . . . it looks pretty interesting . . . Oh . . . My . . . It's wonderful . . . just what I was hoping for. . . . Thank you, how did you know this is what I needed? . . . I'll use this every morning when I wake up' " (1998, 95). This game implies that the bride-to-be is a virgin on her wedding night, surprised by what she finds and experiences between the sheets. It is easy to imagine it as having evolved during the early days of American bridal showers, when sexuality was hinted at with innuendo (Casparis 1979). While most of the women in this sample were not virgins when they married and did not seem to feel embarrassed or ashamed about this, many played along with this game and brides-to-be blushed or giggled appropriately at the idea of the wedding night as a time of new experiences.

All of these games underscore traditional roles in marriage, with romance being the domain of women such that they can readily identify words associated with love and weddings quickly. Cooking and caring for the home were also reinforced as women's pursuits, as such games were never played at showers that men attended. The virgin bride stereotype was also supported, as was the idea that all married women will, can, should, and want to have children. To go along with these games is to implicitly support femininity, feminine role expectations, and gender differentiation. While some women said they didn't like to play these games, none suggested that they refused to do so. Only Abby, mentioned above, resisted being expected to do femininity by not bringing a recipe and suggesting that the bride order pizza instead.

Doing the Right Thing: Submissive and Supportive

A dominant theme in interviews was that many women did not enjoy attending bridal showers; rather, they participated in this ritual out of a sense of obligation. As one bridal shower attendee expressed it, "When it's a good friend, you're going because it's important to them. . . . You usually go for the person, not for the event." In other words, women felt compelled to support other women as members of their community. Brenda, a recent bride, put it this way: "I would consider it an obligation, an obligatory thing. Something that you had to do out of respect for somebody else and if you happen to have a good time while you're there, then yeah. Otherwise you're going thinking I can't wait until it's over." In Casparis's (1979) study of bridal showers, he noted that although many of the women interviewed felt that bridal showers were a social obligation, with 25 percent identifying them as "boring" or "trite," approximately two-thirds felt they could refuse an invitation. The vast majority of the women I interviewed did not share this sentiment. Most felt bound by an invitation to attend, unless they legitimately had a conflict that preventing them from being there. It seems that negative feelings about the bridal shower increased during the twenty years between Casparis's research and mine, consistent with increasing changes in women's roles in marriage and in society. However, comparing Casparis's sample to mine, feelings of obligation seem to have increased, with most women seeing their presence at friends' and family members' showers as required.

Durkheim (1953) argued that obligation is linked with the idea of goodness. One participates in obligatory acts or rituals because she feels a moral compulsion to do so. Failing to do so makes one feel "bad," specifically, bad about one's self. A person who does not go to a bridal shower, when she knows there is a social expectation to do so, may think of herself as a bad person or a bad friend because she has not fulfilled her obligation as member of the bride's community. Durkheim suggested that the concepts of obligation and the doing of good are inextricably linked (1953, 45). One does not act out of duty for the sake of acting out of duty; rather, one performs her obligations because she knows that she will be viewed as and will view herself as good for doing so. Thus, although women felt obligated to attend bridal showers, it was not merely this sense of duty that pulled them to participate. Women realized that they would feel bad about themselves if they did not attend and would be subject to being evaluated as such by others. For women, feelings of guilt or negative self-evaluation may be more extreme due to the cultural association of women with caregiving (e.g., Brownmiller 1984; Cheal 1989; Gilligan 1998; Stein 1992; J. Wood 1994).

Another property of obligation is appropriate emotional expression. One is not only expected to participate in ritual because it is morally right to do so, but one is also expected to convey appropriate sentiments while participating. Durkheim (1912) noted that the expression of grief during aboriginal funeral rituals was induced not necessarily by feelings of sadness, but by an awareness that there was an expectation that family should display this emotion. By mourning the loss of a member of the community, its members paid tribute and reaffirmed their attachment to the collectivity. As Durkheim argued, "Mourning is not the spontaneous expression of individual emotions. . . . Generally there is no relationship between the feelings felt and the actions done by those who take part in the rite. Mourning is not the natural response of a private sensibility hurt by cruel loss. It is an obligation imposed by the group. One laments not simply because one is sad but because one is obligated to lament. It is a ritual facade that is largely independent of the individual's emotional status" (1912, 400–401). In other words, emotional obligation is a component of ritual. At the bridal shower, then, the expressions of joy and gratitude are expected, whether or not one truly feels these feelings. Membership in the bride's gender community—the friends and family members who are close to and responsible for the bride-to-be's development as an adult women and her transition from single to married—carries with it rules regarding how one should react toward the bride and her upcoming wedding. One is obligated to express these sentiments because of her relationship to the bride-to-be.

Despite their discomfort with this ritual, women recognized the important social functions of the bridal shower. Few women expressed an interest in doing away with the bridal shower altogether, and only some suggested that it should be reformed. Why does this ritual continue? Why does the format remain unchanged? Why do women have bridal showers if they are not enjoyed? The answer to these questions lies in the object of the ritual. The objective experience of participating in the ritual can be organized into two broad categories: tradition, and community and care.

Tradition, Tradition!

The power of tradition, or tradition as an unexplainable force, was evident in the responses of many interviewees to the question, "Why do you think women have bridal showers?" Colleen, a then bridesmaid and planner of bridal showers in her early thirties, replied, "That's a good question. . . . It's been going on for so long. Mom had them. . . . I think women like to take care of each other and like to gather all of the gifts. . . . You want to make sure that the women are prepared to take care of the man. They look out for each other that way." Nicole, also a bridesmaid, responded similarly, as she said, "I don't know; I really don't. I guess tradition. They've always done it. And [to] get more presents." Both women noted that bridal showers have been happening for generations, and although they did not know specifically why they continue, it seemed that tradition was a sufficient explanation. Two other shower participants responded to my inquiry this way:

HILARY: I base that a lot on history [and] tradition, dating back ages to the formal role of a woman, and that's the opportunity for her to get her kitchen and her iron and her standard stuff that she might need in her role as bride or whatever. That's what I think. I don't know if I buy into it, but I think that's definitely where it comes from. I think there's a long-standing history.

HEATHER: Tradition. Tradition's very important in the South, and it's a chance to not necessarily show off, but it's a chance to be a hostess; and that's very inbred down here—even in me, and I'm not a traditionalist at all. It's never been a question. It's just that's what you do.

Hilary and Heather also claimed that tradition plays a large part in explaining the existence of bridal showers. For Hilary, the shower is something that she sees as a part of history, evolving from women's traditional homemaker status; and although she was unsure of whether or not it was something that she "buys into," she participated in this ritual and expressed reverence for it. Similarly, Heather found herself getting caught up in tradition and playing along with taken-for-granted roles during the bridal shower. The traditional power of the shower or the repetition of the shower format was not something that many women thought much about. Thus, Hilary's and Heather's comments were indicative of general sentiments toward the shower. Although some of the women who participated felt somewhat ambivalent about what the shower meant for women's status and their identification with traditional feminine roles, few resisted or rejected this classification.

Rituals can be seen as traditions. Inherent in the definition of ritual is the fact that it is an event, ceremony, or activity that is repeated over and over, over extended periods of time. As rituals become institutionalized, they are performed for their own sake. The bridal shower is firmly entrenched as a wedding tradition in American culture. The force of tradition can partially explain why the bridal shower has lasted as long as it has as well as why the structure of the traditional shower is slow to change. Shils argued that "traditions are beliefs within a particular social structure: they are a consensus through time. . . . The structural property of traditional belief is distinct from the substantive properties of the beliefs" (1975, 186). When I asked research participants why they thought bridal showers continued and why the format of events and types of gifts are the same as in previous generations, in spite of changes in women's status, many offered "tradition" as an explanation. Tori, for example, said, "I think because people are stuck in tradition and they feel like that's what they have to do. And not because you don't want to, but because that's just what you do." Other women made similar comments, some lamenting over the fact that bridal showers were no fun, but feeling powerless over a tradition that has existed for hundreds of years. Thus the "structural property" of the bridal shower as ritual is more powerful than the shower itself.

Many women seemed to follow tradition blindly during the wedding-planning process, expressing a sense of helplessness in resisting it. Dawn Currie (1993) noted that for Canadian brides and grooms tradition became a theme that characterized the wedding, as it was encouraged in popular magazines and wedding-planning books. Brides consulted these magazines that directed them to include elements of the wedding that they themselves, in retrospect, would have been happy to do without. When she interviewed brides or couples after they married, many commented that during the planning stages the wedding took on a life of its own, and they felt propelled forward by social convention and normative practices. Not wanting to forget anything or to be too different with their weddings, brides relied on wedding-planning guides, following timetables and suggestions for how the wedding was supposed to be. It is likely that bridesmaids did the same in planning the shower as a majority of the women I interviewed consulted books and etiquette guides, wanting to make sure that they planned a shower that met the expectations of others. Women probably organized traditional showers because doing something different was a risk and, given the template offered by the industry in these books and magazines, it was safer to host an event that followed convention. Although shower-planning books offered many suggestions for different themes and menus, most included extensive rules for the shower and noted that showers were formal, feminine events.

Tradition as an element or guiding influence was pervasive throughout the shower. From the games that were sometimes played, to the decorations, to the format and schedule of activities, to expectations for behavior or compliance with etiquette, an unexpected finding was that women seemed to be somewhat under the spell of tradition. The consequence of this is that the bridal shower experience is not enjoyable. Laura communicated this when she described the atmosphere of a shower she had recently attended. "[It was] stifling. Not to be mean. It was very like rote, actually, which is why I found it so unbearable. It felt like, this is what we're supposed to do; we're doing it. . . . It just didn't feel very genuine at all. It felt very cookie-cutter. All right, this is what we do because she's getting married. That really bothered me." Laura's assessment implies that acts that have the feel of being performed only for the sake of tradition become rather empty. The lack of personalization or individuality associated with this shower made her feel like she was going through the motions of the event, rather than truly feeling the way she felt was expected or appropriate in this situation.

Gender, Care, and Community

It has been argued that women are socialized to care for others and sacrifice their needs to the needs of others (e.g., Brownmiller 1984; Cheal 1989; Gilligan 1998; Stein 1992; J. Wood 1994). Julia Wood (1994) stated that women are socially responsible for caring in Western society. Gilligan, too, suggested that women have an "obligation to care" (1998, 344). Cheal asserted that women are disposed to "sentiments of caring for others and denial of self" (1989, 91). Perhaps related to the myth of maternal instinct, what Michelle Hoffnung calls "the motherhood mystique," is the idea that women are "naturally" suited to care for others (1998, 282–285; see also Chodorow 1978; Brownmiller 1984). In other words, women care, in the ultimate form as mothers, because this is consistent with the enactment of femininity. Brownmiller, writing on feminine emotion, suggested that love is a central element of femininity, as she stated, "A requirement of femininity is that a women devote her life to love, to mother love, to romantic love, . . . to amorphous, undifferentiated caring" (1984, 215). To be a good woman is to be feminine. To be feminine is to love, to care, to be selfless, to be empathic. Thus, good women express care as a demonstration of femininity and goodness.

The bridal shower serves as site where women as family members and friends express care for the bride-to-be by their presence. We can relate this idea of caring as a gendered activity back to Durkheim's (1953) connection of obligation with goodness. To show that one cares by attending a bridal shower and giving a gift to the bride-to-be is a way that goodness can be measured—particularly goodness as a woman. In other words, when women attend bridal showers, they are fulfilling their obligation both as members of a community *and as women* who are members of a *gender* community. This very fact and the related requirement of doing gender at bridal showers may have impacted women's subjective experience at showers.

Discomfort with bridal showers may be related to the ambivalence contemporary women feel toward the wife role. Hoffnung (1998) argued that contemporary women face conflict because they are expected to fulfill contradictory expectations. Women learn that they should be independent and seek out careers but they should also be good, devoted mothers. She argued that women face both an internal and external socially induced conflict between "individual achievement and feminine responsibility" (Hoffnung 1998, 281). Feminine responsibility is implicitly being called for at the bridal shower. For guests at the shower this sentiment may have caused women who did not necessarily identify with this position discomfort. Brides-to-be may have felt ambivalent about becoming wives when they recognized that marriage entailed sacrifice and changes in relationships with friends and family. It is up to the bride-to-be to reconcile any feelings of doubt with the feeling rules associated with her new status. Dalma Heyn noted, in her study of women's transformation in marriage, "Since the joy of the wedding and its aftermath are in the myth we were raised on, . . . any unwelcome feelings simply make no sense. How can a woman be discontented when she's just taken on the very role she's longed for most?" (1997, 15). With respect to the shower, brides-to-be have received the message that they should be thrilled about their impending nuptials, that this is what they have been encouraged to want and achieve (Holland and Eisenhart 1990). Emotions that communicate anything different signify a problem with the individual rather than the social role.

It is important to again emphasize that bridal showers are *women's* rituals. The fact that a primary element of the bridal shower involves showing care and giving care to the bride-to-be can help to explain why men rarely give wedding showers. Berardo and Vera (1981) offered such an explanation as to why this ritual has been primarily women-centered. They suggested that this expression of care is one that men cannot engage in easily because it violates the masculine role (1981, 398). Brownmiller (1984) suggested a similar idea, that being that femininity is centered, in part, on the expression of empathy and sentimentality, emotions that are seen as non-masculine. Furthermore, love is seen as the domain of women (Brownmiller 1984, 215). Love is women's emotion, and thus it seems logical that a celebration of that feeling would be the realm of women.

Related to expectations for women's appropriate emotional expressions and the ethic of care, women are socially responsible for maintaining ties and relationships with extended families. In American society it is women who have been responsible for kin work, for organizing family celebrations, and for remembering and recognizing special occasions (di Leonardo 1987; Brownmiller 1984, 216). Given these role expectations, it is not surprising that women most often give bridal showers and men's involvement in them is minimal (Montemurro 2005). As bridal showers are, in fact, rituals that symbolically and materially express "emotional connection" it makes sense that it would be women and not men who organize and carry out these events. Critically, bridal showers celebrate women's relationships with one another, connections between families, and friends. They reinforce social integration. Since maintaining these relationships is the work of women, women as participants in bridal showers learn that it is their responsibility as women to orchestrate such events and, particularly, that after they marry they will be expected to carry on this tradition. It may be that men do not have showers because it is assumed that their wives or mothers will take care of maintaining relationships with family and friends, thus they need not be concerned with or worried about reaffirming these ties during premarital rituals. Furthermore, the entire wedding-planning process is gendered, with most of the necessary work viewed as women's responsibility (Currie 1993; Otnes and Pleck 2003). Grooms-to-be are discouraged from participating in these activities by the wedding industry, their peers, and sometimes their fiancées. Advice manuals for grooms imply that they are not (and should not be) interested in selecting china patterns, floral arrangements, or wedding attire and thus reframe the least feminine pre-wedding activities (e.g., making decisions about alcoholic beverages, arranging transportation) in ways that make them less threatening to the masculinity of men who participate in them (Otnes and Pleck 2003). The shower is one the many events that must be planned along the way; and as pre-wedding tasks are disproportionately allocated to the bride, her mother, and her attendants, it is logical that it is they who would plan the shower. With the exception of the bachelor party and their own attire, there are few tasks that are specifically designated to men (Currie 1993; Geller 2001).

Interjecting Masculinity into a Feminine Space: Men and Wedding Showers

Men were not completely absent from bridal showers; however, their role at the traditional bridal shower tended to be peripheral at most. When men were present they often congregated together in another area of the home or location where the shower was being held. Interviewees suggested that men were either totally absent or were outside or "in the basement watching TV and drinking beer," thus maintaining a good distance from the feminized space of the shower and participating in activities, like watching sports and consuming alcohol, that reinforced their status as men. At one bridal shower I attended, the groom-to-be was outside with his brothers, father, and other men relatives, where they smoked cigars and sat around on folding chairs surrounding a keg of beer. This groom occasionally peeked into the house, seeming to be interested in the gifts, but did not enter until the gift opening was completed, when he examined the goods that they had received. It was evident that he knew the gifts were for both of them and wanted to see them but stayed out of the way until the women left, perhaps respecting the shower as women's social space. Furthermore, since showers are typically the domain of women, it may be that this man was constrained from expressing full interest in the ritual given the expectation that doing so might compromise his masculinity, particularly in the course of masculine activities such as beer drinking and cigar smoking with other men.

The Fiancé-Only Shower

There were three types of wedding showers in which men were intentionally included. The first type is what I label the "fiancé only," where the shower had the same format as a traditional bridal shower but the groom-to-be was present, usually as the only man at the event. I would not classify this as a coed shower since it was not really comprised of men and women; rather, the groom was there usually to facilitate interaction between his family and the bride and her family. For instance, Josephine's fiancé accompanied her to a bridal shower attended by members of his family. As she said, "It was nice to have my husband there because I didn't know so many of his family—so that was part of the reason I wanted him to stay. Because if I would open a card and it would say [a name], I wasn't able to pick them out in the crowd. So it was nice for me to say this is from Sally and he'd pick her out and say, 'Thank you, Sally.' . . . That made it a lot more comfortable for me."

In this case, like other fiancé-only wedding showers, Josephine's fiancé helped out opening gifts and participated fully in the shower, making it less awkward for her when she did not know who gave certain gifts. However, she commented that even though he had a great time he mocked the feminine aspects of the shower by posing for pictures in a comical manner with the bow hat, wearing it throughout the shower, as well as telling her that when she had a baby shower he would not attend.[4] By treating the femininity of the shower as funny, he demonstrated his masculinity and heterosexuality, which would have likely been questioned if he had engaged in the activities expected in the role of the bride-at-the-shower. Thus, when the usual tools to display masculinity were missing, this man resorted to mocking femininity as a way of showing his status, similar to Leyser's (2003) findings regarding men placed in feminized roles or positions.

The fiancé-only shower does not seem to be common as only three women described showers of this type and all of these women recognized that it was unusual. Helen, a bridesmaid and guest at a close friend's shower, noted her surprise at the groom-to-be's presence. As she said, "The groom was there. I thought that was really weird. And he was there through the *whole* thing." Her reaction to the groom even being at the shower indicated that she defined showers as women's rituals. She further noted his lack of socialization regarding showers and how out of place he seemed at the event: "I made him make the plate with the bows. . . . He had no idea. When I was telling him, 'You gotta do the plate thing,' he said, 'What are you talking about?' Watching him try to navigate where to put all of the ribbons on the plate, that was the best part [of the shower]." These examples illustrate that in this sample men's presence at the traditional bridal shower was rare and certainly changed the atmosphere at least in part by introducing a masculine element into a hyper-feminine context. Men met this situation cautiously and took on the role of naïve newcomer/incompetent or comedian seemingly in order to fit their masculine selves into the environment.

The Groomal Shower

The second type of wedding shower that included men was what Berardo and Vera (1981) labeled as the "groomal shower." This, the least frequent in my estimation—only one interviewee mentioned it—was when the groom was the guest of honor and the bride was not present. Berardo and Vera (1981) described a shower where guests were women coworkers and friends of the groom. While very interesting and potentially a growing trend, with registry available at stores like Home Depot (Walker 2003), this was not common in my research. Only one woman, Abby, described a situation where men friends and family gave her brother-in-law a "tool shower."

The Coed Wedding Shower

The final type of shower in which men are involved is the coed shower, which honors both bride and groom and men and women attend as guests. These showers are notably different from traditional bridal showers in that they are often at night, include alcohol, and have masculine themes such as "Bottle and Bar" or "Lawn and Garden" in order to lure men to participate. Women reported enjoying these showers more than women-only events because they were less formal, less structured, less feminine, and because bride and groom both shared the center-stage position (Montemurro 2005). Gift opening was often a peripheral activity and norms for behavior and appropriate emotional expression were less rigid. Despite media speculation and projections in wedding-planning books, in this sample the coed shower did not replace the traditional bridal shower. Twenty-one showers (14 percent) described by interviewees were coed, and women viewed this trend with ambivalence. While some embraced the idea of men's inclusion in wedding showers, others strongly objected to it. When I asked Jamie (engaged, age twenty-seven) whether or not she would want a shower that included her fiancé, she responded, "I don't like it. . . . I think it's dumb. . . . Maybe I'm more of a traditional person than I thought. I think bridal showers are definitely just for women to get together and have a nice time with each other. The guys are kind of excluded, and they come and pick their wives up and come and pick the bride up afterwards. . . . It's not for men." Lori, twenty-eight and a recent bride, agreed. She said, "I think it's for the girl. I know that's a stereotype . . . but for the main reason that the guy doesn't want to be there. . . . Most guys don't really give a crap about the china or the bedding. They really don't care about any of the gifts they're getting." These women identified the shower as a site where gender was constructed and stereotypes about men and women were reinforced. Due to the feminine environment of the shower and the expectation for the performance of femininity, it seems that these women found it hard to imagine men's involvement or interest. Defining the shower as such and viewing it as women's ritual necessarily challenges the masculinity and, to some extent, heterosexuality of men who participate in it. Perhaps men who appeared to be "into" a traditional shower would have been an affront to the wedding ritual itself. Otnes and Pleck (2003) suggested that men's appropriate performance as groom involves incompetence about wedding shopping and the tasks that need to be completed for a lavish wedding. The groom who projected knowledge or mastery of wedding tasks would be "doing femininity" and thus failing to perform the groom role properly.

However, other women said that they thought that men should be involved in the wedding shower, since gifts given were for both bride and groom. Robin's comments were representative of women who liked the idea of a coed shower: "I think it's a great idea. . . . the older I get, the more appropriate it seems. Nine times out of ten you're going to be living with this person; you're sharing all of the same stuff." And Colleen, who was not sure whether or not she would want to have one herself, mentioned that she really enjoyed a coed shower she attended. She described the atmosphere as "fun," a word rarely heard in describing women-only showers, and said, "It was kind of neat having the men there. It sort of made it a little different. . . . I found myself giggling a couple of times, just to see [the groom there]. . . . But it was just kind of neat that he could be there; and for the guys, you can see what us women have to go through." In theory, many women seemed to be in favor of coed showers. In practice, fewer women had, threw, attended, or even wanted to have coed wedding showers. Even Robin, who thought they were a great idea, was quick to say, "I wouldn't want one."

Some scholars have argued that the women-only shower provides important time for women to come together and support one another and for a bride to maintain her separate identity from her future spouse (Cheal 1989; Geller 2001; Montemurro 2002). Some have challenged the supposed feminist aspects of the coed shower and viewed it instead as a violation of women's individualism and a devaluing of the feminine. As Geller wrote, "the privacy a woman once enjoyed with her female friends, sisters, cousins . . . has now been relinquished in favor of total romantic symbiosis; marital fusion in which nothing is withheld from one's spouse. . . . The new-fangled bridal shower, which eschews the closeness of homosocial friendship for a coed paean to coupledom, does not represent the victory of truly egalitarian values, and it should not be seen as a sign of our progress over the social mores of the past" (2001, 179–180). Geller's critique may articulate some of the sentiments expressed by women like Jamie, quoted above, who felt that showers were about women coming together without men, or other women who could not quite identify why they did not want men participating in showers. Women's dislike or failure to practice coed showers may be partially understood as a desire to hold onto their somewhat threatened relationships with women friends or family members (as many women in this study believed that their relationships with friends and family would change or had changed after marriage). And a few women may resist the coed shower as a means of claiming an event in which bride-to-be as an individual is the guest of honor, rather than having to share that with the groom-to-be. Robin suggested this in explaining why she would not want to have a coed shower: "Because I like all of the attention on me, quite honestly . . . so I wouldn't want to share with anyone, not even him. I'd be like, 'Get away; these are my plates, damn it!' " However, Robin is likely to be in the minority given most brides-to-be's discomfort with the bride's center-stage position at the shower.

Whether or not individual women like the coed shower is certainly interesting, however; the fact that they were not prevalent in this sample is suggestive. This indicates that gender convergence may not be occurring at the pace suggested by the wedding industry press or at least not among white middle-class women. Furthermore, the majority of the coed showers described by interviewees were *supplements* rather than replacements of the traditional shower. All but one of the coed showers described by interviewees were given for women who also had a women-only bridal shower. Thus, the bridal shower remains a ritual in which femininity is enacted and where women are expected to perform or support traditional roles.

Chapter 4

Something Borrowed and Blue

The Bachelorette Party

It is the fall of 1998 and I am attending a friend's bachelorette party. When I walk into Anna's house on the night of her party, the first thing I see is a long white veil on a hanger. On closer inspection, I notice that about thirty silk rosettes have been sewn onto it. Anna's sister, Lynn, the maid of honor, is standing by the sink struggling with a jug, several bottles, and some fruit juice. When I ask what she is making, she smiles mischievously and says it's a little something for the ride. We will be going to one of Anna friend's houses where we will have a "pre-party" before heading out to a nightclub. I find Anna upstairs, applying her makeup, getting ready for the night. We talk for a while about wedding plans until a couple of the other women arrive, and then it is time to go to Sara's house for the pre-party. As we leave, Anna's sister-in-law whispers to me, "So are there going to be strippers?" I shrug because I honestly do not know. Although there has been talk of surprising Anna with a stripper, I haven't been informed of the official plans. Lynn rushes us outside into the car.

When we get to Sara's house, there is a spread of food arranged on the table: cheese and crackers, vegetables and dip, chips and salsa. Sara offers all of us beverages. Anna, who is notoriously a lightweight when it comes to alcohol, starts with a glass of blush wine. Someone distracts Anna in the kitchen when her other sister-in-law, Michelle, arrives weighted down with shopping bags and motions for us to follow her into the living room. She dumps the contents of the bags on the couch and out fall boxes of condoms, edible underwear, a water-gun-shaped like a penis, and a huge phallic-shaped water bottle. She gives Lynn the water bottle. Lynn goes back into the kitchen, where Anna is, takes Anna's cup of wine, and dumps it into the water bottle. "You have to drink out of this the rest of the night," she announces. We all laugh. Anna shrugs, then takes a long sip out of the bottle, making a face as if doing so arouses her. We laugh harder. Sara and I start blowing up the condoms and then hand them off to another one of Anna's friends, who pins them to Anna's waist. Michelle opens a box that says it is an edible condom (but looks like a fruit roll-up) and tells Anna jokingly that she will have to "eat this off the stripper." Anna looks repulsed.

Eight women are here for the pre-party and two more will meet us at the club. We are Anna's coworkers, friends from high school, or family. The atmosphere is congenial and warm. Anna is smiling, playing along, posing for pictures with the penis-shaped water gun between her legs. By the time we are finished with her she is certainly a sight, covered with condoms, holding the water gun and drinking from the penis-shaped bottle, with her pretty white veil flowing down her back. She is innocent and guilty, exemplifying dichotomous images of women's sexuality, virgin and whore.

Soon, Sara announces that the limousine has arrived. We have each given Lynn twenty dollars toward the cost of the transportation. We pile in, and once we are on our way, Lynn brings out the jug with the alcoholic punch she concocted at home. She pours some into Anna's bottle. Beer, wine, and the punch are readily available. The married women of the group talk about how they didn't have sex on their wedding nights. They give Anna advice on how life will be different once she is married, making jokes about not having to perform oral sex after their wedding days.

The club is an enormous warehouse-type place, known as a popular dance club in the region. We each pay another twenty dollars to enter, which includes open bar and access to a "private" area. Anna is let in for free. Once inside we make our way across the dance floor and main bar area to a loft, where we can watch the crowd from above and where our own action will later take place. The private section that comes with the bachelorette party package is, in fact, not at all private. There are maybe ten small bar tables and a few stools scattered around each table. Five other groups are also here in this loft area. A couple of the groups are clearly bachelorette parties, as one member of each is wearing a veil. One of Anna's friends who drove separately told us she wasn't sure that she was going to be able to find us when she first came in—the bouncer told her there were eight bachelorette parties taking place at the club that night.

Anna seems to be having a great time. She continues to pose for pictures with her phallic props and with random men who are pushed toward her by women in our group. Maybe an hour after we've arrived, suddenly there is a great commotion. A man who appears to work at the club starts arranging plastic chairs in the center of the loft area—four chairs, lined up next to each other. Although there is no announcement, "Now it is time for the stripper," everyone seems to know that this is what is happening. I look over and see Anna being pulled through the crowd, her expression both fearful and excited. The man sits her down in the empty chair on the end, next to three other women, two with veils and one who I later hear was there for her twenty-first birthday. I make my way in right behind Anna, so I can see what happens. The women swarm in, friends angling to get a good position. The crowd begins to feel more like a unit than groups, like it has an identity of its own.

He emerges from the crowd with authority, dressed as a police officer, carrying a small radio. Anna rolls her eyes as if to say, "Oh god, here it comes." He struts in front of the four women, as if he's inspecting a lineup, nightstick in hand, handcuffs on his belt, police cap, tight black uniform. As he moves past each woman, he asserts his power, slapping the nightstick in his hand, moving it up and down one of the women's legs, handcuffing another to her chair. He stands before Anna, looks her in the eye, and begins to unbutton his shirt slowly, his hips gyrating to the static beat of his radio. Anna cringes, moving back in her chair and the rest of the women of the crowd squeal with delight. He removes his hat, his shirt, and dances around the next woman, straddling her, moving his chest against hers. She shakes her upper body, chair-dancing with him.

He moves quickly, giving only a few seconds of attention to each woman, doing a headstand between one woman's legs, extending his legs over another's shoulders. He takes off his pants, tank top, slaps his belt on the floor like a whip, stripping until he is down to a leopard print thong. Some of the women in the audience lean over and try to touch his rear end, looking as if they've been dared to do so, then jerking their hands away quickly once they manage to make contact, as if they've touched a hot stove.

Anna is expressing the least enthusiasm of the four women, the most resistance. While the other women are touching and squeezing, Anna is squirming in her chair, indicating that she wants to keep her distance. She is not exactly repulsed. She seems amused and curious, laughing and watching wide-eyed as he wiggles his nearly naked rear end in the face of the woman seated next to her. When the performance is finished, Anna jumps up from her chair and rushes over to talk to her friends about what just happened. She seems relieved that it is over. Still in his underwear, the dancer comes up to Anna, puts his arm around her, and gives her a kiss on the cheek. Cameras flash. Later, when he is dressed, he passes out eight-by-ten photos of himself. He signs one for Anna that reads, "Give me a call if things don't work out."

We spend another hour or so in the club, talking, dancing, and drinking. When Anna says she is ready to go, we leave. On the way home we stop at a diner for a two AM breakfast. We talk more about Anna's wedding plans, though in a more subdued way. It seems the time for innuendo has passed, as the conversation turns to Anna's dress, her hair, and other final details. After our early morning meal, the limousine driver makes several stops, leaving us all at our respective meeting points.

This was my first bachelorette party, both as researcher and participant. And though it was certainly unique in some ways, it bore many similarities to the other parties I attended, observed, and was told stories about during my research. Like other brides-to-be, Anna was dared to participate in certain tasks, most of which she did willingly or with only minimal hesitation. She was embarrassed and tentative with the stripper, although she played along with encouragement from and for the enjoyment of her friends. In my subsequent interview with her it was clear she truly had a good time during the evening and relished the bachelorette role and the opportunity to spend time with her friends. There are many elements of this party, and bachelorette parties in general, to be interpreted. What the example above illustrates is that bachelorette parties are sites where women have the opportunity to express themselves sexually, to play with gender roles and traditional conceptions about what men and women "should" do. Bachelorette parties also provide opportunities for women friends and family members, the gender community of peers, to come together and celebrate friendship and status transition. In this chapter, I describe how bachelorette parties are organized, the main ingredients of typical parties, and what women do on bachelorette parties; then I critically evaluate these characteristic elements.

Planning the Party

In contrast to bridal showers, planning of bachelorette parties was usually accomplished by one or two bridesmaids and seemed to take less time and effort. Because fewer people were involved in decision making and because there were not clear norms for what should happen on bachelorette parties, there were fewer disagreements among bridesmaids about how the party should be. Mothers were almost universally uninvolved in the bachelorette party; therefore, their input and the intergenerational conflicts associated with the bridal shower were absent. In a couple of cases, mothers funded bachelorette parties, paying for a hotel room, or in one case a limousine ride and admission to a strip club, though neither of the mothers who did this participated in the actual events. More often, on the rare occasions when mothers did attend, they went to dinner with the group of women and but headed home before the deviance and debauchery began.

Interviewees related far fewer tales of difficulty in organizing bachelorette parties. It seems that many knew how to plan similar get-togethers (without the sexual elements) and likely had done so before, either in college or among their friends. Although not an event governed by formal etiquette or structure, bachelorette parties were usually well organized, and in most cases there was a specific itinerary for the evening. Those who planned the parties made great efforts to see that the night or weekend would be filled with memorable activities. For example, I attended one party where the hostess had a tight time schedule for all events. The pre-party was supposed to last a designated amount of time and included specific games, drinks, and food. Then the intention was to go out to one club for about an hour, then to another for a couple of hours, and then to another for an after-hours kind of experience. The hostess made mention of the schedule several times during the night, noting that we were behind schedule and that we might have to reorganize the itinerary. Reva had a similar experience on her bachelorette party, noting that her maid of honor had the entire weekend detailed. She said, "Every minute of our weekend was planned. . . . Saturday was planned like, boom, get up. Go out and lay in the sun till whatever time, and then [the hostess] left to go get some cocktail stuff and the lingerie party started right at seven o'clock. And that lasted until exactly nine o'clock and then we were out; the cab picked us up at nine o'clock." Mary Jo Deegan (1989) argued that in American society fun is a structured activity that involves following of rules designed to evoke that particular feeling. Rituals are designed to elicit specific sentiments and types of experiences, and the bachelorette party is intended to provide a fun, memorable adventure. Hostesses planned to include elements of the bachelorette party, such as trips to strip clubs, pre-party lingerie showers or games, or visits to different clubs, because they viewed these as components of a good time. By packing the night with activities that should produce fun, hostesses structured the events in ways that they expected would succeed.

Planning was not always simple, given the lack of available information about such parties at the time. Josephine had a hard time planning a friend's party because neither she nor her friends had much prior experience with bachelorette parties. She said, "I didn't really have any friends to consult. . . . I never heard of having a [task] list until [another friend's party a few years later]. I never thought of wearing the veil." This party occurred in the mid-1990s, and so it would seem that, other than asking other friends what to do, there was little available information for Josephine to consult. As Lori described it, her ideas for bachelorette parties came from "word of mouth. You hear what people have done before you, whether that's through older friends you have or from work. Or just seeing them out. Like just being somewhere and being like, 'Oh look at them. That looks like fun.' " Unlike with showers, women rarely turned to their mothers for ideas about bachelorette parties because their mothers had not had them. So, planning was sometimes a challenge for the bridesmaids organizing showers, particularly in the mid-1990s. Since the turn of the century the proliferation of material on the Internet has probably changed this significantly, as there are abundant sources of information available on line.

In a few cases planning did become stressful. Because the bachelorette party was not perceived to be the responsibility or obligation of all of the bridesmaids, the one or two who took on the task were often logistically or financially burdened. This most often occurred with out-of-town bachelorette parties. Nicole planned a party in the city where the bride-to-be was from, but with which she was unfamiliar. Though not the maid of honor, she assumed responsibility when no one else would. She said, "I pretty much planned the whole thing because the maid of honor basically said to me, 'I'm not a planner, I don't plan anything. If we're going to plan anything, you have to do it.' . . . I've never been to [this city]. I don't know what to plan, so I'm taking everybody's word for it." After talking to different people she organized an itinerary only to be told the day of the party that what she had planned was not acceptable because the area where she planned to go was rumored to be somewhat dangerous. "[The bride] finds out where we were going to go and she doesn't want to go. And I'm like why did all of these people ask me to do everything when all of a sudden that day everyone was like no, and everybody knew what we were doing. I had times set. I had done all of this on e-mail and the phone and I was—I was a little frustrated. I had made the veil. I had gotten presents. I had made up games and now nobody wants to do anything. . . . It was very frustrating for me, very frustrating. I put a lot of time into planning it, and we didn't do anything that I planned." Though few other women reported similar experiences, Nicole certainly was disappointed that her efforts were disregarded and unappreciated by others. A couple of other women experienced difficulties planning bachelorette parties when they assumed the responsibility of paying for hotel rooms or dinners with the expectation that other guests would contribute their share at a later time. Heather, who organized several bachelorette parties for her friends, encountered two situations where women who were slow to pay her back owed her money. In one case, Heather said, "Dinner was like four hundred dollars, and I just paid for that and asked everyone to write me checks for their amount, and [one woman] wouldn't send her twenty-two dollar check. And it just became a four-month drawn-out thing." Fortunately, few women had these types of problems, and overall bachelorette party planning was described as far less stressful or overwhelming than shower planning, primarily because of the informality of the party and the lack of tradition governing its format.

Sex, Drinks, and Just Girls: Characteristic Elements of the Bachelorette Party

Most of the women I interviewed had given or attended bachelorette parties that included three common elements: alcohol, a sex theme, and a gender-homogeneous guest list. Only 1 of the 141 parties described by interviewees included a man as a guest. Although men sometimes acted as designated drivers and were usually involved in the party itself in the form of strippers or random men, the invited participants were mostly friends of the bride-to-be and some family members such as sisters, cousins, or, occasionally, mothers. Grooms were never involved or present during bachelorette parties or pre-parties; however, members of the groom's family, sisters or cousins, sometimes attended as they were often part of the wedding party. Though in some cases the bride-to-be's friendship with the groom's sister predated or even prompted the couple's relationship, in other cases some were uncomfortable witnessing the deviant behavior of their future family member. For example, Gina attended her future sister-in-law's bachelorette party and became upset when she "saw [the bride] dancing with a guy. She didn't do anything like kiss him or anything but I was just kind of like, uh. . . . I guess when you are going out with your soon-to-be sister-in-law who is going to be mother to your nieces and nephews, it's kind of hard to watch all of that." Some women also seemed to feel awkward given the graphic sex talk common at bachelorette parties and uncomfortable thinking about their brothers as sexual beings or hearing details of their sex lives. Bryn attended a bachelorette party where this happened: "Her fiancé's sisters were at dinner. . . . She got really drunk at dinner, talking about the first time she had sex, which was totally bizarre because her fiancé's sisters were like, by then, didn't want to know." Overall, groom's family members were not regular members of the bachelorette party unless they were part of the wedding party, and few brides-to-be expressed discomfort with their attendance. It seems that given the bride's alcohol consumption and level of comfort surrounded by her closest friends, if anyone was uneasy it was the fiancé's family members, although this did not seem to be common.

Bachelorette parties also always included alcohol consumption. Eighty-three percent of parties were described as consisting of heavy drinking, with a bride-to-be who was intoxicated by the end of the night. Every party that I observed took place at a bar or club, and most started with a pre-party at someone's home, where the drinking began. Drinking was a critical element of the bachelorette party because it created a convivial atmosphere and eased women into participating in the deviant activity expected of them (Montemurro and McClure 2005). As

Bridget McClure and I noted, women expected alcohol to alter their behavior and their mood so that they would not be self-conscious or uptight during these events. Gina, for example, said that alcohol is a part of bachelorette parties because "you're more apt to have fun. Like lose inhibitions and this is supposed to be the last wild night. If you weren't drinking, there's more of a chance of that not happening." And Shannon commented that drinking is a part of a bachelorette party "to make people loosen up and less inhibited. Lightens the atmosphere. Makes you more susceptible to doing the things you do at bachelorette parties that you wouldn't normally do sober. You play games, have a better time with the stripper, and [are] more free when you're dancing, . . . more sociable." These women acknowledged that their behavior under the influence of alcohol was different than when sober and that they would not or would be much less likely to engage in the play of the bachelorette party without having consumed alcohol. These statements thus suggest that women viewed alcohol as a substance that could heighten their enjoyment of the party by enabling them to participate wholly in its activities. Part of full participation in some bachelorette parties included being a good sport about being dressed up in a veil or completing dares like asking random men for their boxer shorts. Thus, drinking enabled women to go along with and even enjoy doing things that they claimed they would not do when sober. This was particularly true for the bride-to-be. As Reva said, "It's just a lot easier to go around with a . . . veil on if you've had a few in you. I couldn't imagine being completely sober on a bachelorette party, especially if you're the bachelorette."

Finally, a sexual theme was usually a part of bachelorette parties. In this sample, all of the parties observed and 81 percent (115) of those described by interviewees contained a sexual element or theme. Hiring exotic dancers, decorating the bride-to-be with condoms or plastic penis-shaped items, flirtation with men strangers, and sexualized games were common elements of the parties that I observed as well as those of most of the women interviewed. At many of the bachelorette parties, either during the pre-party or out at dinner, the bride-to-be was presented with sexualized gifts. At two of the bachelorette parties I observed and participated in the brides were given edible underwear, massage oil, penis-shaped pasta, books like *One Hundred Nights of Great Sex*, a penis-shaped water gun, a penis-shaped thermos, and condoms. On a basic

4.1. Pre-party games: Embarrassing the bride with risqué "mad libs"

level this essential element can be understood as related to bachelorette parties' evolution from bachelor parties, the stereotypic purpose of which was to allow a groom-to-be a last night of sexual freedom. This will be discussed in depth throughout this chapter.

A Typology of Bachelorette Parties

Bachelorette parties can be categorized into several dominant forms. While there may be other activities that occur at bachelorette parties, my observational and interview data indicate that there are four main types of bachelorette parties. I call these "Girls' Night In," "Girls' Night Out," "The Women's Bachelor Party," and "Anything Goes." It is helpful to distinguish between types of bachelorette parties to determine the frequency of each type in this research. These different types of bachelorette parties can also be seen as points on a continuum of excessiveness or deviance. The Girls' Night In contained the smallest amount of deviant behavior and the Anything Goes type of party contained the most.

Girls' Night In

The least common type of bachelorette party was labeled Girls' Night In. Of the bachelorette parties described by interviewees, six (4 percent) could be described as this type of party. These parties took place in one location and resembled a girls' slumber party in which a group of women (the smallest of these was four women, the largest about ten) met at someone's home and ate, drank, played games, and told stories. At three of these parties the women stayed in because the bride-to-be (in one case) or some of the guests were under twenty-one and thus were unable to go out to a nightclub or a place where alcohol would be served. Only one of these parties included a stripper. Other reasons for staying in included bad weather or lack of finances. Some interviewees described these parties as "mellow or boring." One recent bride's friends planned this type of party because the bride-to-be was not a big drinker and was not interested in a stripper.

Although some women challenged the idea of the Girls' Night In as a "real" bachelorette party, for others it was an ideal way to spend quality time with girlfriends. For example, Joanna's bridesmaids threw her a laid-back bachelorette party weekend, which involved renting a condominium in the mountains, where they stayed in and spent time talking and reminiscing. She described it as a very special time for her:

> I made it quite clear to my bridal party—they pretty much knew by knowing me—that I didn't want to do anything outrageous. I didn't want to go to a strip club; I didn't want a stripper, you know, nothing like that. For me it was more important just having the girls get away and, you know, have total quality time and hang out. . . . [My bridesmaids] rented out a condo [in a ski resort town]. . . . And it was really nice. . . . It seems like a lot of time we're all so caught up in our jobs and you know. . . . So for me, I was just very happy because obviously these are very important people in my life and I was like, 'I'm so excited that we get to go away and we get to spend that time together.' So we drove up, and we did like little—we played board games; we drank; we made brownies; we did our nails; we watched . . . all of these movies that had bride themes. . . . We did girl stuff.

For Joanna, like most women, it was important to have the bachelorette party be primarily about a last night of quality time with "the girls" rather than a last night of sexual freedom. In fact, regardless of the type of party they had, most women mentioned that spending time with friends was the best part of the night. Because women demonstrate their friendship through sharing with one another (Oliker 2001), the Girls' Night In party gives women space to do so as they tell stories about and recollect their shared past. As Tom Driver has suggested, one of the "gifts" of ritual is to bring people together, to reinforce bonds among members of the community, to "unite them emotionally" (1991, 152). While most women who marry retain their friendship networks, for many the amount of time spent with friends changes after the wedding day. Joanna had lived with her bridesmaids during and after college, and so, for all of them, this was a real separation and change in terms of the frequency of contact. The bachelorette party can be seen then as a way of both acknowledging the change in relationship and mourning it. By coming together women reinforce their ties to one another, they strengthen their bonds by reminiscing about the past while at the same time implicitly accepting their soon to be redefined friendships. Gina communicated this in explaining why she would want to have a bachelorette party when she marries: "You share so much with friends, but you rarely get to have all of them together, to be there. And it's fun to just sit there and be excited and talk about all of the different things. . . . I think it's fun, even for the single girls, to sit there and kind of dream with her and just hang out." While most bachelorette parties include some activities that implicitly facilitate bonding among women friends, the Girls' Night In party places the most emphasis on this and involves more explicit reflection on relationships.

Girls' Night Out

One of the more popular types of bachelorette parties was the Girls' Night Out. This party involved going to a bar, restaurant, or dance club. The Girls' Night Out was often similar to a regular night out with women friends. The bride was rarely dressed up in any fashion (e.g., with a veil). Similarly, she was usually not made to carry around any type of phallic items, and the sex theme, though usually present in some form, was minimized. In some cases, at the beginning of the night, women gave risqué gifts such as massage lotion, books with sexual advice, or sex toys. But these were usually left behind when the party changed locations. While drinking was common and an important element of the party, like the Girls' Night In the focus was usually equally, if not more so, on spending quality time with friends. One-third of the parties (forty-seven) described by interviewees fell into this category. Women who had Girls' Night Out bachelorette parties went out to dinner and then to one or two bars for a few drinks. These bachelorette parties were seen as "tame" according to interviewees. Still, these parties were relatively common. It is important to acknowledge the prevalence of these parties because they are contrary to the stereotype or image of the bachelorette party. Several women mentioned that bachelorette parties were (or at least should be) designed with the bride's personality in mind, consistent with the cultural rhetoric that instructs women not to feel it necessary to do what men do (see chapter 2). Some interviewees suggested that the women who had Girls' Night Out parties were more "laid back" or "mellow" and so these parties were more their style. Samantha, for example, a twenty-five-year-old woman in a serious relationship, described her ideal bachelorette party as a Girls' Night Out: "I think I'd like something calm. I'd like to go out to dinner, I think . . . just kind of hanging around bonding, talking, just doing whatever, maybe shopping." Samantha saw such a celebration as consistent with her personality, and she thought of bachelorette parties as a time to share with close friends.

The Women's Bachelor Party

The Women's Bachelor Party was a copy of the stereotypical bachelor party. The image of the bachelor party, as discussed by interviewees, was that it nearly always included a stripper. Thus, in the Women's Bachelor Party women tried to replicate what they perceived men did on bachelor parties by either going to a strip club or hiring a stripper to perform in someone's home or hotel room. Thirty-five (approximately 25 percent) of the parties described were characterized as Women's Bachelor Parties.

Carol's bachelorette party would be described as a Women's Bachelor Party. At Carol's party, about eight women met at a bridesmaid's house and had drinks and snacks while waiting for the main event. Somewhat unbeknownst to Carol, a stripper had been hired to come and give her a private dance.[1] She described what happened when the stripper arrived:

> I guess after maybe an hour . . . the doorbell rang. And [the hostess's] husband is a cop . . . and somebody came to the door and nobody

> wanted to answer it. And one friend got stuck answering and said to the hostess, "I think it's for you." And she said, "It's a cop." . . . I just assumed it was somebody her husband worked with or somebody that really was a cop 'cause I wasn't expecting it then. . . . I said, "Shit, I am so sorry I asked for this because I am way too sober and mortified." So everybody ran away [*laughs*] and left me standing there, and he told me I better chug my wine. And he sat me down in a chair, handcuffed me . . . and, uh, everybody sat in the back, laughing at me, pointing at me, leaving me there mortified . . . and [he], uh, stripped and danced, and I barely touched [*laughs*] anything. He made me touch his chest.

In this example, Carol's friends imitated the idea of the bachelor party by having the focal activity of the evening be the exotic dancer. While the party continued afterwards—Carol and her friends went out to a bar where she was encouraged to drink heavily via a straw with a plastic penis on it—it was clear that the stripper was the highlight of the night. Some of the guests did not go out to the bar, but left after the stripper performed his routine.

Some women went to a male strip club for their Women's Bachelor Parties. There were two major male strip clubs observed during this research, one in the Northeast, the Hideaway, and one in the South, the Regal Room. Interviewees identified these places as popular sites for bachelorette parties. And in my observational research this was clearly evident. For example, during one night of observation at the Regal Room in August of 1999, I observed eighteen bachelorette parties over the course of three hours. I reported in my field notes: "By 10:00 PM the place really started to fill up. Another half a dozen bachelorette parties came in, easily identified by their veils. . . . After that the bachelorettes began coming in so quickly I was losing track of all of them. Some came and left quickly. Most seemed to come in after 11:00. There were two wearing hats that said bride, one had a veil attached to the back of it. . . . Another one just had a ribbon that said bride. One was wearing a button that said bride-to-be."

At the Hideaway bachelorette parties were given special treatment. The dancers paid extra attention to these women since these groups made up a large portion of their clientele. Most of the bachelorette parties that took place at male strip clubs, as described by interviewees, included a private dance or lap dance either on stage, at the table, or in a private area. Both the Hideaway and the Regal Room had private VIP rooms. I observed bachelorettes entering these areas with dancers, always accompanied by their friends. Descriptions of other strip clubs suggested the same type of area was present in other clubs in other cities. Several women who hosted or attended Women's Bachelor Parties said that they gave the bride-to-be single dollar bills and encouraged her to tip the dancers when they approached. Not surprisingly, when I asked women for their image of the typical bachelorette party, most described the Women's Bachelor Party. However, many bachelorette parties did not include strippers.

Anything Goes

The final type of bachelorette party was by far filled with the most deviant behavior. While I was surprised by some of the interactions between women and strippers, as described above, I was equally amazed by some of the activities of what I call Anything Goes bachelorette parties. I labeled this type of party Anything Goes because there was little that was off limits for the bride-to-be's task list and the activities of the night. Based on descriptions from interviewees and my observations, these parties included very heavy drinking, where shots of alcohol were often consumed and the bride-to-be and many of the guests were described as or observed to be quite intoxicated. All of these parties featured a bride-to-be who was dressed up in some way, usually so that she was identifiable as a bride and with some type of phallic or sexual paraphernalia strewn about her. Brides-to-be wore veils or hats or white ribbons in their hair, white T-shirts, or T-shirts printed with phrases like "Jane's bachelorette party" or "Jane's final fling." During my observation in clubs like the Regal Room, I noted, in my field notes, the various costumes that brides-to-be wore:

> [One] bride-to-be was . . . given a veil to put on. She also had a ball and chain around her wrist, the ball said "bride" on it. . . . I could see two [brides-to-be] who were wearing veils with condoms on them. Lots of condoms. One had the condoms in their wrappers, the other had opened multi-colored condoms all over it. Another

> [bride-to-be] sitting at the bar had a kind of see-through chemise on over a short black dress. The chemise had like feathers in it. She had a penis straw that she was drinking out of. . . . A bachelorette party came in and sat at the bar next to us. This bride was wearing a veil and the veil was decorated with multi-colored condoms, opened. Then she also had on a T-shirt that said, on the back in glittery, puffy paint, "A Buck for a Suck" and had multicolored lifesavers taped all over it. . . . She also had penis straws, which were regular . . . straws with penis-shaped tips on them. And she was carrying a white book that looked like a photo album that said, "[Her name]'s last stand, yeah right" in letters cut out of magazines.

On many parties brides-to-be were required to carry around phallic paraphernalia. At the Regal Room, in addition to the penis straws, I noticed quite a few phallic-shaped drinking devices, some like the one Anna used at her party and other similar variations. Josephine described how a friend was decorated on her bachelorette party: "We did make her wear a veil and . . . we all wore matching shirts for the day, saying, 'Jane's bachelorette party,' and we made her wear one. And we made her wear penis glasses and eat penis gummies and we made her carry penis mug. She had to wear a penis around her neck. Oh, it was horrible [*laughs*] what the maid of honor did to her!" These parties were the most common of any of the four types of bachelorette parties described by interviewees. Fifty-four (38 percent) of bachelorette parties would be described as Anything Goes.

The Anything Goes party often included strippers, like at the Women's Bachelor Party; however, the stripper was not the main event but rather an element of the party, something that added to the wild and festive atmosphere of deviance and play. The Anything Goes bachelorette party involved barhopping, where women patronized several different types of drinking establishments like taverns, large nightclubs, (both male and female) drag clubs, strip clubs, and, in a few cases, S and M clubs. These parties also often featured a scavenger hunt or task list. The scavenger hunt was a list of tasks or dares for the bride-to-be to complete during her party. Common tasks included receiving a dance from a stripper, drinking a shot of a sexually named drink such as Sex on the Beach, kissing a man with the same name as the bride's fiancé, obtaining a con-

4.2. Completing a bachelorette party task: Removing the tag from a random man's briefs

dom, asking a man for his boxer shorts or a tag from his underwear, dancing on stage or singing with a band, and having men sign the bride's shirt or some part of her body. Completion of this list often required approaching strange men, interacting with strippers, and almost always some form of ritualized embarrassment. Usually, the bridesmaids or party attendees helped the bride in acquiring the materials she needed, and often this provided an excuse for single women to approach men in bars or clubs. Claire described the task list completed at a recent bachelorette party. She said, "[The bride-to-be] had to get a condom, get a kiss from a guy named [same as her fiancé], and she did have to get a pair of boxers–that was interesting." I asked her if the bride-to-be got them. Claire laughed, "Yeah, yeah. He took them off right there in the parking lot."

What is interesting about this type of party is the degree of intimacy the bride-to-be is expected to share with strangers. At one bachelorette party described by an interviewee, one of the bride-to-be's tasks was to have a certain number of men sign her underwear—while she was wearing them. While this activity did result in the bride-to-be being ejected from a club (when she pulled up her dress to allow a man to sign her underwear), the closeness necessary to successfully perform this task is apparent. Even the comparatively tame activity of approaching strange men and asking for their phone number or business card seems to require the bride to attain a level of intimacy that a person in a committed relationship would not consider doing at other times. Many of the tasks were like this in that they involved a faux "pickup" or flirtation characteristic of a single woman looking for a man. Asking men for kisses or boxer shorts—approaching men strangers at all—is a suggestive activity and one that women saw as a critical part of the Anything Goes party because it was a way of symbolically articulating the idea that this is the bride's last night of freedom. Even if the bride had no regrets about commitment or monogamy, it was important for her to pretend or go along with the idea that she would miss flirting with or having sexual relationships with other men because doing so expressed equal status with men. In a way that was not that explicit or even conscious, it seems that women's participation in these activities, particularly as a part of the Anything Goes and Women's Bachelor Parties, was a way of resisting sexual repression or the idea that women should not express their sexuality in public.

Like Anna's party, summarized above, another one of the bachelorette parties I observed and participated in would be described as Anything Goes. This party occurred in a large Northeastern city. The night began with a pre-party at the maid of honor's apartment, where we snacked on appetizer foods and the bride and guests consumed wine, margaritas, beer, and Jell-O shots. Though no one was specifically watching television, the film *My Best Friend's Wedding* was playing in the background. The seven guests were friends from college, work, and high school, all of whom were about the same age as the bride. While people ate, there was talk about plans for the wedding, specifically, what the bridesmaids' dresses were like. After we ate, the hostess told us that we were going to play a game, and she had the bride sit down on the couch and the rest of us sat in a circle facing her. She directed the bride to close her eyes and then produced a veil on a headband that she had made. She put the veil on the bride, who knew from its feel what was happening and remarked, "I'm not going to wear this all night. Do I have to wear this all night?" To which the maid of honor replied, "Yes, you do" (and she did). The maid of honor then presented the bride with gifts, including a book about sexual techniques, which the bride read portions of out loud, and "dirty dice," which have instructions for different sexual activities depending on how they are rolled. There was a lot of joking about sex, with some of the single women making comments about how long it had been since they had been intimate with a man. The next activity was a game where the bride-to-be was expected to answer questions about her future husband, such as What is his favorite movie or favorite song? Where did he go to high school? and What did he wear on their first date? Each of the guests was given an index card with a question and answer on it. We were each to ask the bride the question, and if the bride was correct, she received a prize. If she was incorrect, we received the prize. This game was a lot of fun and involved a great deal of laughter and joking among the women. Several women complimented the hostess of the inclusion of this game and remarked how they liked that it gave the bride and her friends a chance to learn little things about the groom-to-be. When the game was over, we talked for a long time, reminiscing about college and high school. Although the hostess had planned for the first stop of the night to be a local strip club, she discarded the idea when she realized that everyone was having a really good time talking and playing games at home. She had made a reservation to see the first show of the evening at that club, but noted that we missed the chance to do that. One woman expressed her disappointment about that, saying that she had never been to a strip club and was really looking forward to seeing what it was all about. With that plan abandoned, we left the apartment and took taxicabs to a popular bar area. The club we went to was located in a huge warehouse with five distinct areas with different themes. For example, on the waterfront was a "beach" area, complete with a sand volleyball court. Inside there were jazz rooms, a dueling piano area, and a large techno-music dance room. This club was like going to several different clubs in that the atmosphere of each room was different. When we first arrived in the club, the bride-to-be, aided by her friends, ordered drinks. While waiting for the drinks, she and several of the other women in the group drank shots of liquor. After the drinks arrived, the bride-to-be was given several tasks to do. The first was to find and kiss a man with

4.3. Bachelorette party games: Suck for a Buck

the same name as her fiancé. Her friends, particularly the single ones, started approaching men they thought were attractive and asking them their names. Finally, the bride-to-be found a man with the right name, verified by her friends, who examined the man's drivers license, and she kissed him on the cheek. Although the maid of honor, who planned the party, had ideas for other tasks, the group became quite caught up in the dueling piano bar and then went to the dance room and danced for a while. Relatively early in the night, the bride got sick and the party ended without the intended visits to other bars.

On other Anything Goes parties women described brides kissing men strangers, men taking off their underwear to give to brides-to-be, and women removing men's brief tags with their teeth, doing body shots, patronizing strip clubs, and receiving lap dances. Additionally, I observed a few women having their stomachs or chests signed by men or touching a stripper's genitalia or having the men's genitalia touch them in a direct, skin-to-skin manner. There were also several intimate, sexualized games that women played on Anything Goes bachelorette parties. The popular Suck for a Buck, also documented as a standard party element in Atlantic Canada (Tye and Powers 1998), involved women wearing a shirt covered with hard candy. The idea of this game is that men pay the bride-to-be a dollar to suck a piece of candy from her shirt. At her sister-in-law's bachelorette party, Anna watched this play out: "She had to wear a T-shirt and it had candies, hard candies, taped all over it. At the end of the night she had to have all of the hard candy off. And each hard candy had to be taken off by a different guy—for the most part with his mouth. That's what she had to do." Ashley suggested that Suck for a Buck resulted in some humorous moments captured on film because of the compromising positions it involved. "Some of the pictures we got in the bar are really funny. I got this one, this guy's biting this lifesaver and it's like a little below her belly button, like right crotch level, so he's down there with his face like on her crotch like biting off this lifesaver." This game can be viewed as comical, sexualized, and humiliating, and brides expressed such reactions to it. Some enjoyed the attention and played it up, others seemed uncomfortable with it, and a few refused to play along altogether—wearing the shirt for pictures and then taking it off before they went out or soon after arriving at a club. As a sort of variation on Suck for a Buck, a couple of women went on parties where the bride-to-be was given a candy necklace to wear. As Kristen recalled, "We had candy necklaces and I think people were supposed to eat the candy necklace off." Her friend Jane, who I interviewed at the same time, added, "Right. A guy paid a dollar and he got to bite her necklace." Like the faux-pickup, Suck for a Buck is very suggestive and intimate and is something that most people would rarely do under other circumstances for these reasons, as well as for the fact that it would be seen as deviant, overly promiscuous, and probably embarrassing to do so without a legitimate excuse.

The Anything Goes bachelorette party was described as "wild," "fun," and "naughty" by interviewees. Binge drinking, sexualized interaction, and ritualized embarrassment were all elements of the Anything Goes bachelorette party. Additionally, this type of bachelorette party was characterized by liminal deviance, which I discuss further below. While most women who participated in these parties reported enjoying them and having a lot of fun, several of the single or engaged women reported a lack of interest in having such a party themselves. Kate (single and twenty-seven) explained why: "I think they're silly. I'd like to go out to dinner with my friends and maybe even do a cooking class, something in that regard. But not going to bars and getting drunk. No." Jorden suggested that while she knows the bachelorette party planning would be out of her hands, she would be sure to make it clear that the Anything Goes type is not for her: "[I] would be particular about not doing things like body shots off of strange men. I'd rather it just be kind of a bunch of girls getting together." When I asked her why, she replied, "It doesn't really seem like my personality to—I've always been kind of shy. I don't like being the center of attention, so I don't know if I'd really like being put in that situation." Finally, Hilary suggested that what she would most like to do for her bachelorette party would be to have her girlfriends get together for a paint-your-own-pottery party and then to go out for a nice dinner. She said she wanted a party that was "kind of simple, maybe wear the veil to dinner, 'cause that's sort of fun. But, um, not really other crazy stuff." I asked her if she had a need for strippers or heavy drinking. She said, "No, no, not at all. . . . Without the stripper—just going out and getting me to drink or drawing attention to the fact that I'm getting married. I could see a night like that taking place, but not as my key bachelorette evening." Hilary's image of her party is that it should be a time when she brings her friends together. Although she could picture a night out on the town, it is interesting that she would not want such an outing to be her "key bachelorette evening." What these comments suggest, like Joanna's and Gina's above, is that women look at the bachelorette party as a night for coming together as friends and recognizing the importance of their peers. Women's relationships are of crucial importance, and women want those close to them to support them during this major status transition. Perhaps on some level, women are ambivalent about the changing nature of their friendships and recognize marriage as a threat to relationships that they have cherished. This is not to say that women lose, abandon, or are abandoned by their friends when they get married, but that there are changes in relationships after marriage that may be subtle in some cases, dramatic in others. And the bachelorette party provides a forum to ritually express conflicting emotions about this transformation.

A Note on Age

Although there was not much variation in age in my sample, it seems that age did have an influence on what type of bachelorette party women had or wanted. Colleen, in her early thirties, made this comment about age, "As I get older they're taking it on a different tone. It's more of a more becoming let's go to a bar and talk with my friends, or like this is what I want to do; I just want to hang out and be a little mature. . . . I think when you're younger you're in more of a party atmosphere [like] college; you've had sisters or brothers [get married]; you've started to see what they're all about. And the tendency there is to be a little more immature and reckless or whatever. As you get older, you don't want to stay out as late. A lot of times people at bachelorette parties have children . . . at home and husbands and responsibilities on the weekends that they can't afford to be shut out all weekend." Other women expressed similar thoughts. Bryn, in her mid-twenties and engaged at the time of the interview, said she was not having a bachelorette party: "I've done it. Like that was my life for a long time [*laughs*]. So both my friends from high school and my friends from college, we've all been out drinking together a hundred times and don't really have a need to do it."

Many of the single or engaged women in their late twenties or early thirties commented that they might have wanted a different type of bachelorette party had they been younger when they got married. Kristen, a recently engaged woman of twenty-nine, said that if she had any type of bachelorette party, she would want it to be more of the Girls' Night Out than the other "more excessive" types. She said, "If I was twenty-one I might be like, 'Let's go and get ripped and get a limo.' But–not that I'm old, but I've done it. I've seen it. I don't know if I'd feel different if I was younger, but it's like I don't want to go to those clubs and say I'm the bachelorette and people be like, 'Wow, look how old she is. Look at that old lady getting married.' " And Robin, a single woman in her late twenties, remarked that if she gets married when she's older than thirty she doesn't want to have a bachelorette party because she thinks it would seem "silly." Her comment reflected the similar idea of having outgrown the bachelorette party and the activities commonly or stereotypically associated with it.

More Than a Fling: Analyzing the Bachelorette Party

Organizing a wedding is time-consuming, often stressful, work (Currie 1993). The bachelorette party is a time away from the constraints of everyday life, from the anxiety of wedding planning. Philip Rieff (1966) noted that modern life is characterized by periods of restraint, where formality constrains behavior, and release, where one is able to "let her hair down," to let go. The bridal shower and the wedding ceremony would be periods of restraint, but the bachelorette party is definitely a time of release. Women are expected to lose their inhibitions, to unwind, and some have argued that this is a much welcomed experience after the stress of wedding planning (Tye and Powers 1998). It is a time to express excitement and joy about marriage. It is also seen as an appropriate time for playing with the ideas of commitment and the sanctioning of sex within marriage. In this section, I discuss the meanings underlying behavior common at bachelor parties. Primarily, I focus on the actions of those at the Women's Bachelor Party, Girls' Night Out, and Anything Goes parties, as they were the most popular types (comprising 96 percent of all parties) and featured the common elements of alcohol and, in more than 80 percent of the cases, sexual innuendo or play. Though I acknowledge that not all women engage in this type of behavior at bachelorette parties, the majority of the parties I observed and attended and those described by the women I interviewed met these criteria. Furthermore, popular cultural representations, print media coverage, and planning guides for bachelorette parties often present the bachelorette party as such.

Deviance and Liminality

For some women, the deviant activity consistent at bachelorette parties—going to see strippers, kissing or flirting with strange men, getting intoxicated—was part of the fun. John Lofland (1969) suggested that some deviance is performed for the fun or thrill generated from participating in what he called "the adventurous deviant act." He wrote, "Some kinds of prohibited activities are claimed by some parts of the population to be *in themselves* fun, exciting, and adventurous. More than simply deriving pleasant fearfulness from violating the prohibition per se, there can exist claims that the prohibited activity itself produces a pleasant level of excitation" (Lofland 1969, 109). Drinking was clearly fun for many of the women at bachelorette parties. Brides-to-be were more comfortable engaging in embarrassing and otherwise deviant acts, such as being dressed up in a costume or watching a dance by a stripper, when they had con-

4.4. Friends buy a bride-to-be shots of alcohol

sumed a substance that made them less self-conscious. Dwight Heath suggested that because alcohol is associated with lowered inhibitions, it is sometimes used as an excuse to deviate: "Others who claim to drink, 'just to get drunk' or 'to be totally out of it' subsequently take great pleasure in recounting their outlandish behavior, suggesting that they may . . . have been drinking primarily in order to misbehave while enjoying the temporary suspension of certain social expectations (time-out) that is often accorded to the inebriate" (2000, 171). Though for some women the subsequent hangover was described as the worst part of the party, it was clear that drinking with friends and feeling the effects of alcohol were quite pleasurable. Alcohol is associated with increased sociability and solidarity (Trice 1966), and this heightened feeling of camaraderie was enjoyable for and important to women on bachelorette parties.

Since play is seen as time off or time out from the responsibilities of everyday life and adulthood, the focus on having a good time or giving the bride-to-be a night she will never forget may imply that she sacrifices this type of play when she is married. Play, particularly in the form of binge drinking and having a "girls' night," is associated with youthfulness and a more carefree lifestyle. To some extent, the freedom to do this frequently is something that is given up upon marriage. The idea of going all out for the bachelorette party can be explained in part, then, by the idea that this is the bride's last chance to free herself of urges to do so in the future. As Jamie, aged twenty-eight and engaged, noted, "Your bachelorette party is supposed to be a crazy, uninhibited time, and you're supposed to act like you wouldn't normally act. . . . [I]t's kind of like your free pass for the night. . . . As we become adults, we don't do that, and we can't because we have to get up the next morning. We have to go to work. . . . Like every other night, you really can't because—not because you have a husband at home, but because you have a job or you have kids." For many women this transition from single to married is not merely that but also a symbolic transition from childhood to adulthood. Since we do not have any secular rituals expressly designated to mark this status passage, exactly when this transition is completed is ambiguous. Not only is marriage about the union of two individuals; it also functions as recognition of adulthood. In this sense, the drinking and play of the bachelorette party are opportunities for brides-to-be to act not as children or responsible adults, but somewhere in between.

There is little doubt that the activities engaged in at bachelorette parties are defined as deviant by the participants in this ritual because this is exactly the point of these parties. Although some women called their own behavior "bad" or "naughty," they did so while grinning, seemingly proud of their transgressions because such acts meant they had accomplished the goals of the bachelorette party. However, a couple of women said they felt regret for what happened or described friends who felt guilty about what they did on their bachelorette parties. April, for example, described the aftermath of a friend's bachelorette party in which pictures were taken of the bride-to-be kissing random men. She described her friend's feelings of remorse, saying "When she showed me the photos at work the next week and she had to censor them for her fiancé, you know, I think she felt bad about that. I'm sure there's a lot worse things that happen at bachelorette parties then just kissing a couple of guys because your friends egg you on to do it. I'm sure horrible things happen. But she felt guilty, I think, about that part of it. I think overall she had a good time . . . but I do think she had a little bit of regret."

Most women, however, recognized their behavior as deviant but felt it was excused or legitimated within the context of the bachelorette party. David Matza (1969) argued that all members of society have periods of nonconformity and, as a result, develop justifications or accounts in order to explain why they violate the norms, rules, and laws of society at certain points in their lives. Matza argued that we all "drift" in and out of conformity; yet, we still like to consider ourselves conforming, moral members of society. Since these deviant acts are subject to evaluation and judgment by others, when otherwise rule-following members of society deviate, they account for or defend their rule or norm breaking by using what Sykes and Matza (1957) called "techniques of neutralization." Jamie employed the "denial of responsibility" technique in her comment above when she called the bachelorette party a "free pass," indicating that because it is the bride's special night, she is not responsible for her actions. One way women employed this technique was by saying that their actions were the result of their friends' pressure or instruction. The friends at the bachelorette party create the task list or scavenger hunt and the bachelorette, as the submissive initiate, knows it is her duty to play along. Pam, for example, was instructed to have two dozen men sign her shirt. When her fiancé saw her shirt after the bachelorette party and asked about it, she responded, "Hey, it wasn't my doing." April, who was quoted above regarding the guilt her friend felt after her bachelorette party, defended her friend, explaining to me that her behavior was not really her fault. She said, "I mean she was forced to wear and do these things, but she's such an easy going person that she just went along with it. . . . She has this group of friends and they do a lot of things together, and I guess a few of them were married and they had gone through this exact same thing, so they were determined to put [this bride] through it all. . . . But it was very familiar and there was a whole set way they had to do all of this." In this case, April attempted to neutralize her friend's deviant behavior by suggesting that she did what she did because her friends pressured her to do so. Related to this, the bachelorette party calls attention to the transitory or liminal status of the bride-to-be at this point in time. Victor Turner argued that liminality is when one is between statuses, and those who experience it "elude or slip through the network of classifications that normally locate states and positions in cultural space. Liminal entities are neither here nor there; they are betwixt and between" (1969, 95). At the bachelorette party the bride-to-be is no longer single but not yet married. She is spoken for but not legally committed. As Tye and Powers suggested, part of the successful bachelorette role is the communal understanding that "while she is available, she is not available" (1998, 58). Because of this special and ambiguous status, the bride-to-be has a degree of freedom that she will not have again.

Erikson (1966) noted that some societies, like ours, sanction this type of behavior, what I call "liminal deviance." He stated, "There are societies which appoint special days or occasions as periods of general license, during which members of the group are permitted (if not expected) to violate rules they have observed during the preceding season and will again observe during the coming season" (Erikson 1966, 27). The bride-to-be is not in a constant state of back and forth during the engagement period, kissing strange men, going to strip clubs, and then being devoted to her fiancé. Rather, she is offered one opportunity during this time to act out feelings of ambivalence or doubt (whether she has them or not). She is given one chance to play and behave as a single woman before returning to her role as a faithful, committed romantic partner. This "special period of license" is when the bride-to-be is both allowed and expected to cross the boundaries of acceptable behavior for a girlfriend, fiancé, or (especially) wife. Thus, the bachelorette party itself, given the liminal status of its central participant, functions as an excuse for deviant and excessive behavior.

Strippers and Seduction: Interpreting the Meanings of Sex Symbols

The majority of bachelorette parties described (81 percent, or 115) and all parties that I observed included a sexual element or theme. Sex was a major component of the bachelorette party, and some of the women I interviewed questioned the legitimacy of bachelorette parties that omitted it entirely. Much of the deviant behavior at bachelorette parties involved sexualized interaction and play. Brides-to-be danced with strippers. Random men sucked candy pieces that were suggestively attached to brides' shirts. Women carried around giant phallic-shaped novelty items. Why is the bachelorette party sexualized? How can the use of sex symbols and props be interpreted? The association between sex and marriage is certainly a partial explanation. Traditionally, sex was expected to be reserved for marriage, and thus the bachelorette party could be interpreted as a means of socializing women into marriage by giving them sexual advice and showering them with symbols of sexuality so that they are prepared for a sexual relationship with their husbands. However, since the majority of women who marry in contemporary American society are not virgins (Laumann et al. 1994), and since the bachelorette party appears to have emerged in the United States after the sexual revolution of the 1960s (see chapter 2), this rationale is insufficient.

A modern explanation would be what I have suggested thus far, that women have dated different men prior to marriage and that many have had more than one sexual partner. Like men have for decades with bachelor parties, they see the bachelorette party as a way to acknowledge the termination of their single life. It is a symbolic means of showing that they are "off the market." Similarly, part of the sexual element comes directly from bachelor parties, from which the bachelorette party is certainly derived. Stereotypes about bachelor parties suggest that they are hyper-sexualized and that men frequent strip clubs or view pornography as a part of their "last night of freedom" (Schultz 1995). Luanne, a bride-to-be in her mid-twenties, expressed this when she stated why she felt sex talk and imagery are involved. She said, "When . . . girls were copying the bachelor party into the bachelorette party, they really were just kind of copying the same thing. It's not that girls are as interested in [sex] when they're just sitting around—not that, I mean shoot, [you] can't get a group of girls together without it coming up eventually, too. But I think . . . we can certainly find other things to talk about. I think it was more copycatting the whole bachelor party thing." Luanne's comments, coupled with an examination of the structure of the bachelorette party, particularly the Women's Bachelor Party or Anything Goes types, suggest that a major reason women include sexual elements is that they are purposefully replicating their image of the bachelor party.

One prominent element of bachelorette parties, the inclusion of a stripper, seems to have been copied from women's perceptions of men's parties. The stereotype of strippers as a part of bachelor parties is certainly dominant in our cultural history. Films depicting bachelor parties, such as *Bachelor Party* (1984) and *Very Bad Things* (1999), include strippers as central elements. However, while strippers were often included in bachelorette parties, and bachelorette parties made up a large portion of patrons of strip clubs like the Hideaway and the Regal Room (Montemurro 2001), women's interactions with and feelings about strippers conveyed ambivalence. In trying to replicate the bachelor party, it seems that some women ignored their own indifference to or even dislike of

4.5. Male exotic dancers often wear costumes that exemplify hyper-masculinity, such as this one, who made use of handcuffs and a nightstick during his routine

strippers in order to do what they felt was appropriate for a bachelorette party. Several women admitted that they really did not want to have strippers at their parties or did not care about having strippers but did so because they thought that was what was supposed to be done. Luanne communicated this as she told me about the first bachelorette party she attended. She said, "It almost seemed like we were trying to chase down that novel idea, but weren't really having a good time with it. Like you think you are going into a strip club with a bunch of girls and you're going to hoot and holler and it's going to be great. And we did, but after about thirty minutes it's like, 'This is getting boring. Let's go and meet some real men.' "

Strippers (and the sex theme) at bachelorette parties may also be included simply for the novelty of male strippers and male strip clubs. Many interviewees stated that their first exposure to a stripper was dur-

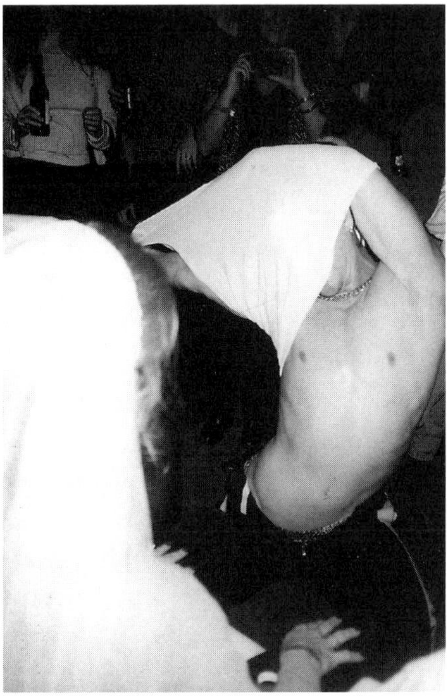

4.6. An exotic dancer performs for a group of bachelorettes at a nightclub

ing a bachelorette party. Thus, women may be curious about strippers and take advantage of a situation in which patronizing a strip club is considered to be an appropriate activity. When I asked Laura what she would want for her bachelorette party, she replied, "I don't necessarily need a stripper or anything, but if it's funny and we end up doing that. . . . I've never seen a male stripper, so I don't know if I'd be offended or not. I'd probably be embarrassed, but you should probably do it once and then you don't have to do it again." Laura's response implied that in some cases the inclusion of a stripper seemed to be less about wanting to see a naked man, or expecting to be aroused by him, and more about finding different or unique entertainment and being able to say that one had done it.

Also, most women said that the stripper part of the bachelorette evening was funny rather than sensual. Women's reactions to strippers rarely involved appearing "turned-on"; rather, women suggested, among other things, that strippers were "disgusting," "mortifying," "humiliating," and "funny" or that they made them "uncomfortable." In my observations, I watched as women howled with laughter as dancers straddled their friends. These women seemed to find amusement in the shocked or embarrassed expressions on the bride-to-be's face. The association with the stripper as a sex object (or subject) was secondary to his use as a source of humor. Colleen, for example, made this observation, "Well, I mean—I've heard some bad stories about bachelor parties where people follow through with stuff. And I think for women—at least for ones that I've been associated with—it's more like, 'Hee-hee, isn't that funny?' And it's more like to entice the man, like, 'Oh, I went and saw a stripper tonight.' It's never like—we're not like turned on by it, We're actually turned off by it. It's more just kind of like we're actually disgusted by it."

The idea that men exotic dancers are more humorous than sensual is consistent with research on women's interaction patterns with strippers in general, which suggests that patronizing a strip club is more often about having a good time with friends than it is about seeking a sexual experience (Montemurro, Bloom, and Madell 2003). Colleen's words also communicate another interesting and provocative theme, women's disinterest in and discomfort with men strippers. Whereas some women seemed to be "into" the strippers, like Sloane's friend at a bachelorette party at the Hideaway—"She [the bride] was up there dancing [on stage with strippers]. And she was so into it. She loved it. She loves being the center of attention, you know, in a good way"—more reported feeling embarrassed, indicating that they were not wholly at ease with the deviant environment of the strip club or presence of a stripper. Several quotes from brides and party attendees further illustrate this theme. First, at a bachelorette party she attended, Maureen (single, twenty-six) became uncomfortable with the stripper's level of intimacy. She commented, "[The stripper] just basically had a very thin see-through G-string on. . . . He, you know, laid her down and laid down on top of her and actually did kiss her on the lips, and so that's probably what surprised me the most."

I later asked her what the worst part of the night was, and she said, "I think it was when he laid down the bride and laid on top of her. I just had a weird feeling about that, and I remember thinking I don't want a bachelorette party, at least not like that. I thought it was pretty fun up until that point. But then everything just kind of got quiet and I was just like all right, [enough]."

During her friend's bachelorette party, Claire noted that the bride-to-be seemed not to like the "lap dance" her friends purchased for her at a strip club.

Claire: We got her a dance, but I could tell that was like yuck for her. . . . She did not enjoy that at all. I mean she was laughing with everybody; she wasn't upset. Just like I could tell she was uncomfortable.

Beth: Did you feel at this party you needed to have the stripper element?

Claire: I was just kind of up in the air with it. A lot of people feel like you've just got to do that. And I've gotten to the point, now, to me, you don't. . . . Now I have no desire to have any of it. I don't know what guys get out of it either, but to me, it does humiliate—some women are very uncomfortable with it.

Finally, Vicky's friends hired a stripper to dance for her bachelorette party. Her reaction was that "it was embarrassing when the stripper came in. . . . It was definitely embarrassing, but it was fun and funny." Unlike the first two women, Vicky had a good time with the stripper; yet, her response that it was fun and embarrassing, rather than hot or sexy, conveys the message that the experience was at least somewhat desexualized. Anecdotal evidence from the popular press showed that some strippers were aware of and careful about women's potential discomfort with them. When reporter Jenny Lyn Bader covered a bachelorette party, she watched an exotic dancer whisper in the bride-to-be's ear as he danced. She later asked what he had said, expecting to hear a smooth pickup line. The bride laughed and told her, "He just kept asking me if I felt comfortable. . . . He kept saying, 'If any of this makes you uncomfortable, I can stop' " (Bader 1999). These examples suggest several things. First, most of these women did not find the strip show or the dancers themselves to be sexually appealing or arousing. Second, women were uncomfortable or uneasy about the intimate contact involved in lap dances or interactions with exotic dancers, which may mean that women were uncomfortable with acts that they considered private being done in public or with strangers. Like Carol, quoted earlier in this chapter, who suggested that the stripper at her bachelorette party "made [her] touch his chest," women were tentative and few eagerly or aggressively responded to strippers' advances. It may have been that women were uncomfortable with the sexual aggression shown by the strippers. In most of the interactions that I observed between strippers and brides-to-be at bachelorette parties and in strip clubs, unlike that described by Bader (1999), the women were passive, and the men aggressive. Women sat with their hands at their sides—or, in some cases, handcuffed by the ever popular police-officer stripper—while dancers gyrated on them, thrusting themselves against women's bodies or encouraging women to touch them. At one strip club, Lucy's, I noted that the dancers pushed the women's chairs against the wall, pinning them in, displaying their strength and masculinity by physically positioning themselves as powerful or dominant. This culturally approved masculine sexual aggression may have made some women feel ill at ease because it put them in the position of being dominated and controlled by a stranger, which is unlikely to be a positive experience.

Furthermore, women may have found the sexualized atmosphere of the bachelorette party to be awkward given the cultural ambivalence about women's sexuality in contemporary society. As Susan Douglas articulated in her study of images of women in popular culture, American media have presented conflicting images of girls and women, images that paint them as either innocent or promiscuous, resulting in "schizophrenic [ideas] about women's sexuality" (1995, 15). The women in this study have grown up with a sexual double standard that suggests that men who have multiple sexual partners are to be congratulated while women who do so are to be punished. They also have learned from American culture, through media and other agents of socialization, that men are the sexual aggressors while women should be sexually passive (Spade and Valentine 2004). At parties, engaging in the various tasks positioned the bride-to-be as object more often than aggressor. When women played the Suck for a Buck game or had men remove pieces of candy from necklaces, or when they had men sign their underwear, this placed them as sexual objects, selling or making themselves available for men's pleasure. Rather than representing their sexual confidence or participating in acts that were sexually titillating as a means of celebrating their last night of sexual freedom, instead, some of the bachelorette party games were about offering themselves up one last time to interested men. Some tasks called for brides-to-be to play aggressor by approaching random men and asking for their phone numbers or other items on a scavenger hunt. Thus, it is not surprising that the women's response to exotic dancers and the general sexualized atmosphere of the party was ambivalence because, on one hand, women are told to claim and embrace their sexuality, but, on the other hand, much of the expected sexual expression is based on making themselves available to arouse and entertain men.

The bachelorette party is based on the idea of the non-virgin bride who has had sexual experiences and is acknowledging, even lamenting, the end of her freedom. Yet the sexually experienced woman is not a privileged position in Western society. Leora Tanenbaum (2000) argued as much in her study of female sexual activity. She noted that teenage girls and women face pressure both to have sex and to preserve their reputation as "good girls." Having grown up in the wake of the feminist movement, the women I interviewed received the message that they can do what boys or men do. But in terms of sexuality, when women of this generation listened to such rhetoric, they would quickly be made aware of the consequences of promiscuity (Tanenbaum 2000). Furthermore, women received mixed messages about how they should express this sexual liberation. The bride-to-be at the bachelorette party exemplifies this contradiction with the props she carries, the way she is costumed, and the expectations for her behavior. The party itself is indicative of this incongruity as women play along with a male-defined image of feminine sexuality in terms of the show or performative aspect of bachelorette parties.

Many of the women in the study talked about boundaries for appropriate behavior at bachelorette parties and implied that there were definitely lines that should not be crossed. Vanessa, a married woman who helped plan two bachelorette parties, said that those parties were "crazy, silly, fun, but never stepped over the line, if you know what I mean. Neither one of [the brides] did anything that they would have been embarrassed about. Maybe the body shots. But everything else was just good, clean fun. It never went over the line—a lot of drinking and innuendo but never anything that we would have worried about fiancés finding out about." Anna, recently married, also suggested that bachelorette parties should be fun, but under control. In reflecting on a party she had been to, she said, "The bride did not do anything inappropriate, but I could see where there could be a tendency where she could do something very inappropriate. And if you have any kind of conscience—I don't see how you could just forget, just do something that one night and then saying,

'Oh, it was my bachelorette party. I don't have to worry about it.' If you have any kind of conscience it should bother you."

Some women made a point of stating their boundaries while the party was still in the planning stages, so that their friends were clear on what they considered acceptable behavior. Kristen, for example, told her friends that she was not interested in going to a strip club, a request that was honored: "They asked me. The one thing I definitely did not want to do, I did not want to go to the Hideaway, where there's like male strippers. I didn't want a male stripper. That's just not my thing. I do draw the line there. Cheesy games I'll do, but not that." None of the interviewees reported that any sexual acts occurred at any of the bachelorette parties in which they participated. The most extreme behavior described in two cases involved brides-to-be kissing other men. In one incident, the kiss was closed-mouthed and the bride-to-be was described as feeling terrible about it afterward. In the other, the kiss was more intimate and the interviewee who told of this expressed stern disapproval over the bride-to-be's actions, even suggesting that maybe she should not be getting married. These actions, seemingly minor transgressions, and the responses to them demonstrate again this ambivalence toward sexuality. While some women believed that men were more sexually licentious than women and had the attitude that anything goes on bachelor parties (several women described bachelor parties that their husbands/fiancés/boyfriends told them about in which there were sexual encounters between grooms-to-be and exotic dancers or prostitutes), it was clear that they did not believe that the same held true for women. Sexual arousal from watching male strippers or from the general sexualized atmosphere was not expected and likely would have been seen as inappropriate by the other women, consistent with cultural norms about women's sexual passivity and arousal. Furthermore, women clearly communicated the message that the sexual element, while fun for some and less so for others, was really secondary to the real reason for the party, spending time with one's closest friends. Nicole, who had planned an Anything Goes party for a close friend and attended several other libidinous bachelorette parties, even suggested that the sexual element detracted from quality time. She said:

> I'm not big into the whole big stereotypical bachelorette party—you have to have all of the games, and when you go to the bar you have

these T-shirts, Suck for a Buck. I'm not into that. I think that's cheesy and disgusting, you know? I'm not into having to have a penis as a straw or having a stripper or having anything like that. I think that it should be just a fun evening out for the girls. Not that you're getting married and it's the last time you're going to go out with the girls, but at least it's an occasion to just say, all right, all of the girls we're getting together we're just going to have a good time—either get dinner or not and just have a fun evening out. Yeah, make her wear the veil, be a little embarrassed . . . [and] that's what I would consider an ideal bachelorette party. Have all my friends . . . there and everybody have a good time.

In addition to strippers, another way sex was included in the bachelorette party was with the games, such as Suck for a Buck, described earlier. The games played at most bachelorette parties were notably different from those at the bridal shower. Even though some of the bridal shower games were laced with sexual innuendo, most were dated and sustained the assumption of the virgin bride. As in the game where the maid of honor records the bride's reactions as she opens her presents, then reads the list back as if it is what she might say on her wedding night, the bride at the shower is sexually naïve. Knowing older relatives and married peers introduce her to the adult world with advice or lingerie, communicating their approval of sexual activity within the bounds of marriage. These older family members often tease the bride about her future sexual activity, communicating that they hope it will soon lead to procreation. When the bride-to-be is told that the number of ribbons she breaks when she opens her gifts is equivalent to the number of children she will have, she receives the message that motherhood follows marriage. Simply, the sexualized games at the shower connect sex to marriage and childbearing. In contrast, the games at the bachelorette party assume an opposite identity for the bride-to-be. Sexually experienced women do things like "Pin the Macho on the Man" or ask men strangers to "suck for a buck." Women here play with the idea of a sexual pickup or their knowledge of male anatomy. The bride's friends encourage her to play these games as if she has before and should enjoy this final opportunity to flirt or seduce or be approached by random men. No mention is made of becoming pregnant; instead, sex is framed as a pleasurable, youthful activity that the bride will enjoy less after she marries. Brides are often decorated with condoms; either still in their wrappers and taped to veils or shirts or blown up and pinned all over their clothing, or in some cases as earrings or made into corsages. Condoms seem to be associated with single women or singlehood, with sexual relationships among less-committed partners or virtual strangers on one-night stands. When the bride is adorned with condoms it seems to communicate the idea that such days of sexual experimentation or adventure are over.

Mocking the Bachelor Party and Images of Inhibition

While the above discussion implies that traditional gender roles and expectations for sexual passivity are subtly and implicitly reinforced, I suggest that the bachelorette party is not wholly repressive. Rather, it represents women's agency as well. Women were not only mimicking the bachelor party, but mocking it as well. With the hyper-sexualized atmosphere of bachelorette parties, with women carrying around giant "blow-up men" dolls and, in a couple of cases, giant, five-foot, "blow-up penises" or consuming alcohol out of oversized phallic-shaped containers, it seemed that women were making fun of the sexual element of the bachelor party. Though not necessarily consciously, many of the women appeared to be mocking the idea that men feel it necessary to have a last night of freedom that involves the viewing of pornography or patronizing of strip clubs. Women went overboard in sexualizing bachelorette parties. On some of the bachelorette parties observed and described, the sexual element was almost comical. The women who were adorned with dozens of condoms or penis paraphernalia were sources of entertainment. At Anna's bachelorette party, described in the opening of this chapter, women friends giggled as they inflated condoms and filled a penis-shaped water gun, joking about how they were going to embarrass the bride. This bride had condoms pinned all over her, and she, like her friends, responded by laughing at and playing with these items in a jovial manner. This over- or hyper-sexualization actually desexualized these objects, such that the symbols no longer represented sex but humor. They became funny and their manifest function became irrelevant.[2]

The fact that these symbols of sexuality were treated with humor and that sexual arousal was inappropriate at the bachelorette party is telling. Modern women are expected to be sexy, but not too sexy, to like sex, but not too much. For "good" women, sexual activity is expected to take place within the confines of a committed, monogamous relationship. Since the bachelorette party flagrantly defies and ritually enacts opposition to these cultural prescriptions, the use of humor may in fact serve to minimize the deviance associated with going against society's moral code (Tye and Powers 1998). If women treat the sexual objects and atmosphere as something that is fun and funny, then they cannot be accused of being "bad" or labeled with some other pejorative term. In their study of in-home sex-toy parties, McCaughey and French reported that these parties were characterized by "uproarious laughter" because looking at and touching sex toys embarrassed women (2001, 80). Dealers of these products used carefully chosen words to describe the female and male sexual organs and anatomy as a way to draw the line between being sexy and being "dirty" (McCaughey and French 2001, 81). So, like the women-only sex-toy party, also a modern invention, the bachelorette party communicates ambivalence about the nature of contemporary women's sexuality, drawing moral lines between good women and bad women. In other words, good women could play bad women at bachelorette parties but were sure to make it evident that this was an act, not an element of their true identity.

Women seemed to be mocking not only the bachelor party, but also the idea that women are sexually repressed or that it is inappropriate for women to express themselves sexually in public. The bachelorette party can be seen as a form of rebellion on the part of women in that they acted in a feminized masculine manner, as sexually aggressive. Women approached men strangers, danced with exotic dancers, and made the first moves. In doing these tasks, even when pressured by their women peers, it was still women who were controlling or directing women's sexuality. Thus, women resisted the stereotype that men should be the only ones who initiate sexualized interactions and, through the use of sexualized objects, that women are (or should be) sexually inhibited. And while some women objected to or were offended by such activities, others relished participating in them, flaunting themselves and enjoying the attention they received for being "naughty." It is here, in part, where we can see the transformative power of this ritual. Kertzer (1988) suggested that symbols can be seen as representative of power, such that those who are more powerful have the ability to define and control the meaning of symbols. The redefinition and manipulation of symbols can be seen as a means of taking hold of or expressing power. When women seize and mock the phallus, a symbol long associated with men's power, this indicates a questioning and challenging of that power. In this sense, bachelorette parties can be seen as evidence of changes in women's roles. Whereas women's public sexual expression was considered inappropriate in the past, in some ways contemporary women claim the right to be sexual and sexually aggressive, particularly in this context. The relative acceptance of bachelorette parties is a significant marker of changes in gender roles, marital roles, and expressions of masculinity and femininity.

Anything You Can Do . . . : Liberal Feminist Ideology and the Bachelorette Party

In addition to understanding why the bachelorette party ritual is what it is, why women do the things that they do, and why sexuality and deviance are critical elements of this ritual, it is important to discuss how women who participate in these parties interpret their significance. During the bachelorette party section of the interview, two of the last questions I asked were, "Why do you think women started having bachelorette parties?" and "Why do you think women continue to have bachelorette parties?" What surprised me was how many women suggested an association between these parties and the women's movement. Gretchen, for example, said this about why bachelorette parties started: "It appears to have grown out of the bachelor party phenomenon, where the women want to say that they can party just as hard as their fiancé. Sort of growing out of the feminism, seventies, women's liberation thing." Several other women mentioned feminism explicitly. Brittany, in response to my question about why bachelorette parties started, said, "It could have something to do with the feminists. It really could, 'cause women didn't really stand up for what they want. And now they're saying they want to go out." Alicia also suggested that women's rights were important in the evolution of the bachelorette party when women began to recognize that they were missing out on a fun time. She thought this ritual started "just to feel equal with the men, 'cause it wasn't fair for the men to go out and then the women just be sitting at home like, 'We're so lucky to be getting married, [we] shouldn't go out.' So when women's rights started picking up, I think they just kind of felt it was about time."

At first I dismissed the connection, thinking that feminists would not endorse the sexual objectification often standard at bachelorette parties. However, although the link is not as direct as interviewees suggested, there is certainly a connection between the idea of the bachelorette party and liberal feminism. Liberal feminists are primarily concerned with equal employment opportunities, yet are more generally concerned with equal rights for women, concisely, that women have access to the same opportunities as men (Lorber 1998; Tong 1998). The implication of the comments made by the women who suggested that bachelorette parties started "because of the feminists" is that women wanted to be able to have the same type of pre-wedding celebration as men. They saw the bachelor party as more fun than their gendered ritual of the bridal shower and wanted to be able to go out with their friends in a less restrained, more jovial atmosphere. Josephine made this point in saying, "I think we started it because men always have their bachelor parties. I think they had to have been around before bachelorette parties. And all we had was a bridal shower. Getting stuff for the home–and you never hear of them having a man shower where they get hammers and tools and things for the home that are needed. It seemed like theirs was something more about sex and drinking and partying. And it's not fair for the women to miss out on that." Josephine's comments communicated the idea of "equal rights." This sentiment was by far the dominant idea expressed by interviewees as an explanation for why bachelorette parties started. Nearly 73 percent (thirty-seven) of interviewees mentioned "getting back at men" or the idea that women deserved to celebrate with their friends in the same manner as men. April, for example, stated, "I think it is a part of kind of wanting to match what they think men are doing. If the men are doing it, we can too. Why shouldn't we? I think it's probably why it evolved . . . to, um, kind of show up the men; if they can do it, we can too." Emily made a similar comment, saying, "I would say it would probably be a reaction to the fact that men do. Not that necessarily [women] think they would be missing out but that if the men do it, the women think they should be able to do it—that whole argument." Finally, Carol also concurred that strippers seem to be involved in bachelorette parties because they have been a standard at bachelor parties. She remarked, "I think because bachelor parties . . . have been going on forever and guys get to see naked women, and so now . . . the girls feel they should get to see naked men."

Although several women expressed reservations about their fiancé's bachelor parties, very few women suggested that their bachelorette parties bothered their husbands-to-be. I asked each bride-to-be if she had talked with her fiancé about their respective parties. Several women stated that they made agreements with their fiancés that neither would include strippers in their festivities. Most, however, said that they were fine with what their husbands-to-be were going to do and that the grooms "didn't care" about what they were going to be doing. For those whom I interviewed after the fact, most reported that they exchanged details with their spouse soon after the parties ended. A few did not share details and hid mildly incriminating pictures (e.g., the bride-to-be with a stripper). Most seemed to joke with or playfully tease their spouse about what they did on their parties. Although it would be necessary to interview grooms to know how they really felt, their fiancés and wives suggested that for the most part they were unconcerned. Given this, how women use the bachelorette party to get even with men is complicated. More women suggested that they were worried about what their fiancé would do on his bachelor party than vice versa. Discussion on Internet message boards on Web sites like The Knot.com supports this. In a January 2005 search on the topic bachelor/bachelorette parties, I noted many posts from women who were "freaking out" about the bachelor party but none about how the groom was reacting to the bachelorette party.

Interestingly enough, many women planned their bachelorette party intentionally on the same night as their fiancé's bachelor party so that they would be distracted from thinking about what he might be doing. For several women, the bachelorette party was an afterthought, organized by friends who did not want the bride-to-be sitting home while her groom-to-be was out on the town. Janet's friends started organizing a party for her "as a distraction" when they found out that her fiancé was having a bachelor party. Pam, too, said she had not given the bachelorette party much thought, but her friends threw her a party when they learned the date of her future husband's party. And April hadn't intended to have a bachelorette party and actually did not know that she would until the night that it took place. As she said, "There was no planning. It actually happened—and I didn't even know if I was going to have one. . . . The plan was the guys were going to go out and have their bachelor party after the coed shower and then the girls are going to go out. Well, since none of my friends were [in state], I really didn't know if anything was going to happen or not. And I kind of hoped, to save face, you know, I wanted to do something. I didn't want to be sitting home doing nothing while the guys were going out. So it just kind of happened that some of the women who were here and me decided to go out that night. And I didn't even know, until that night, whether I was going to go out and do anything." Several women even suggested that if their fiancé would agree not to have a bachelor party, then they would gladly pass up the bachelorette party. Mary, for example, said, "I would be happy with that mutual decision [not to have bachelor/ette parties] completely, 'cause I don't like the thoughts of them—whether she be a stranger or not, I don't like the thoughts of another woman coming on to my man kind of thing." I asked her what she would do if her fiancé planned a bachelor party. She replied, "I think I would almost do it out of spite." Though many women said they would have bachelorette parties no matter what their fiancé did, the comments of these women whose bachelorette parties were afterthoughts or organized as a distraction suggest that the ritual is not standard practice. Their involvement does, however, bolster the power of the ritual as expressing women's status. In all of these cases, friends of the bride-to-be rallied to make sure that she would have a night out like her future husband, to show that she could and would do what he was doing.

Some women had a specific agenda when playing the "anything you can do" game. Several interviewees who went to strip clubs or hired strippers said they did so specifically because they knew their fiancé would or was doing so and they wanted to "get even." Jamie, for example, expressed this opinion, saying, "I don't know if I want a stripper—like I'm kind of like, 'Ew, that's gross!' I think the whole reason maybe I would want a stripper there—a lot of it is because [my fiancé] is gonna have a bachelor party. And this probably sounds really bad, but if he's gonna do it, I'm gonna do it too." Jamie communicated the message that she could look at semi-clad men if he was going to be looking at semi-clad women, even though the idea of strippers in general was not particularly appealing to her. Carol noted that she had some concerns about her fiancé's party, as did he about hers. She said that given his friends she knew he would have a bachelor party that involved strippers and resigned herself to that. But she decided that if he was going to do that, she would too. It seems that she and other women who made similar comments were asserting their ability to do what men do, and thus, in a sense, asserting their equality. In their study of Canadian "stagette" parties, Tye and Powers made a similar discovery. The women they interviewed saw the stagette as a "feminist statement" made by women who were tired of seeing men have all of the fun (Tye and Powers 1998, 554). While equality in this sense is difficult to measure, the fact that women feel that they deserve a night of deviance and play with their friends is indicative of the fact that women are now entitled to publicly express ambivalence toward marriage. They are able to acknowledge the changes this transition will produce in terms of loss of sexual freedom and relationships with friends, sentiments previously reserved for men. It is likely that these sentiments of equality are based on women's equality in other areas of society. The bachelorette party, as part of a changing climate in terms of women's independence and sexual expression, redefines women's appropriate "feeling rules" as brides-to-be. Instead of only having a forum to eagerly welcome their new status as wife, the bridal shower, women now have the opportunity to publicly demonstrate that they have made a choice to get married, that they considered other men and selected a spouse, rather than merely having been selected.

Women's desire to have bachelorette parties was not just about getting even with men for their supposed sexual escapades. What was more important to women was the chance to have a fun night or weekend with their friends, as men have on bachelor parties. It seems that a major part of what women felt they were missing out on when they only had bridal showers was the chance to have a memorable, carefree evening, characterized by an ethic of release rather than restraint. While research suggests that men and women value friendship equally, women tend to be more concerned with expressing their feelings about friendships (Fox, Gibbs, Auerback 1985). Women seek to create more intimacy in their relationships by engaging in sharing behaviors (Oliker 2001), and the bachelorette party is a forum for creating mutual memories. In the same way that women express care at the bridal shower by attending and giving gifts, women's presence at the bachelorette party was indicative of the importance of friendships as well as a means for women to show their

4.7. Women bonding at a bachelorette party

feelings for the relationships that they built over the years. Women showed how much they cared for one another by making the effort to attend this pre-wedding party, even when doing so was costly or time consuming. It was evidently very important to women to recognize and express how much they cared about one another. Jorden communicated this when she talked about a party for one of her close friends. She said, "I just really enjoyed being out with her and trying to make her feel special because I imagine she was pretty overwhelmed with being a bride. I think you want to make it her day and about her. I was just glad that we were finally able to do something together, and she seemed happy with the whole thing. I guess the best part was just spending time since she's been so busy the last couple of months." Laura, too, enjoyed seeing her friend having a good time, identifying that as the best part of her night. She said, "I had never seen her drunk before, so for me . . . to see her like [that], it seemed to me she had this huge smile on her face the whole night, and she was just having such a great time being in this club of her youth, you know, that she used to go to a lot. . . . It was fun to see that, see that she was having fun." Nearly every bride-to-be and party attendee told me that the highlight of the bachelorette party was the quality time they were able to share with their friends. It seems that while women may acknowledge and play along with the idea that their sexual freedom is terminated when they marry, more important to them is that their relationships with friends are likely to change when they marry. Some had already experienced the beginning of this transition when they graduated from high school or college and became geographically distant from friends. So, the bachelorette party is also important to women as a vehicle for bonding and showing the bride-to-be how much her friendship means. And through their calling attention to the rarity of occasions during which the whole group of friends is together, through their reminiscing, creating memories, and expressing their love and care for their friends, these women communicated the significance of the party as an event that celebrates relationships. The responsibilities of adulthood and careers prevented women from spending as much time with their friends as they would have liked, and in many ways the bachelorette party allowed women to express that they sacrificed regular girls' nights when they married.

Close examination of women's behavior at bachelorette parties and the use of sexual objects suggest that these women still view their own sexuality with ambivalence. In some ways they ritually enact sexual equality and reject the sexual double standard. However, in other respects, women reinforce and express traditional gender norms for sexual expression. The brides in this sample embraced monogamy and had few regrets about saying farewell to their days of sexual freedom. They were clearly not infusing the bachelorette party with sexual symbols because they had qualms about monogamy. None of the women interviewed communicated any regret or disappointment about no longer being able to be sexually intimate with men other than the groom-to-be. Like most women in American culture, they wanted to get married and were looking forward to their wedding days. They recognized the wedding as a special day where they would receive heightened attention and marriage as a status elevation. They participated in the bachelorette party as a symbolic gesture, communicating that they could do what men do and have done. Here again, it is evident that the bachelorette party is not only about changes in women's sexuality, but also about changes in gender roles as well. So, while television shows, such as *Sex and the City* and magazines like *Cosmopolitan* and *Glamour*, suggest that modern women are (or should be) in favor of sexual experimentation and that they enjoy controlled and responsible promiscuity, this research reveals the opposite.

Women interviewees enjoyed playing at the bachelorette party because the sexual encounters were just that—play. The faux pickup of a man, getting phone numbers or kissing men as part of a scavenger hunt, the intimate dance from an exotic dancer, all were safe ways to be sexually promiscuous. These acts simulated sexual liaisons and were often viewed as "naughty" in and of themselves. For women in this study, the idea that any real sexual encounter would occur on a bachelorette party was unthinkable. The fact that women talk about sex and hyper-sexualize this ritual with a playful, mocking, humorous tone within the safe, sanctioned framework of the bachelorette party indicates that women are confident about their sexuality within this context where it has been deemed appropriate. Outside of the bachelorette party ritual, it is unlikely that many of these women would be seen publicly with these sexual objects or would host parties in which they could buy sex toys or learn sexual techniques. In fact, very few women were willing to share their photographs from their bachelorette parties for inclusion in this book because they considered the pictures to be embarrassing or incriminating and saw themselves as wives as different from whom they were as brides-to-be. The bride at the bachelorette party seems to be a time-bound role, where the bride can play roles with which she does not truly identify. But once the party is over, once she is married and fully transitioned into the wife role, the image of the bride at the shower is much closer to her self-definition. There is change, certainly, in women publicly talking about sex and joking about it; and, critically, women are claiming a night out with their friends and acknowledging that their relationships will be altered when they become wives. Yet there is still stigma associated with women who are too sexual or are sexually expressive out of the appropriate contexts. Thus, the bachelorette party is emblematic of the contradictory expectations for contemporary women's sexuality and gender roles.

CHAPTER 5

Something New

CONSUMPTION, MATERIALISM, AND EXCESS IN PRE-WEDDING RITUALS

BETH: Do you think showers are becoming any less common with people living together before they get married?

BRYN: No. They just ask for more. And more elaborate things—like register for beds. . . . It usually seems like people have so much with their weddings, it doesn't seem like anything is getting replaced.

In 2003 Trista Rehn, star of ABC's popular reality dating show The *Bachelorette,* signed a deal with the network to have her (and then fiancé Ryan Sutter's) pre-nuptial preparations and wedding filmed and aired on national television. Representatives for the show boasted that they spent nearly four million dollars on the ceremony, reception, and related festivities. Rather than public outcry at the ridiculous lavishness of the event, more than seventeen million viewers tuned in to watch the stars of this made-for-television romance wed. The Hollywood-style nuptials included a fifteen-thousand-dollar wedding cake, a twenty-five-thousand-dollar gown, and custom-designed platinum-and-diamond-encrusted shoes worth approximately fifty thousand dollars (Tresniowski, Wang, Wihlborg 2003).

Though not quite on the same scale, couples all over America are getting married extravagantly, sparing little expense, and even going into debt to create a memorable and indulgent event (Otnes and Pleck 2003). Due to the increased emphasis on consumerism in Western society in the latter decades of the twentieth century, the ideal of the "perfect" wedding (Otnes and Pleck 2003), and the emergence of the "superbride" (Boden 2003) who is expected to put in the necessary time to create this event, there are specific expectations for how a wedding is supposed to be. And while in many ways the modern wedding ceremony is very traditional, the notion of the lavish wedding as an entitlement is a relatively recent construction, purposefully encouraged by the wedding industry as such ideals sustain and enhance it (Otnes and Pleck 2003, 54). Brides-to-be and those who finance their weddings are encouraged to spend excessively on this "once in a lifetime" event, and such indulgence is justified because weddings and romance are viewed as sacred in Western culture (Geller 2001; Holland and Eisenhart 1990; Ingraham 1999).

Thus, the wedding industry is booming. In the late 1990s the wedding industry garnered over thirty-two billion dollars annually (Ingraham 1999), and more recent estimates report that it is currently at least a fifty-billion-dollar industry (Wallace 2004), with some suggesting the figure of seventy billion is more accurate (Lagorce 2005). In 2002, the average amount of money spent on a wedding in the United States was twenty-two thousand dollars (Otnes and Pleck 2003), which was more than half of the median household income for that same year (U.S. Department of Commerce 2004). Costs have continued to increase in wedding spending as well, the 2005 Fairchild Bridal Infobank recently reported that the average cost of a formal wedding is now more than twenty-six thousand dollars (cbsnews.com 2005). Weddings are not merely about love and romance; they are cultural products weighted by materialism and consumerism and the usually unspoken yet pervasive belief that the more money one spends the greater the celebration and the greater the level of love or commitment of the couple (Otnes and Pleck 2003). Given this trend, it is logical that the events associated with weddings would also become grander and more elaborate. In the three-episode series *Trista and Ryan's Wedding*, ABC devoted a full episode to the bridal shower, bachelor party, and bachelorette party. Trista, Ryan, and dozens of friends and family were flown to St. Martin for luxurious send-off festivities. It is not just weddings that fuel the industry, but the process of preparation and the activities that both build and maintain momentum for the big event also act as opportunities for consumption.

Furthermore, weddings serve as markers of social class. As people spend excessive amounts of money on lavish weddings, doing so becomes a means by which the couple or the family of the bride, groom, or both display their social standing. Americans consider money to be an indicator of status, and most of the women in this study, particularly in the Northeastern United States, where wedding spending is highest

(Ingraham 1999, 28), directly or indirectly classified wedding showers and the weddings that followed by the amount of money spent on them. In this chapter, I detail the significance and role of consumerism and the wedding industry in setting standards for contemporary bridal showers and bachelorette parties. Additionally, I discuss the importance of social-class display and the relationship between a middle- or upper-middle-class lifestyle and the materialism that is explicitly celebrated at bridal shower and is implicitly a critical part of the bachelorette party.

THE RISE OF THE BACHELORETTE PARTY INDUSTRY

The bachelorette party seems to have become popular in the United States in the 1980s and 1990s, yet it was not until the end of this time period that these parties were considered to be a normative part of the wedding routine (see chapter 2). The surge in popularity and prevalence of bachelorette parties is explained not only by changes in gender roles, but also by the focus on lavishness and excess characteristic of the larger wedding experience. Additionally, the increasing emphasis on consumerism and materialism and the rising prosperity that characterized the late twentieth and early twenty-first centuries (Otnes and Pleck 2003) are likely to have contributed to the normalization of the bachelorette party. As Otnes and Pleck (2003, 55) wrote of the activities during the engagement period, "These rituals have become more elaborate in recent years as if a fancier wedding somehow requires or deserves a more dramatic and magical warm-up." Bachelorette parties such as the "Anything Goes" and "Women's Bachelor Party" type, described in the previous chapter, illustrate the spread of lavishness from the wedding ceremony and reception to the events that precede them. These parties took place at multiple locations, involved the consumption of many goods and services, and often included a gift-giving portion as well. Most bachelorette parties lasted at least six hours, many turning into slumber parties for at least part of the group. The bachelorette party was not just a party; rather, it was a ritualized event with many components, most of which involved spending money.

During the course of this research, I watched the bachelorette party industry grow. When I began collecting data in 1998, I did not find a single Web site offering bachelorette party-planning information (although some sites featuring male exotic dancers, or limousine rentals would list bachelorette parties as part of their market). In 2005, there was an abundance of these sites, ranging from those that sold gag gifts and novelty items to those that advertised weekend trips to places like Montreal and Las Vegas, with custom-designed itineraries for bachelorette parties. And women are using the Internet as a tool for planning parties. One advertising company that monitors Web searches reported that during the month of September 2004 there were over forty-seven thousand searches for "bachelorette party," compared to only slightly more than nineteen thousand for "bachelor party" (Owens 2004). In addition to information on the Internet, books advising bridesmaids about how to plan an appropriately indulgent "last night of freedom" have also increased in number. One desktop-published volume, *How to Host a Hilariously Fun Bachelorette Party*, was listed on Amazon.com in 1998. By 2004, more than a dozen books on the topic of bachelorette party planning were available. As authors of that original volume noted, since 1998 bachelorette parties "have gone from not existing to having their own Web Site category," and they personally have gone from selling a desktop-published book to creating their own online store (Palmer 2003).

The industries that fuel bachelorette parties include travel and tourism, media, transportation, entertainment, dining, alcohol, and retail goods. From strip clubs and dance clubs to limousine companies and trolley rentals, capitalists have recognized engaged women and their friends as potential customers and have encouraged bachelorette parties as a means of increasing their revenue. With the same pseudo-feminist rhetoric used by dieting, beauty, self-help, and even tobacco companies (Douglas 1995; Hochschild 1994; Stinson 2001), women are fed the message that having a bachelorette party or going to a strip club is a means of expressing their "equal rights." Thus, nightclubs and clubs featuring male exotic dancers have taken advantage of the bachelorette party trend by offering incentives and package deals to women. The clubs in which I conducted observation provided such packages and goods. A popular dance club in the Northeast included a "Bachelorette Bash" in their monthly schedule. One Saturday night each month this club invited bachelorette parties, offering an open bar, free admission for the bride-to-be, and a dance from an exotic dancer for the charge of

5.1. A bride-to-be wearing a tiara receives lingerie at her bachelorette party

twenty dollars per guest. Women mentioned taking advantage of similar offers at other clubs in the North and Southeast.

Additionally, as described in chapter 4, the bride-to-be is often adorned with phallic or sexual paraphernalia or a veil. Women also often bought phallic-shaped food items for the pre-party gatherings that they hosted. Several women reported serving "gummy penises" or penis-shaped cookies, cakes, or chocolates that they made with molds or pans that they had purchased over the Internet or in adult or novelty shops. Bachelorette parties thus also provide a new and expanded market for gag or novelty gifts. In fact, a few of the bachelorette party-planning books listed Web sites where one could purchase these items, and one even included an order form for items like playing cards with pictures of naked men and straws with "rubber penises" on the end of them. The women I interviewed reported that they purchased these items on the Internet, in novelty stores like Spencer's Gifts, in adult entertainment stores, and sometimes at places where the party took place. A strip club in a Northeastern city sold "Bridal Survival Kits" that included a veil, a "condom corsage," and pictures and novelty items from the club. This club, named "#1 bachelorette party location in the country" by a local newspaper, catered to brides-to-be by offering special seating and attention. I interviewed one of the managers from this club who indicated that they increased their offerings of bachelorette-party-related merchandise since the late 1990s and created an online store in addition to selling such goods at the club.

National club chains also offer special perks for bachelorette parties. At the 1970s-themed Polly Esther's, for example, bachelorette parties could bypass admission lines and brides were granted free entry and a T-shirt. Or, for twenty-five dollars per person, guests could have access to a two-hour open bar and a private room where they could host a dancer that they hired (at their own expense). In 1998, it was estimated that more than fifty parties would take place at Polly Esther's Chicago location on Saturday nights during the wedding season (Navratil 1998). Party planners also advertise bachelorette party packages in major cities in the United States, offering things like dinner, limousines, open bar at particular clubs, and exotic dancers (e.g., www.partypop.com; www.ultimatebacheloretteparty.com), with costs ranging from $120 to $250 per person for the bachelorette evening. One Washington, D.C., entrepreneur, for example, created a company through which he hosted bachelorette parties by designing itineraries for the evening including trips to bars and strip clubs (Brace 1999). He chauffeured women from destination to destination in a rented van, taking advantage of his numerous connections at different nightspots in the metro area and working deals for bachelorette parties. He looked out for the women while they were in the clubs, took care of them when they were sick, and claimed that he generally afforded them a worry-free event. Women paid approximately $300 for his services, which included club admissions but not drinks.

In addition to the standard activities of the bachelorette parties, some include additional opportunities for spending money by combining the bachelorette party with a lingerie shower or by having a demonstration of some type of material goods that party guests are encouraged to purchase, like a Tupperware party. Several entrepreneurs offer their services to bachelorette parties (among other groups of women); however, the products they sell are for use in the bedroom rather than the kitchen.

Companies like L.O.V.E Parties, Tasteful Treasures, and Slumber Parties market their wares on site with elaborate sales pitches and demonstrations of sex toys (Brodsky 2004; Copeland 2000; McCaughey and French 2001; Rouvalis 2002). The expectation is that guests will order something for the bride-to-be and maybe themselves as well. Ashley, who included this in a bachelorette party she hosted for a close friend, described how it worked:

> A lady comes and she displays all of her goods, which are like sex novelties—everything from like these cups that have funny things on them to actual vibrators and dildos . . . and all these massage creams. . . . So she displays them all on the table and . . . everybody had a sheet that they fill out. She goes through and describes every product and you write like how many you want. And at the end, after she goes through everything—[I had said in the invitations] that you didn't have to buy [the bride] a gift—you could give her money towards this purchase. So everyone when they made their purchases, they could buy her gift certificates . . . and then [the bride] could buy whatever she wanted to, 'cause they had lingerie and things like that as well. . . . So everyone went in individually, and if they wanted to buy the bride a gift certificate it could all add up. . . . 'Cause I was the hostess, I ended up getting like forty dollars free, . . . like 10 percent of everyone's sales. And we were talking to the lady about how much she made or whatever. She said, at this party she sold like eight hundred dollars and she actually made half the profit . . . like four hundred dollars for three hours . . . so she makes good money. . . . The bride had like two hundred dollars of gift certificates accumulated so she raked the stuff in. And half the stuff, like some of the people, half of the stuff they got they're like, "I know my husband or boyfriend he won't ever use this, but I'll just get it anyway. Just 'cause it's fun and maybe he will sometime." So some of it was a waste of money, but a lot of people told me later that they liked it, people who wouldn't like go to a store and buy this stuff. This was kind of discreet.

Ashley's comments suggest several interesting things about the sex toy demonstration and its inclusion in the bachelorette party. On one hand, it is an example of new expressions of sexuality for modern women. When women buy and sell sex toys, though giggly and embarrassed during the presentation, they are claiming their status as sexual beings. However, the secretive and humorous nature of the parties suggests that this sexual liberation is time and place bound and thus not really exemplary of sexual freedom (McCaughey and French 2001). Those in the industry noted that the success of these in-home parties has much to do with women's reluctance to patronize adult book stores, which are perceived as "sleazy" and where women fear leers from sex-crazed men (Copeland 2000; Rouvalis 2002). This change in norms for women's sexual expression, this being able to express interest in sex and a desire to spice up sexual activity with erotic aids, remains a private activity where women play brash or bashful within the safety of a friend's living room. Furthermore, women are put in the position whereby consumption is what functions as a means to liberation. Women can show their sexuality by purchasing sex toys or related goods, feminizing them by using shopping as a means of sexual expression. It is noteworthy that even when at a party, women have included the opportunity to shop, to spend more money on the bride-to-be and, while they are at, themselves. At this party, in addition to spending money on drinks and cover charges at clubs, women spent an average of forty dollars each on sexual novelty items that many even said that they would not use. From Ashley's description, it seemed that women got caught up in the excitement and fun of the party and wanted to buy *something* because others were doing so. One sales agent for such a company reported making twelve thousand dollars in one year, for eight hours a week worth of work (Copeland 2000). Though clients were not just women at bachelorette parties, women spent considerable sums of money on sex toys in the late twentieth and early twenty-first century. Having these types of parties, particularly in conjunction with a bachelorette evening that is costly on its own, is certainly indicative of a middle- or upper-middle-class status in that these women had money to spend and, arguably, money to waste on items that they themselves deemed useless.

Exercises in Indulgence: Lavish Bachelorette Parties

Bachelorette-party-related businesses encourage women to consume their many services and products, filtering more money into and expanding the already booming wedding industry. While many of the women interviewed bought veils or patronized strip clubs or rented some form of transportation, some, like Ashley and the women at her friend's bachelorette party, took things to another level in terms of consumption of goods and services and the locations of these parties. Lavishness in the bachelorette party is not just about how much money was spent, but also about material display and the apparent need for the bachelorette party to be an event with many elements, rather than just a regular night out. Careful planning and effort is undertaken in order to create a memorable and sometimes unique once-in-a-lifetime experience. Many women had parties that fit these criteria. Not only did these brides-to-be and their friends rent party buses or limousines, they also traveled to major cities or resort areas, in some cases by plane, rented hotel rooms, and had both pre- and post-parties. About one-third of the bachelorette parties described by interviewees were like this. The bachelorette party was not just a night out with friends but an opportunity to show the bride-to-be how much she meant to them. Part of the way that was expressed was by sparing few to no expenses, being willing to do whatever the bride wanted (or the hostess perceived that she wanted), whatever the cost. Though not as obvious as with the shower, it was apparent that being a good friend meant being willing to spend, particularly for bridesmaids or those who planned parties, to go all out celebrating the bride's last night of freedom. Using the same mentality common in justifying wedding spending, the idea that this was a once-in-a-lifetime experience, women spent freely with few complaints about the cost of participation. As Lori commented, when I asked her about differences between bachelorette parties and regular girls' nights out, "Just the excessive drinking and the excessive money being spent. Like you think nothing about spending fifty dollars for a limo. . . . [On a bachelorette party] you'd never think, 'Oh, we can only go one place, so we don't have to pay cover.' As a guest, you don't care. You think, you know, this is their night and you don't want to be cheap about it." Lori, who was one of few women who mentioned expressing concern to the friends who planned her bachelorette party that it not to be too expensive, communicated that she was happy to spend money for a friend's party. She essentially wrote off such expenses as expected and justified given the special circumstances.

Tourism professionals from popular vacation destinations for bachelorette parties recognize brides-to-be and their friends as potential customers and have begun to target advertisements and services specifically to them. Evidence suggests that some women go on cruises, spending upwards of six hundred dollars each for a three-day trip, or rent cabins in the woods for some quality "girl time" (Fischler 2004). Others have even more exotic vacations, taking the bachelorette party and bridal shower on the road to places like Hawaii or Florida (Boston 2004). The travel and tourism commission of Las Vegas has developed a series of print and television advertisements featuring the tag line, "What happens in Vegas, stays in Vegas." In one of these television commercials a group of women is shown riding in a limousine. The women are dressed as if they had been out for a night on the town, one with a white veil attached to her head. It seems as if this is the end of the evening, and all the women are giggling and looking at one woman who looks away, embarrassed and shaking her head. The tag line follows. This ad suggests that crazy and embarrassing things can and do happen on bachelorette parties. The viewer is asked to use her imagination as to what such activities may be, but rest assured, Vegas offers the opportunity for guiltless indulgence in deviance and debauchery. Bachelorette parties are big business for this city, and in the early years of the twenty-first century approximately one hundred parties took place there each month. Bachelor parties used to outnumber bachelorette parties at a rate of ten to one, but the spokesman for the Las Vegas Convention and Visitors Authority suggested that since the turn of the twenty-first century there were almost as many brides-to-be partying in Vegas as grooms-to-be (Fischler 2004). In 2000 a company called Final Fling was created to plan bachelor and bachelorette parties in Las Vegas, and three years later the owner and president noted that the majority of requests for assistance came from women (Barker 2003). For a group of twelve women, a night out including limousine rental, a scavenger hunt with a champagne reward at the end, and VIP club entry, but excluding food, drink, and gratuities (not to mention lodging or airfare), cost approximately $140 (Barker 2003).

Though none went to Sin City, some of the women I interviewed went on elaborate get-away weekends to celebrate, including places like Cancun, Myrtle Beach, and New Orleans. Tammy, a recent bride and a travel agent from the Northeast, arranged such a trip for a friend's bachelorette party. As she said, "She wanted to go away for her party. That's what she wanted to do. She wanted to go to Cancun for a couple of days. . . . We went for like three days. . . . We were all older [in their thirties], so basically we just wanted to go away for a few days. So, we sunned and had a lot of tropical drinks and we just did some shopping. It was just like a mini-vaca[tion]. [That] was what she wanted to do for her last bachelorette-type thing." Although Tammy mentioned she was able to get a good deal on the weekend package because of her job, this was not an inexpensive celebration. The women who participated in this party had to have sufficient financial means and the ability to take time off from work. The party Tammy described was most like a Girls' Night Out bachelorette party; however, other women who did get-away weekends had more stereotypical bachelorette parties, like the one Heather planned and hosted for her best friend in a Southern coastal resort area.

> It was an entire weekend instead of just one night. . . . We had two condos at a resort. . . . We all met there on that Friday, and everybody kind of trickled in that night, and we went to dinner, which everyone paid for themselves. . . . Everybody kind of just chilled out that night. The next day we kind of laid out at the beach for a while, but then I had to get up and start running around. I had to get the T-shirt, food, alcohol [and] to set up and decorate. . . . Since it was springtime, I had this flower garland stuff that I hung up on the walls. I had some confetti that I threw over, and I lit candles . . . all around the room. . . . I had the lights off and let the candles do it. And then we had some serving trays with pizza and Subway sandwiches. . . . We had a lot of beer, vodka, bourbon, and mixers. Oh, and little drink umbrellas. We had a lingerie shower, and we served drinks and food for her at the lingerie shower and, um . . . we had a lot of alcohol. After that I called two cabs to pick us up. . . . They took us to a place that was having a Chippendales revue. . . . After that the cabs came back and took us to a place [with] a piano bar. . . . After that we went dancing and then the bars closed and we all went back home and passed out.

In this case, it seems that Heather considered and attended to every possible detail in planning this bachelorette party. From the decorations in the room to the multiple sites, food, drinks, and lodging, this was clearly an elaborate event that she said cost her alone (other guests made contributions toward the bride's expenses and each paid her own way) about $350. Known among her friends as the "bachelorette party queen," Heather may have felt it necessary to organize a memorable event in order to live up to her reputation. Heather's example, like that of other bridesmaids and party planners, also indicates that the bachelorette party provides an excuse for indulgence. The bride and her friends, mostly middle- and upper-middle-class women, justified their spending, time off from work, in some cases, and general extravagance by noting that their friend deserved a special send-off. Of course, it is not just the bride who indulges at the bachelorette party. Guests seemed to take advantage of the once-in-a-lifetime experience as well, and the bachelorette party provided an excuse for excessive drinking, spending more money than usual on a night out, and engaging in deviant behavior. Thus the bride's liminal status of being not single but not yet married, "betwixt and between" two statuses and thus accorded special privileges (Turner 1969), seemed to extend in some ways to her friends during the bachelorette party. Of course, this once-in-a-lifetime experience is relatively frequent for women in their twenties, as friends and family members marry and they participate in multiple bachelorette parties. Furthermore, the idea of the wedding as a once-in-a-lifetime experience has been constructed and promoted by the wedding industry to sell more goods (Otnes and Pleck 2003, 18). It seems that women—brides-to-be, bridesmaids, and friends—have internalized this message and used it as a justification for their behavior at the bachelorette party.

More common than the out-of-town weekend were the bachelorette parties in which women traveled to a close major city in order to take advantage of the nightlife. For these parties, women rented hotel rooms or suites for the night and, when not in an area where they could walk from bar to bar, limousines or party buses were standard. Women reported spending from one hundred dollars to two hundred dollars per person at these events, which usually began with a pre-party of cocktails and appetizers in the hotel room and a lingerie shower. Guests were expected to bring presents for the bride-to-be, and even when gifts were gag gifts, such as the sex toys and related items described in chapter 4, they still were an added expense. The party described by Ashley that included the sex toy demonstration would be an example of this type of

5.2. At a pre-party in a hotel room, the bride-to-be poses in her veil

event. Ashley hosted the event in a hotel suite (that the bride had won a night's stay in during a bridal show) in a downtown area of a mid-sized Southern city. She chose this location so that the women in the party could walk to the bars to go out for the evening. She began her preparations the day of the party by making chocolate covered strawberries and penis-shaped chocolates. She decorated the room with tissue-paper wedding bells in the colors of the wedding. After she finished decorating and setting up the food and drinks, she and several other friends of the bride took her out to a nice dinner. Then they returned to the hotel and met up with the rest of the party guests, about twenty women in total, and went upstairs to the penthouse suite where the party was to officially begin. In addition to the candy, Ashley served fruit and other light snacks, as well as beer and champagne. As she was working in a restaurant at the time, Ashley borrowed champagne flutes: "So we wouldn't be drinking out of plastic or anything." The next activity was the sex toy demonstration, then sales and games facilitated by the saleswoman. After that, there was a cake for the bride-to-be, which the women enjoyed while drinking more champagne. Even though Ashley had suggested gifts were not necessary, some women brought lingerie for the bride-to-be and so gifts were also opened during that time. Most of the women then continued the party out at a dance club where the bride-to-be, dressed in a veil and a Suck for a Buck shirt that Ashley made, was given a list of tasks to complete. After the dance club they went to another bar, and then five of the women went back to the hotel and spent the night there.

Even bachelorette parties that were one night only and did not involve a hotel room were often extravagant, certainly more so than a regular girls' night out. Many women rented transportation, and most included a pre-party with some gifts (rather than an organized lingerie shower), drinks, and snacks and then went out to clubs or bars, as described in detail in chapter 4. An example of a local yet lavish bachelorette party would be one depicted by Grace that took place in the Washington, D.C., metropolitan area. This night, she noted, cost approximately two hundred dollars per person and involved a pre-party at someone's home, a rented van and driver, gifts, and stops at multiple night clubs, including a strip club, most of which had cover charges and what she described as expensive drinks. And Bryn, who lived in the Northeast but was from the South, also attended an extravagant bachelorette party in Washington, D.C.

> We took a bus and a driver. The man she was marrying was very wealthy and the family had a van pick us up [in another state, more than two hours away] and drive us to a crab place in Maryland, and we all had crabs and Bloody Mary's during the day. Then the van drove us into D.C. and we got together at one of the bridesmaid's homes, and then we watched a videotape where questions had been asked of her fiancé and recorded and she had to guess what he would answer and then they'd play his answers. . . . We were very dressed up. We had very civilized drinks and that type of stuff at the house. And then we went out to dinner. . . . We all brought presents. . . . And then we went out to several bars that she used to hang out at when she was in college, this whole circuit of bars. . . . It was all day and then it culminated in the whole drinking binge of the evening. And . . . we all had hats that said, "Jane's getting married."

This was an expensive and long celebration. Bryn was picked up in the morning on a Saturday and was out until early the next day. The groom's family funded the party, complete with custom-embroidered hats so they would be identifiable as part of a group as well as for a souvenir to take home. They had a pre-party, two meals out, went to four different night clubs, and gave gifts to the bride-to-be. This was certainly an elaborate affair.

There were interesting regional differences in the degree of excess. Women from the Northeast rarely had as lavish bachelorette parties as those from the South. Only two described weekends away with rented hotel rooms, both within driving distance of the bride's home. One of these was a trip to the beach, where the party guests stayed in a "disgusting, dirty," inexpensive motel, obviously indicative of the limited budgets of the women who were recent college graduates at the time. Rarely did women in the northeastern region have lingerie showers before going out, and most felt a gift, novelty or heartfelt, was not required. Although party planners usually purchased a lot of props for the bride-to-be to use and limousines or other forms of transportation were arranged for the night, it seems that the northern women spent less money and time on bachelorette parties when compared to the women from the southeastern region. Furthermore, the bachelorette party was more likely to be an afterthought, planned as a distraction for the bride while her fiancé was out for his bachelor party, for women in the North than in the South. Why did the southeastern women have more excessive bachelorette parties? Perhaps they did so because in the South there is a greater emphasis on manners and etiquette, and bachelorette parties, though often risqué, are still parties and opportunities to display status and demonstrate proper upbringing. If these women were taught that a gift was expected when going to a party, then they may have felt inclined to bring a gift, albeit one that matched the licentious nature of the event. Furthermore, there remains a greater emphasis on traditional gender roles and displays of masculinity and femininity among southern women, as was evident in their descriptions of the bridal shower and the behavior expected there. Thus, it may be that the southern women were complying with similar feminine expectations of expressing care by hosting elaborate bachelorette parties and spending money. Or, these women may have had more to symbolically mock or express regret over during their last days of being single as their status as wives is more defined and carries more traditional expectations than is the case for most of the women in the Northeast.

Another explanation is that, overall, more of the southern women were from wealthier backgrounds than the women in the Northeast. Even though most women in this study self-identified as middle class, variations in class position were apparent in discussions of the bachelorette party, even more so than for the bridal shower. And it seems that, given the greater amount of money spent by the southern women, this is likely to reflect their higher social standing. Because the bridal shower is more bounded by traditional feminine structure and has a standard time frame, there was less room for a clear identification of class, although class was certainly relevant, as will be discussed below. Additionally, since bachelorette parties were nearly always funded by the bride's peers (in contrast with bridal showers that were often supplemented by the bride's, hostesses', or groom's families), these events were more telling in terms of the class status of the interviewee herself rather than the status ascribed to her by her family.

Thus, not only an expression of changes in women's sexuality, the bachelorette party may also be explained as a part of a larger trend in making the wedding into an extravagant and memorable celebration, extending from the time of the engagement through the honeymoon. The presence and popularity of the bachelorette party seems to have increased as the emphasis on the lavish wedding has increased. It may be that the party is a way to further the excitement and to display one's class status by equating materialism and the ability and willingness to share one's wealth with care or love for the bride-to-be. Also, it seems likely that the format of the bachelorette party has been influenced by the developing industry. It is certainly easier for women to express sexual "liberation" or to flaunt their sexuality when there are places, like male strip clubs, and companies, like those that sell sex toys, that facilitate and increase the social acceptability of doing so.

Social Class and the Shower: Consumption and Status Displays

Over the course of her year-long engagement, twelve pre-wedding parties (mostly showers) were thrown for Reva and her fiancé. Though this was not typical, most women in this study, particularly those in the South, had more than one shower. Overall, the average number of showers per bride was 2.46; however, southern brides had an average of 3.63

showers compared to 1.60 for northeastern brides. Occasionally, having multiple showers was a practical idea when, for example, the bride's family lived in one state, and the groom's in another. In a couple of cases, brides were given multiple showers because of divorce or remarriage and a desire to avoid conflict between mothers and stepmothers. Also, sometimes friends would throw a shower separately from family. But equally as often, multiple showers seemed to be given for no logistical reason. Rather, many people wanted to celebrate the bride and groom's upcoming wedding and offered to throw parties for them. These showers became opportunities to display status through location and details of the event and gifts given. Some showers could be described as lavish, paralleling wedding receptions. One interviewee described a catered bridal luncheon held in the late afternoon in a tent set up in the backyard of the hostess. Another told of a shower in which guests were treated to a multicourse meal at a country club. About half of the bridal showers attended by the women I interviewed could be described as "lavish," meaning that they were formal and elaborate in terms of the location or food. Nearly all showers featured extravagance in some way, primarily via the presentation of gifts. All participants in the bridal shower were called to display their social status in one way or another, and for certain participants, heightened attention was given to their focal role. Specifically, for some mothers of the bride the shower was an opportunity to show off their daughters and themselves.

Mother of the Bride: The Wedding She Never Had

While I was engaged and making decisions about dresses, reception location, and other elements of the wedding, my mother, who married in the mid-1960s, often commented that her mother made all of the decisions about her wedding, yet brides of my generation determined how their weddings would be. She lamented not having the opportunity to plan a wedding, and it seemed that the shower, held at her home, was one place where she could aid the bridesmaids in coordinating a wedding element which I was uninvolved in planning. Most of the women in this study had mothers who were contemporaries of my mother and may have felt similarly. Mothers often involved themselves in hosting the bridal shower, even when traditional etiquette dictated that they should not. Brides and their mothers often have different ideas about how the wedding should be, which creates tension for both parties (Otnes and Pleck 2003). The shower is a space where mothers often have or claim more influence than in other aspects of wedding planning, and they may see it as a way of living out their own wedding fantasies that may have been rejected in other areas.

Several women in this study noted that the bridal shower was a big day not just for the bride, but for the mother of the bride as well. Somewhat surprisingly, these women were not referring to the significance and marking of daughters growing up and moving into the next stage of their lives (although some women did mention this). Rather, these women commented on how mothers saw the shower as momentous because it was an opportunity to show off, to display their homes or class status to other women friends, family members, or to the groom's family. Even though traditional etiquette dictated that the mother was not expected or supposed to host the bridal shower, most interviewees suggested that mothers were very involved, making suggestions about elements such as the menu, shower location, or decorations. As Brenda, a bridesmaid who planned a friend's shower, noted, the bride's mother had very specific ideas for how her daughter's shower should be. She said, "The mother, she just had to be in on everything. And, to me, to plan the bridal shower is more of the bridal party does that, not the mom. And she just had to have everything her way, which was very frustrating. It was beautiful, but it was ridiculous. My idea of a bridal shower is in the house where you grew up and maybe twenty people at most. And to rent a hall and have forty-plus people there and all catered and this huge cake and the decorations and the party favors. . . . She ended up doing it all anyway. All that I ended up doing was getting food. And then even when I made the menu she didn't like it."

Brenda indicated that she thought this shower was too extravagant and that, had she been in charge, as she felt she and the other bridesmaids should have been, she would have done things differently. But for the bride's mother, this seemed to be an important event, one of the prewedding pep rallies that would set the tone for the type of wedding she and her husband would throw for their daughter. It may be that this bride's mother had a vision of how her daughter's shower should be, how her wedding should be, and for her it was consequential to see that vision realized. Perhaps, she had been imagining her daughter's wedding—the whole spectacle and process of events—for some time. The mother of the bride is, after all, a star player in the wedding and is afforded "celebrity status," given her close association to the happy couple (Otnes and Pleck 2003, 271). Thus, she may feel entitled to execute the perfect shower, or at least have her hand in doing so, because it is her big day as well. As Turner noted, rituals of status transition are significant not just for the initiate but also for the community. A daughter's transition from single to married brings change not just for the couple but for those in their community as well, and it is likely that mothers are among the most impacted.

Josephine had a particularly lavish wedding shower, almost on par with an afternoon wedding reception, held in a banquet room at a country club. For her shower, planned and hosted by her aunt (with much suggestion and behind-the-scenes assistance from her mother), a great deal of time and special effort was made to provide an elegant ambiance. This included the on-site construction of a gazebo for the bride (and groom, the only man at the shower) to sit in while opening gifts. Josephine described it: "For [my mom] it was a chance to show off to people at times. Hundreds and hundreds of yards of tulle was brought in and wrapped around the gazebo and around the tables and was just brought around the room. They worked from seven in the morning until the shower started around noon. And I think to her that was a chance to show people how much she cares, and what she can do." When I asked her if she talked with her mother before shower about what she wanted, Josephine quickly replied that she had "no say, whatsoever." When I asked her if this was because she thought her mother wanted to surprise her, she responded by saying, "I think she had an idea of what she wanted my day to be like. Even for my wedding, she knew what she wanted my wedding to be like and how it was to be. And I was just part of the package."

Tammy, who married when she was thirty-four, said that the shower was important to her mother for similar reasons. Since she was from a large family, she and her mother had attended many family members' weddings and showers. Tammy believed her mother was happy to finally have the opportunity to host a shower herself. She said, "It was a big deal to my mom. She had just finished remodeling the house the week before the shower. My mom is very big on appearances. Not necessarily one-upping relatives, but putting on a good show, having a good party, and doing at least just as good as everybody else. 'Cause I am older, so pretty much all of the cousins have been married at least once, . . . so we've been to all of the weddings over all of the years, so, for once, she was happy that people were coming to us. I think it meant a lot to her to put on a good show." Although Tammy suggested that her mother wanted to show off her new house, it seems that she also appreciated the opportunity to have her family celebrate her daughter, particularly her success in the romance department. Tammy's mother, like Josephine's and Brenda's friend's mother, appeared to want to display her daughter's success in having found a man, maybe because in so doing she showed her success as a parent. As a society consumed with heterosexual romance, and one that places the majority of responsibility of child rearing on mothers, it would seem that the mother's role in encouraging and supporting traditional romantic expectations and relationships is not insignificant. Because women's success is more often defined by marriage and family as opposed to career achievements, the shower is the first (or one of the first, if couples have engagement parties) time for the bride's family to demonstrate and show off their daughter's accomplishments. So, it may be that the shower is significant for the mother of bride because it symbolizes her mothering ability as well as her class standing. Furthermore, women are expected to express an ethic of care, and one of the primary ways this care is expected to be conveyed is through mothering (Gilligan 1998). Thus, mothers of the brides may create lavish or extravagant showers because they see the shower as an expression of care for their daughters. Spending more money or attending to detail seems to be a way to demonstrate love for a daughter, conveying the attitude that a daughter's wedding and happiness in love is an occasion where no expense should be spared, as being thrifty might come across as a lack of care. Parents justify spending exorbitant sums on weddings because of the emotional rewards they receive from doing so and because there is a cultural association between the amount spent and the perceived level of care or love (Otnes and Pleck 2003). The shower is part of this overall spending and is legitimized by the same ethic.

The Gifts: Materialism and Status Display

The mother is not the only one who displays her social standing at the shower. Each shower guest has an obligation to present a gift, and those gifts function as indicators of status. As Bourdieu (1984) noted, gifts are essentially about connections between individuals, families, and other social groups. They are markers of who one is and who one perceives the recipient to be. Annually, more than eighteen billion dollars is spent on gifts for the bride and groom (Ingraham 1999, 48). The current custom of the bridal registry, a list of preferences from selected department or specialty stores, is usually used as a tool for the purchase of shower gifts. As many people shop from the registry for bridal showers, and as the bride herself has registered, there is a general awareness about how much registry items cost. Spending more money, or the ability to spend more money, can be used as a way to display social status, both in terms of financial comfort and in terms of relationship to the bride. Most women reported spending approximately twenty-five to fifty dollars on shower gifts, with those in the wedding party often spending more. Interviewees from the Northeast reported spending more money on gifts than those in the Southeast. The greater number of showers held in the South may explain this. If women attend multiple showers, it may be that they spend more money on gifts overall, but less for each shower. At many of the showers described and several of the showers I observed, it seems that some women used gifts to display their social-class standing, their creativity in personalizing registry gifts, or their abundant affection for the bride.

For example, Josephine described a situation in which a mother of a groom and a mother of a bride tried to use shower gifts to "one up" each other. She said, "The mothers went berserk. [The bride's] mother and mother-in-law had a contest, who could buy more. One bought her eight Lenox place settings and the other bought her eight pieces of the silver and then put everything in a hatbox with all the side platters for the Lenox. They had a contest to see who could pay more." In this case, the mother of the bride and the mother of groom seemed to be using the gifts to display both their social positions and affection for the couple. Fine china and silver are very expensive, and giving large quantities of these items gives the impression that the giver is well off. Furthermore, Josephine's analysis of the interaction as a "contest" also suggests that these two women were competing with one another for the bride's reaction and gratitude as well as, perhaps, a positive evaluation by the guests at the shower. In his analysis of the rules for giving Christmas gifts, Theodore Caplow suggests that "the economic values of any giver's gifts

5.3. An abundance of gifts at a bridal shower

are supposed to be sufficiently scaled to the emotional values of relationships" (1984, 1313). Thus, the mother of the bride may have wanted to give her daughter more gifts or more expensive gifts than anyone else to demonstrate that she is closest to and cares for her child more than anyone else and is thus entitled to spend the most. The mother-in-law-to-be may have used gifts to build or bolster her relationship with the bride. She may have seen gifts as a way of showing her feelings for her future daughter-in-law and the bride's relationship with her son. Thus, she may have bought more because she felt that the amount of money spent would be seen as representative of her feelings for the bride and the impending marriage. Also, as it is more often those closest to the bride who host the shower, mothers of the groom-to-be may perceive their gift as a representation of their family's status. Because the bride's family also traditionally pays for the wedding, the groom's mother may view the shower gift as needing to be expensive so that they do not appear cheap or ungrateful for the amount of money being spent on the entire wedding. After all, unlike wedding gifts, shower gifts are opened in public and displayed or passed around so that others see who gave what. Each participant looks to the shower as an opportunity to symbolically express relationship, connection, and status. The gifts function as symbols of these sentiments.

Brittany, a lower-middle-class woman who was engaged at the time of her interview, noted that she liked to give unique gifts, rather than items from a bridal registry. She commented, "[I like to give] personalized items, like wineglasses with their names on it or something. It all depends on the person. Like it—it's a cousin, it might be a little different than a close friend. . . . Very rarely do I do house gifts 'cause I like to make something special for them. . . . I don't like to spend a lot of money 'cause I don't have it, especially when you go to like twenty [showers]." Rather than display her lower-middle-class status with an obviously less expensive registry gift, Brittany opted to do something different. She demonstrated how much she cared by making special efforts to give unique gifts. Other women, however, like the mother and mother-in-law described by Josephine, seemed to see spending more money, giving more expensive items like place settings or small appliances, as the primary means to communicate relationship. These people seem to have been guided by the same sentiments that Otnes and Pleck (2003) described in making sense of why people spend so much money on weddings. People want to show who they are, and they justify wedding spending as necessary because it is for a once-in-a-lifetime event. Generally, most women stated that they spend less on the shower gift than the wedding gift; however, I received some items at my shower, like china place settings, that I also received as wedding gifts, as did women whose showers I observed and whom I interviewed.

When brides had multiple showers and bridesmaids were invited and expected to come to more than one shower and purchase multiple shower gifts, it seems that the meaning of each gift and the shower itself diminished into empty presentations of material goods. The structure of the shower, with gift opening as the focal activity, made it difficult for brides to show appreciation for each gift, particularly at large showers. At Claire's shower, she was upset because the gift opening became like an assembly line activity, "We had people handing 'em, opening 'em, and it was like a machine. . . . We opened like forty-nine gifts, and then I almost felt like it was forced because we didn't even have time to chat 'cause we were going to the next one." She felt badly that she had not given proper recognition to each gift giver, making it seem that her concern was just on getting goods rather than appreciating the graciousness of the gesture. Guests and bridesmaids also noted the banality of the ritual and the gift giving as an obligation and sometimes even a burden. Stacey, for example, was a bridesmaid for a sorority sister who had multiple showers. When I asked if the bride-to-be had more than one shower, she said, exaggerating somewhat, "She probably had fifteen. We gave her just a plain [no theme] shower. She had the lingerie shower. She had a house and garden shower, a Christmas shower, a Tupperware shower, um, . . . bath and linen shower. She had a whole bunch." And, as bridesmaids, Stacey and many of her sorority sisters were invited to most of these showers and expected to bring a gift to each event. By one of the last showers, Stacey implied she was losing interest and growing resentful of the expectation. She said, "It almost seemed like the only reason was to give her a present because as soon as the presents were opened, everybody left." Stacey continued, saying that in the beginning she had enjoyed being a part of this friend's wedding, but "it got really old, really fast. After the third it was enough. I had already been to four or five by March, so I was pretty showered out by then." Later in the interview she returned to this subject and this bride and said, "I feel bad [because] I made [this bride] seem like all she wanted was the presents. But I think that was very important to her. She was very concerned that she wasn't going to get all of her china. She actually wanted our theme to be china. And her china was really expensive. There was no way we could ask other college students to buy her eighty-dollar plates. So I think towards the end she was just looking for the gifts. Maybe in the beginning it was a celebration, 'Oh, we're getting married,' very exciting. But probably after the fifth shower [it was] 'Are we going to get any good stuff?' " It would seem that this bride was concerned with material accumulation and having all of the right goods to start her new household. Not just basics, but also china, crystal, and silver were on this bride's registry; and, as Stacey noted, it was important to her to acquire these things. As a woman in a materialistic, consumerist society, Stacey's friend may have viewed these goods as symbolic of adult status and wife status. Because wives are more often expected to be responsible for all aspects of home, china and silver may have been props that facilitated her transition from single woman to wife. So, Stacey's friend, seemingly a very traditional bride, may have been raised with the expectation that she would receive her china and crystal when she married, and this may have been a symbolic step toward becoming a woman who would be the hostess of

5.4. To make the shower efficient, bridesmaids assist the bride in opening her gifts

formal dinners and parties. Some southern women even mentioned that they or their friends began registering for such gifts before they were even engaged. Heather, a bridesmaid, noted this when she talked about a friend whose shower she attended: "[Her family is] very Old South. And they wanted to start buying her something nice . . . when she got [to be] about eighteen. So she actually had about half a set of the holiday china and just used her wedding to complete that."

While women in the South, like Stacey's and Heather's friends, may be more concerned with etiquette and may be more inclined to use formal dining wares than those in the North, several women in both regions remarked that they had registered for fine china, crystal, or silver flatware although they admitted that they did not know why they did or when they would have the occasion to use such items. They seemed to feel it important to register for them and, more importantly, to have these goods anyway. Like the brides in Currie's (1993) study who felt caught up in following the standard wedding preparation script, it seems these women were simply acting on the basis of tradition and norms. Consistent with the current ethic of consumerism and the accumulation of material possessions, most brides registered, and they registered for unnecessary items. Some recent research suggests that a growing trend for couples is to register for more exotic or extravagant items such as "a $500 crystal ice bucket," vacations, major appliances like washing machines or clothes dryers, large furniture items like sofas or beds, or even mortgage payments; Otnes and Pleck noted that contemporary couples make use of wedding Web sites where they can let guests know where they are registered, and these registries now include "everything from traditional items to Blockbuster video vouchers, stocks, mutual funds, frequent flier miles, down payments for a mortgage, and hiking treks to Nepal" (2003, 77). In some ways the bridal registry seems to empty the meaning of gift giving, and this may be another explanation for women's dislike of bridal showers. Rather than selecting a personal gift on one's own, the registry transforms gift giving from a personal gesture to one that would more accurately be interpreted by guests as the couple saying, "Here's what we want; this is where you can find it; buy it for us." And women like Stacey did not miss this message, nor did others who reported growing tired of their friends' materialism. Geller (2001) made a similar assessment. She argued that the registry and the requirement of shower gifts produces resentment among guests not because they are not happy for the bride (and groom) but because of the expectation that a certain type of gift be purchased and a certain amount of money be spent as an expression of that happiness. Some shower themes take the depersonalization of gift giving to an extreme, making no pretenses about the real purpose of the shower. Though none of the women here had or attended such showers, some mentioned the existence of "money tree" showers, where brides-to-be were given cash or gift certificates rather than gifts. Shower-planning books note that if the bride lives far away, that doesn't mean she shouldn't receive a shower. In *Bridal Showers: 50 Great Ideas for a Perfect Shower*, Dlugosch and Nelson (1984, 79) encouraged bridesmaids in this situation to instruct guests to send gifts to the bride and groom for them to open at a designated time. The party planner invites guests over to call the couple at that time to wish them well as they open their presents. This focus on gifts as the primary reason for the shower may have been more readily accepted if brides-to-be had only one shower or if there was a demonstrated need for such items. However, as the majority of the women in this sample and the brides-to-be whose showers they attended were middle or upper middle class, there were few showers given for a bride-to-be who truly needed the gifts she received in order to start her household.

The Right Way Is the Middle Way: Taste and Distinction

Many interviewees suggested that there was a proper way for a shower to be "done" and thus implied or stated explicitly that some showers they had attended were not up to par. Like mothers of brides, many of the women communicated their middle- and upper-middle-class status and biases when they described the way a shower should be. Anna, for example, suggested that she preferred showers that were held in restaurants to those held at home because the latter seemed to express a lack of care for the bride. She said, "I personally like the showers that are . . . at a restaurant better. . . . You kind of know what you're there for. . . . One I went to at the house. It was real informal, and if I were her I think I would have been a little disappointed." The shower out at a restaurant is considerably more expensive than the shower held at home. One shower that I observed was a luncheon held at an Italian restaurant. It included a champagne fountain, several kinds of appetizers, and a four-course meal in which we could choose what type of salad, pasta, and entrée we wanted. Another that I attended and helped organize was also held in a restaurant, and there were more than fifty guests at a cost of approximately twenty dollars per person. It would seem that financial status would influence one's ability to host such a shower, suggesting that the shower held out was probably more common among those of higher social classes.

Some women were more straightforward about variations in showers they attended, labeling some showers as "working class," with a tone that suggested that they did not approve or that they would have done things differently. One recent bride, describing a friend's shower, noted, "[It] was in a fire hall. That was the only one I went to that I think was in a fire hall. . . . You walked up yourself, and they had paper plates . . . and you sat on big long, long metal tables with metal chairs and just watched her. And they had a U-Haul waiting outside. There was eighty people there. I think they gave out a sponge as a favor. It was very, um, working class. . . . The tablecloths didn't even cover the table all of the way. . . . So that was a basic, bare bones shower. No wishing well, no recipe cards." While this woman enjoyed her friend's shower, her tone of voice and labeling it as "working class" demonstrated her awareness of class levels and the idea that middle-class and upper-middle-class women do things differently when they host a shower. It was also apparent that she felt that the middle-class way was the right or better way, as to her it seemed to indicate a greater level of care for the bride-to-be. Heather, who described herself as being from a "middle-class/working-class" background but whose friends were upper middle class made some interesting observations about the differences between the showers her family had and those of her friends. She said, "My family is very middle class/working class, and when they give a shower it's usually at the church, in the fellowship hall. . . . And the showers that I have with my girlfriends now, those are always at someone's house. There's always a big spread of food. China is used. Silver is used. People are more dressed up. It's almost like church-wear. Whereas, these other showers, there's people in blue jeans. There's sometimes alcohol served at my friends' showers, like mimosas or stuff like that. And our showers always have a theme." Heather seemed easily socialized into the upper-middle-class shower as she reported spending a lot of money on shower gifts, different from what her family does for showers. She said, "I have a budget I set for my friends . . . around $100 . . . [to] $140. [For one friend] I broke it up for her shower[s]. . . . I got her an ice cream maker that she registered for and rock salt and ice cream mix and little ice-cream fountain glasses from Crate and Barrel and sprinkles. And . . . that night I got her the blender that they registered for and some tequila and triple sec." Heather's comments indicate that rather than fitting the shower to her budget, as she was a student and unemployed during several of these weddings, instead she stretched her finances to match the social class of the recipient and other guests at the shower. She knew what types of gifts were appropriate and spent accordingly, even when it was more than she could afford. Heather's internalization of upper-middle-class expectations was apparent when she described her reaction to a shower she attended in a rural area in the South. She noted:

> Small town people just do things differently. [A friend] had one shower like with about eighty guests, hosted by nine people. Those

> nine people went in together and bought her one place setting, at nine dollars a piece. I thought that was tacky. And that's just me going to showers in the city, though. Also for that shower, for her flatware, stainless, somebody just gave her a spoon. I didn't even know you could buy them separately. I didn't know they were sold open stock like that. And she was just kinda, "Thanks for the spoon" [*laughs*]. That's bitchy, I know, but . . . you've got to have a decent gift . . . and I go to one and somebody actually thinks dishtowels is an acceptable gift. . . . And I mean some people I do take into account their financial situation; you know, it's nice that they can come. But you know who's financially hurting and who's not. And who should know better. Let me just say that.

It was apparent that Heather followed middle-class etiquette in attending and hosting showers and used those as standards to evaluate others. Like other women interviewed, Heather noted the difference between "cheap" and "tacky" gifts and those purchased by people of higher social standing.

Gifts were not the only way middle-class bias was evident. Décor and food also factored into women's evaluations of showers. For example, Bryn, an upper-middle-class engaged woman with friends whom she described as very wealthy, also noted the variations in class tastes and distinction, particularly when she and her fiancé hosted a coed shower for friends.

> The couples shower that we hosted . . . the girl getting married is marrying one of my fiancé's friends. She's very, I don't know, Fifth Avenue, Manhattan. We set them up . . . but he, his family, his dad's a truck driver—very completely different background than what she's from. His sister and her husband . . . helped us a little bit with the shower, and her sister's husband was like, "Why am I at the shower?" Like just didn't get it. I mean I don't think [couples showers are] the greatest idea ever, but it seems to be common, and I wonder if maybe they are common among a certain group of people, a certain income-class expectation type. I don't know how to describe it. . . . [While setting up for the shower] he was also like, "What do you want me to do with this brie?" And I was like, "*That's* the goat cheese; *that's* the brie." [His wife] wanted pepperoni. I was

> like, "No one's going to want pepperoni," [but] I didn't say that. She was like, "Everyone wants pepperoni; I'm getting pepperoni." No one ate the pepperoni, but everyone ate everything I made.

Bryn implied that she considered this couple to be working class and that maybe class affected what type of shower you had and your expectations for what type of food should be served. Middle-class people, particularly upper-middle-class people, pride themselves on their awareness of and ability to distinguish between items considered to be less mainstream, particularly food (Bourdieu 1984). Thus, Bryn's ability to differentiate between goat cheese and brie served as a marker of her status and, consequently, of the groom's brother's working-class status. In her world and in that of her friends such distinctions are obvious, as is the idea that serving pepperoni at a shower would be inappropriate. Bryn's suggestion that coed showers are more of an upper-middle-class activity is consistent with my research findings, as the coed shower seems to be an addition rather than a replacement for a traditional wedding shower. It makes sense that the higher one's social class, the more likely one is to have multiple showers or supplemental showers. This is because some of the same people are often invited to multiple showers, bridesmaids, close friends, and family members; thus, these people are expected to spend more on gifts. It is likely that hostesses would be aware of this and this would affect one's decision to host an additional shower.

Otnes and Pleck noted that throughout history weddings have functioned as opportunities to demonstrate class standing; however, as the lavish wedding has become common among most social classes, those in the higher classes focus on finding ways to personalize their celebrations. As Otnes and Pleck suggested, "Where there is great affluence, people then search for individualism and self-expression. . . . Distinctiveness is now as important as luxury, because taste becomes as much a marker of class as money" (2003, 5). One of the ways this is evident in pre-wedding events is in the ways that women, particularly younger peers of brides-to-be, modify the shower format by giving "theme" showers. Like the coed shower, the theme shower is a supplement rather than a replacement for the traditional shower. And in many cases themes are focused on nonessential items such as holiday decorations (Christmas shower) or consumables (bottle and bar shower), indicating that the couple either already has or has been given necessary items. Reva, the bride who had a dozen pre-wedding parties, is an exaggerated example of this emphasis on personalization and consumption. When we began talking about bridal showers, she started by giving an overview of the showers that were given for her:

> Lawn and garden—we got a lot of stuff for the house and outside stuff. His aunt and uncle gave us that one at their house. We got a lawnmower, a couple of weed-eaters . . . big things. . . . The next one was bed and bath, and that was given by two of my friends, two of my bridesmaids, and that was just like sheets and towels and pillows. . . . The next one was stock the bar. And my [husband's] sister and her husband threw that one . . . and that one we got a ton of, you know, we got a bunch of beer; we got a bunch of liquor; we got nine or ten bottles of wine, . . . a blender, cosmopolitan cocktail set, wine glasses, stuff that we registered for. . . . I had three miscellaneous showers. . . . [One] at my church, another at home that there was about eighty, eighty-five people there, and that was given by eight hostesses, all my parents' friends. . . . And the next one we had a cocktail party . . . where my husband's from, and that was given by his parent's friends. . . . [I had another] miscellaneous shower at [my husband's] parents' neighbors' house. . . . After that then I count my lingerie party, and that was like fifteen people there. . . . And then I had a kitchen and brunch shower. It was given by two of [my husband's] aunts . . . and then that same night . . . it was a stock-the-pantry party that night. We got a hundred-dollar gift certificate to the grocery store, like napkins, mustard, and pepper. Just stuff that you have to buy but we won't have to buy for a long time. . . . The next one I had was just a weekday night, and it was a Pampered Chef party that was given by [my husband's] mom's people that she works with . . . and that was cool because I picked out the stuff I wanted and people bought it for me.

These showers were far from the original purpose of the shower, in which friends and family gave the bride-to-be, who had very little, basic household items so that she would be able to marry. Reva and her then-fiancé were self-sufficient, successful people in their mid-twenties, both of whom worked and were enjoying an upper-middle-class lifestyle.

They purchased a home that they moved into after the wedding. Clearly, they did not need people to buy them household basics like pots and pans or salt and pepper. And while they were certainly the exception with the number of showers held in their honor, many of the brides-to-be in this sample were from similar backgrounds. All worked at the time of the interview and either alone or with their fiancés or husbands were financially stable. It is certainly conceivable that any young couple might need some household items, as about half of the brides in this sample did not live with their fiancés prior to marriage. Yet, this could be and usually was satisfied by the traditional miscellaneous shower.

So, what then is the purpose of these additional showers? First, it seems that they serve as social occasions. They provide an opportunity for family and friends to come together, and this fosters connection and relationships among gender communities and families in general. Second, as materialism becomes the dominant way that care and support for friends is expressed, particularly during the wedding process, it gives people a symbolic way to show their affection for the bride-to-be and/or the couple. Additionally, the theme shower becomes a way for the hostess or hostesses to express their social standing and creativity. If middle- and upper-middle-class people know that people of all social classes have lavish weddings and pre-wedding parties, a way to further distinguish one's social standing would be to have more and better parties. By hosting a shower that is fun and unique, like, for example, a coed cocktail party or tailgate-themed pig roast attended by fellow university alumni football fans, one gives the impression that one is creative and knows how to produce a good, memorable event. From the descriptions given by southern women, who were more likely to have multiple showers, theme showers, and coed showers, it seems that this self-presentation and concern with the image given through the shower are important to hostesses, families, and friends of the families of the bride and groom. Brides like Reva and Bryn, bridesmaids like Heather and Stacey, all southern women gave examples of this concern with the image and either explicitly or implicitly called attention to the shower as a way of demonstrating one's class position. Similarly, brides and guests also seemed to use the bridal registry as a way to display their status and individuality. Brides (and grooms) who registered at upscale stores like Bloomingdales, Nordstrom, or Williams Sonoma sent different messages to guests about who they were, what they liked, and the image they planned to project in their homes than did those who registered at places like Target; Bed, Bath, and Beyond; or Sears.

The Expense of the Shower: A Middle-Class Shower on a Working-Class Budget

Not everyone was happy about the lavishness of weddings. Bridesmaids who were encouraged to plan extravagant bridal showers by mothers of the bride or brides sometimes felt resentful or even hostile about having to do so, since the financial burden was on them. Megan, who was unemployed and struggling financially part of the time while she was maid of honor for her best friend, felt compelled to spend more than she could afford in order to live up to her friend's standards. She said, "There is still a lot of bitterness about the amount of money that was spent. Everywhere I tried to cut corners and save money, she wanted to spend that money someplace else. I was just giving in to it. I wasn't sure how it was going to work. Traditionally, the maid of honor paid for everything. Her mom said she'd split it with us. The whole wedding, being in the wedding, cost me $1,500. For her shower gift . . . we gave individual gifts; I spent like $200 to $250." While being in her best friend's wedding might have been a meaningful experience that they enjoyed together, instead, Megan felt their relationship was harmed by her friend's disregard for Megan's financial situation and the bride's reluctance to cut corners and avoid what Megan deemed unnecessary and extravagant expenses. Why did Megan not put her foot down or simply explain that she could not afford to spend what was being asked of her? It seems that being maid of honor was a privilege for which she felt she should be grateful and that she owed it to her friend to help make her wedding fantasies reality. Additionally, like the bride-to-be, Megan probably subscribed to the cultural norm of the lavish wedding as a right (Otnes and Pleck 2003) and on some level assumed that she was bound by custom and would not have grounds to seriously protest. If she had, it is likely that it would have been Megan who would have been viewed as the bad friend, rather than the indulged bride.

Other women found the excess and lavishness unnecessarily formal or indulgent and objected on those grounds. It was not (or not only) that they could not afford such a shower, but women like Nicole suggested that they were just "too much" with all the extravagance already associated with the wedding. She said, "I prefer [to have or go to showers at] a house. I think it's just cozier, nicer. You don't have to spend all of that money to go to a restaurant." And Hilary described the divergence in views between her mother and herself on what to spend on a shower gift. Unable to attend a shower, Hilary planned to send a small, inexpensive item. Her mother thought she should do more. She noted, "I was just going to go Victoria's Secret and pick something up and my mom was like, 'Where is she registered?' and I was like, 'Mom, you want me to go and get a $50 shower gift for a shower [I] didn't go to?' So I was like, 'No, just a token $25 Victoria's Secret thing,' and my mom, traditionalist in her own way, was like, 'Oh no.' At my age and my generation, I don't have to go and get her a $50 or $100 vacuum. We had such different ideas, really different ideas."

There was a notable tension, which seemed to be related to both age and generation, between those who planned the showers and mothers of brides. Mothers of the bride were often overly involved in the wedding shower, even though most of the bridesmaids and shower planners viewed the orchestration of the shower to be their responsibility. Much of the intergenerational discord seemed to relate back to these financial issues when a mother of the bride encouraged bridesmaids to plan showers that were beyond their budgets. Some bridesmaids expressed frustration at this lack of awareness of the financial situations of college students or recent college graduates with student loans.

In summary, showers function as a means by which people express their social-class standing. This is accomplished by both their evaluations of showers that others give and by what they deem appropriate in terms of gifts, food, and atmosphere of the shower. Some bridal showers are lavish, with catered meals or rented halls and excessive decorations. With both the bridal shower and the bachelorette party, it seems that women connect spending money and giving the bride material goods with the level of care of a party planner or hostess. Spending more money is both explicitly and implicitly read as a sign of affection and considered requisite for these once-in-a-lifetime celebrations. Such spending bolsters and fuels the wedding industry, as most of the goods and services consumed at bachelorette parties and bridal showers are provided by the wedding or supporting industries (see Ingraham 1999 for discussion of the different tiers of the wedding industry). As women have more indulgent pre-wedding events, showers with themes, and bachelorette party overnights or weekends, the industry expands, furthering the social rewards associated with and the commercial emphasis on love and marriage.

Chapter 6

Something Different

Variations in Pre-wedding Rituals

This book focuses primarily on the bridal showers and bachelorette parties of middle- and upper-middle-class white American women. Other women and men celebrate such events differently, if at all. There is great cultural variation in the way weddings are constructed and executed around the world; thus, it makes sense that there would be variation in pre-wedding rituals as well. In this chapter I explore variations in pre-wedding rituals from around the country and around the world. Some rituals have strong similarities to bridal showers or bachelorette parties. Others are very different, reflective of different conceptions of marriage and the roles of bride and groom, wife and husband. However, at their core all have a similar function; to prepare the bride (and in a few cases the couple) for her new status by having her explicitly or implicitly acknowledge what she is to leave behind and what she is to expect for her future.

Examples of Hispanic American Bridal Showers: Explicit Socialization into the Wife Role

Among several ethnic groups of Hispanic women, the bridal shower is treated as an opportunity to prepare the bride-to-be for her future roles as wife and mother (Bahn and Jaquez 1997; West 1988). As Hispanic cultures tend to be more likely to adhere to traditional gender roles than other racial groups (Bahn and Jaquez 1997), it is understandable that bridal showers within these cultures commonly assume an old-fashioned, virginal, sexually naïve bride. It is expected that she will be her husband's caretaker and that children are wanted and will be conceived shortly after the wedding. This emphasis on domestic responsibility and children is not unlike the bridal showers of the middle- and upper-middle-class white women whom I interviewed; however, it seems that this theme is more explicit and pronounced at Hispanic American bridal showers. And, particularly because of the assumption of a lack of sexual experience, these showers also seem to be more raucous and feature more teasing or "hazing" of the status initiate than do those held and attended by the middle- and upper-middle-class white women in this sample.

Based on participant observation at seven bridal showers and interviews with Dominican women living in New York City, Bahn and Jaquez (1997) stated that the shower functioned as a means of socialization into four normative roles for traditional Dominican wives. These are "(1) The role of a woman among women, (2) the sexual role; (3) the homemaker role, and (4) the subservient role of the female in the marital relationship" (Bahn and Jaquez 1997, 195). Like the showers of the women interviewed for this study, the Dominican showers were women only and women of multiple generations were present. However, because of the expectation of sexual socialization, sometimes, as with bachelorette parties, the mother or grandmother of the bride was not included, as it was believed she might spoil the fun. Interestingly, the Spanish word used for "bridal shower" among Dominicans translates as "goodbye to singlehood" (Bahn and Jaquez 1997, 196), a sentiment more consistent with the tone and activities of the bachelorette party than the bridal shower. In fact, this type of bridal shower shared as many similarities with the bachelorette party as it did the traditional wedding shower. A sex theme was normative and activities and decorations were suggestive. Guests brought sexually explicit gifts and pornographic pictures decorated the room. As Bahn and Jaquez described it, "The refreshments may consist—besides cakes and sandwiches . . . of sausage and hot dogs arranged to look like the male sex organs and served to the guest of honor. Sometimes a root vegetable . . . is arranged and decorated with corn silk and two small potatoes to resemble male genitalia" (1997, 196). Like the brides at their bachelorette parties, guests of honor at Dominican showers were sometimes adorned with phallic paraphernalia such as "a 'corsage' made of stockings in the shape of male genitalia" (197). Dominican brides-to-be were hazed, like at the bachelorette party, though more dramatically, as a means of preparation for their supposed first sexual encounter. During the initiation, the bride-to-be "may be forced to eat the sausage or . . . she may be undressed to her underwear and told to put on a 'baby doll' nightgown. A vibrator may be used on her breast and intimate parts but no penetration occurs. The bride is shown pictures of a variety of sexual scenes and is told that this is what she may expect. . . . Typically, one of the participants dresses like a man and imitates the groom's actions on the wedding night. . . . Aside from these overt 'sexual' acts, there are guests who give her 'tips' about how to please a man sexually, such as how to perform fellatio successfully" (197).

What was notable and different about the Dominican bridal shower was that it was the other women guests who were involved in the sexual hazing. At bachelorette parties, men strangers and strippers were used to perform these tasks and socialization was much more symbolic than was the case at these showers. Furthermore, while brides in both situations were expected to be embarrassed about the sexual elements of the parties, Dominican women were expected to be passive, virginal, and surprised by what they encountered. In contrast, the bachelorette parties I analyzed called for a sexually experienced bride who acknowledged the end of her sexual freedom. In a more conservative culture it may be safer and more appropriate to have women whom the bride-to-be knows perform these sexualized acts and games as a means of preparation for her wedding night, rather than random men strangers. Cultural norms in Hispanic cultures would likely view flirtation with men strangers as deviant and the woman who engaged in such behavior as committing acts of betrayal. The role of the bride at the Dominican shower calls for a feminine performance, in this case in terms of sexual passivity, in the same way as the traditional bridal shower described in previous chapters. As Bahn and Jaquez wrote, "The role of the bride-to-be at the shower is very clear, underscoring the appropriateness of her reaction to the sexual aspects of the proceedings. She is expected to scream and show horror and surprise. The response of the girl is scripted and socially prescribed. She is expected to cry and scream to be let go, and to beg for her mother to rescue her. She is expected to be modest and maidenly. Should the bride not show the proper surprise . . . the shower becomes more conventional [as she] is believed to by many to be perhaps 'experienced' " (1997, 198). This type of sexual socialization is similar to that reported by Johan Casparis in his 1979 study of American bridal showers. Casparis found that young brides were assumed to be sexually naïve, and so their friends and family members provided them with advice, teasing them about what might happen on their wedding night. However, few of the women I interviewed mentioned explicit sexual socialization as part of the bridal shower. Occasionally, women played games such as "The Wedding Night" (chapter 3) or mothers gave lingerie to brides. It seems that once the bachelorette party became popular and women began to have separate celebrations with their friends, it was unnecessary to provide sexual socialization during the traditional shower. The part of a woman's status transition that was related to sexuality was covered during the bachelorette party when friends talked about sex or played games with sexualized themes. The bridal shower became a time for dealing with other elements of women's status transformation, particularly learning or preparing for the domestic obligations associated with becoming a wife.

The greatest similarity between the Dominican showers studied by Bahn and Jaquez and those of my interviewees was the socialization into the wife-as-homemaker role. Older family members and friends at both types of showers provided advice on keeping house, and the Dominican brides also received household items related to cooking and cleaning. With all elements of the shower it seems that Dominican women were more overt and decided about the wife role, particularly their subordinate status in relation to their future husbands. Although this idea was an implicit theme at the traditional bridal showers given by the women I interviewed, it was certainly not one that was readily accepted. Rather, women seemed to resist the idea of their subordinate status and the traditional wife role, as was evident in their resistance to the traditional shower overall. At the Dominican showers, in contrast, women were expressly told that marriage involved transitioning to a status in which they were subservient. It is important to mention that Bahn and Jaquez noted that this was one type of shower and that Dominican women sometimes had other more formal and feminine showers. More Americanized, less sexually naïve brides-to-be had more conventional showers, as there was less of a need for preparation for sexual activity. Furthermore, the Dominican brides who had been raised in America tended to be more educated, more likely to pursue a career, and less likely to accept a subordinate role. As the American and Dominican ideals and values merged with one another, the showers held for these brides transformed to reflect their social status.

Though not as ribald as the Dominican showers studied by Bahn and Jaquez, Mexican American showers also focused on preparing the bride for her change in status (West 1988). At Mexican American wedding showers women played games that reinforced the traditional wife role, simultaneously mocking and supporting it. Women played "fertility games" in which a blindfolded bride-to-be had to remove cotton balls from a bowl with a spoon. She was given a designated number of tries to accomplish this and was told that however many cotton balls she removed indicated the number of children she would have (West 1988). Similar to the superstition about breaking ribbons at American bridal showers, this game reinforced the association of marriage and motherhood. Other games that Mexican American women played further underscored this, treating brides-to-be as mothers-to-be by testing them on their ability to handle multiple tasks at the same time. For example, one game called for women to hang a load of laundry while blindfolded and holding a plastic doll. Another had the bride-to-be dropping toothpicks or other small items into a bottle while reading and never taking her eyes off of the book (West 1988). These games were designed to tease the future wife and mother as a way of preparing and socializing her for what was to come in these new roles.

Ukrainian and Polish Canadian Hall Showers

Among some ethnic Canadian women a different type of bridal shower exists. Sociologist David Cheal (1988, 1989) observed two large-scale "hall showers" in Winnipeg, one for a Ukrainian and the other for a Polish bride-to-be. These showers were held in rented halls and attended by approximately 75 and 115 guests, respectively, although he noted that some hall showers included hundreds of guests. Guests were family, friends, and neighbors of the bride-to-be, and the events were planned and orchestrated by women relatives or friends, although, like the bridal showers I studied, etiquette prohibited the mother from hosting. These events were unique due to their "banquet" format, with the bride, her mother, her attendants, the hostess, and the groom's mother seated at a head table and an announcer narrating the events over a public address system. According to Cheal, Polish and Ukrainian showers are very similar, with the exception of the type of food served and a few other minor details. Both are structured and begin with an introduction of and toast to the bride-to-be, followed by a traditional song of "hope for future happiness" (Polish or Ukrainian) and then cheers and a round of "For She's a Jolly Good Fellow" from the guests (Cheal 1988, 88). Following these "welcoming ceremonies," guests eat and then open gifts. As his focus was on the shower as a life-course ritual, Cheal did not provide much detail on the type of food or gifts characteristic of these events, so it is difficult to make comparisons between them and the middle-class white American women's wedding shower. He did observe that the mistress of ceremonies (usually the maid of honor or a close family member) announced each gift as it was opened, identifying both the gift and giver. Also, he noted that there were many gifts and the unwrapping took between one and two hours. At both bridal showers the bows and ribbons from the presents were collected; they were assembled into a hat at the Ukrainian shower and tied to a chain and worn around the neck at the Polish shower (Cheal 1988, 89). This ritual of adornment and embarrassment seems to transcend cultures, although Cheal did not have any more of an explanation of its significance. The hall showers concluded with thank-you remarks from the bride-to-be, her mother, the groom's mother, and the hostess (89).

One other element of the Polish shower is worth mention, a ritualized embarrassment of the bride-to-be. Balloons were used to decorate the room, and as a prank balloons were placed on the bride's chair, hidden underneath pillows. When the bride was seated following the introductory remarks, her attendants popped the balloons, startling the bride, who was embarrassed by her surprise and by having been tricked. Her response generated laughter from the guests, who were in on the joke. It is interesting that, like the Mexican and Dominican showers and the bachelorette parties that I studied, embarrassing the bride is an important part of the experience. The status initiate is hazed by her community and is expected to participate in this ritualized teasing as a means of acknowledging her status transition. Her liminal status as neither single nor married places her in the position to follow the dictates of the community, to accept and even appreciate their actions, even if they humiliate or distress her. As Turner noted, status initiates or "neophytes" must submit silently to the authority of the community (1969, 103). Bridal showers and bachelorette parties are rituals of transition, the goal of which is to prepare the bride-to-be for her new status either explicitly or implicitly. And even though there is cultural variation among ethnic American, Canadian, and immigrant groups in how this is accomplished, that it is present in all cases is significant evidence of ritual expression in contemporary society. These events also elucidate the gender community's awareness of the importance of preparing the initiate for her new status.

The Work Shower

The work shower is usually an additional shower, held by coworkers of the bride-to-be often at the work site during the workday. Shower-planning books offer the "office shower" as a theme (e.g., Dlugosch and Nelson 1984; Warner 1998). Warner labeled it "Not Your Average Coffee Break Shower" and noted, "An office party takes very little in the way of planning, decorating, and expense. It's the thought that counts! Set out extra-special bakery treats in one of the meeting rooms or in someone's office, decorate with a simple balloon bouquet, and invite the bride for an extended coffee break. . . . Another option is to bring the party to a nearby restaurant where everyone can order their lunch 'Dutch Treat' " (1998, 45). Dlugosch and Nelson (1984) advocated a similar format but also provided advice about gift giving, encouraging coworkers to band together and give a joint present. One interviewee who had recently attended work showers noted that the office manager or secretary often took the initiative in planning a work shower and passed around an envelope for donations, ranging from five to ten dollars per person.

There is evidence that the work shower has been an important cultural practice for employed women throughout the twentieth century. Vicki Jo Howard (2000, 2001) noted that both white-collar women and women working in factories hosted showers for coworker friends and that such showers were significant in developing and maintaining relationships among women. Despite this history, work showers were not common among women in this study, perhaps due to the work situations of these particular women. Only three brides reported that they were given a work shower. I observed one work shower that was given for a bride-to-be by another woman in her office. They had worked together for about a year at the time the shower was given. Eight people attended and all were current or former coworkers, two of whom were men. For this shower, guests went out to lunch at a moderately upscale restaurant.

The bride-to-be opened gifts, but since there were few guests and few gifts, unwrapping gifts was not the focus of the event. Rather, discussion alternated between the upcoming wedding, wedding traditions, and "shop talk." I noted this in my field notes: "This shower was more like going out to lunch with friends for no particular occasion than like a shower, perhaps because these coworkers are not really good friends. . . . It seemed very unstructured. There were no games or traditions" (April 30, 1999).

Lori had a work shower that she described as meaningful. She said she felt touched that her coworkers cared enough about her to have a celebration for her, even though she had only been with that company for a short time. She described it: "A couple months before the wedding I started a new job, and they threw a little shower for me. It was very small; there were like maybe ten of us, 'cause I hardly knew anyone. . . . So they had it for me at Pizzeria Uno, since they knew I loved that place. And they got me gifts. Everyone chipped in; like they got me a nice gift certificate for Macy's. I remember being very touched by that. . . . Not only did they like get me gifts, they took me out and surprised me."

The work shower is sometimes a surprise, where the guest of honor is called into someone's office or into the break room to complete a work-related task and then surprised with a cake and gifts. Tori's coworkers planned an event like this for her; however, there was no food, only drinks (nonalcoholic) and gifts opened in a room in her office. Most interviewees noted that work friends were most often included as guests at the showers given by the bride's family or bridesmaids. And those who did have work showers seemed to regard them as in a separate category from those organized by family or bridesmaids. As Tori remarked, "We had one for a girl we worked with which was like guys and girls. We all chipped in and got her a gift certificate to Home Depot, 'cause they were working on their house. Got like ten pizzas and a cake. That was kind of not like a real shower, but we called it a shower." Work showers seem to be less formal surprise parties and more often include men. It may be that work showers are common among other women, particularly those working in occupations where there are large numbers of women employed, or among women who are more geographically distant from their families and friends from other times of their lives. Anecdotal evidence from women who work in office settings supports this.

For example, because the women in my sample had few experiences with work showers, I informally interviewed one woman, Anne, who has worked in both hospital and corporate office settings. She remarked on their popularity and suggested that she attended at least ten work showers (both bridal and baby) during the past five years. She personally organized three wedding showers for coworkers. Anne noted that these showers were always surprises held in a conference room on site and involved a group gift. Coworkers contributed approximately ten dollars each for a gift and for the food for the shower, which consisted of pizzas or tomato pies and a cake and drinks. People often brought extra food such as salads, chips, or cookies. It was also noted that these were sanctioned parties; supervisors or managers participated as well, and Anne remarked that it seemed her coworkers looked forward to showers as breaks from the standard operation of the day. When I asked her about the differences between work showers and non-work showers, she commented, "The work showers are attended by people that you may not know too well or you may not even consider them your friends. It's a little bit overwhelming. Whereas non-work showers are usually people you've known for many years, like friends and family." Thus, it may be that work showers also involve feelings of obligation, as coworkers may feel their absence would be obvious. However, when faced with a choice between routine work and attending a work shower, the shower may be a more appealing option. Another difference is the presence of men. In fact, Anne noted that some grooms-to-be were also given showers by their women coworkers. Anne observed that men did seem a bit self-conscious about their participation: "The men are the minority, but they're always participant[s]. I think they also like to get away for a little party. By way of contributing to food, they usually volunteer to bring the silverware or cups and plates, or bags of chips. One man I worked with in the hospital . . . brought a plate of chocolate chip cookies to a wedding shower. We were all so impressed until we learned he just opened a bag of Chips Ahoy and arranged them on a plate! At the showers, the men usually congregate together. The last wedding shower we had at work only had about three men. They all sat together, but they still socialized with everybody else." This gendered behavior at office showers is consistent with that at coed showers or showers where only the groom is present (Montemurro 2005). It seems that even when men are included and on equal status (as in their relationships as coworkers), their behavior is differentiated. Similar to the men at coed wedding showers, the men that Anne worked with recognized the shower as feminine, even within the work context.

The Church Hall Shower

Another shower that was less common among the women I interviewed, but prevalent enough to be merit mention, was the church hall shower. This was more often practiced among women in the South, who reported being more religious than women in the Northeast. The church hall shower, often held on Sunday afternoon, following religious ceremonies, in the basement or meeting room at the bride's or groom's parents' church, was usually open to all members of the congregation (most often only women attended), thus resulting in a large number of guests and gifts. Emily, who attended church showers as she grew up, noted that they were announced in the church bulletin, presenting an open invitation to women in the community.

I interviewed Alicia during the week following the shower organized by women from her church. She told me that it was held in one of the classrooms and cookies and punch were served, although there were no decorations. Alicia remarked that she was surprised that more than forty people attended that shower since most did not know her well. She said, "It was big. And I was totally shocked because it was an open church kind of thing and . . . my mom's been to these in the past and she was like, 'Don't be upset if a lot of people don't come from the church.' So they had invited like a lot of my extended family members as well. . . . I was really impressed [with the turnout] and I got a lot of nice things." The hall shower was often described as a "drop-in" event, where people came and went as they pleased and there was not an expectation for guests to stay for the duration of the gift opening (which in Alicia's case took about two hours). People also talked among themselves at the hall shower, and Alicia said that not all of the guests were focused on her while she opened presents.

Reva, a southern bride like Alicia, had a church hall shower that was given by her parents' Sunday school class. Similar to Alicia's, the theme for the shower was miscellaneous and it was also held on site in the church fellowship hall. Reva commented that in her small town everyone who is a member of the church is thrown a shower when they marry.

There were about thirty people at that shower, the majority of whom were fellow church members. Only southern women from small towns mentioned church showers. This makes such showers seem to be consistent with the norms of traditional gemeinschaft-type communities (Tonnies 1887), where residents know most other residents and maintain involvement in their lives. In modern gesellschaft communities, characterized by instrumental relationships, large populations, and less sense of community membership, members of the same church are less likely to know one another and thus unlikely to be involved in each other's lives.

Same-Sex Couples

Though there is a growing body of research on same-sex commitment ceremonies or weddings in the United States, there is not much information on pre-ceremony activities. In other words, it is not evident in current research whether or not or how often same-sex couples have wedding showers, bachelor parties, or bachelorette parties. However, the information available suggests that some lesbian and gay couples include some of these events. Tess Ayers and Paul Brown, authors of *The Essential Guide to Lesbian and Gay Weddings* (1994), noted the heterosexism inherent in the shower, given its origin; however, they supported the tradition and encouraged its practice. As they wrote, "Yes, it reeks of straight tradition, but a shower is a great opportunity for small groups to celebrate, so why not skew tradition to your own situation? A lesbian or gay shower can be given for the couple together, or individual parties can be thrown for say, Groom One and Groom Two, which can be a healthy break from the constant pre-wedding togetherness" (1994, 214). Ayers and Brown offered suggestions for shower themes and activities, some of which replicated the traditional format, but most of which called for significant differences. Notably, they recommended giving inexpensive gifts, such as following the theme of the "Cheap Thrills Shower," where guests were to bring gifts that "cost five bucks or under; free is best of all," like "a story about the couple during their earlier days" or "a decorative gift [made] using found materials from around your home"(214). Seemingly tailored for couples who have already established a household and have most of the essentials, themes were more humorous than serious. In this way, the hyper-feminine aspects of the shower were minimized and even mocked under some circumstances. By including the presentation of gag gifts, these wedding advisors communicated the message that the shower is supposed to be a fun, informal event. These authors commented that rather than having a separate shower, most of the couples they consulted "combined a shower with another tradition such as the bachelor or bachelorette party or the pre-wedding luncheon" (214). However, the bachelor/bachelorette party was given less attention in their guide than the shower. Ayers and Brown downplayed the significance of this event, indicating that it is not popular among the gay community; they stated, "Maybe because many gays and lesbians had years and years of 'boys' and girls' night out,' they just don't feel the need to kick out the jams at this point" (216). Rather than offering advice for what to do on a bachelor/bachelorette party, the authors instead summarized what they perceived to be typical activities for heterosexual parties.

As far as empirical study of the popularity of wedding showers or bachelorette parties among same-sex couples, information is also limited. In her study of marriage and commitment among gay and lesbian couples, Gretchen Stiers (1999) offered some confirmation of participation in conventional pre-wedding events, although she argued that most couples did not partake in these parties. Based on interviews with approximately forty lesbian, gay, or bisexual individuals who had or were planning commitment ceremonies, she reported that none of them had "traditional" bachelor parties. She suggested that this was because the meaning of that type of party implied that the groom-to-be was taking the opportunity to enjoy his last night of "freedom," whereas men in same-sex relationships did not perceive their commitment to be indicative of a loss of independence. Stiers observed that the sexist nature of the stereotypical bachelor party likely made it unappealing to those in same-sex relationships. One man in her study did report going out to a strip club with friends; however, rather than going out with his men friends he celebrated with women friends instead. Since this man had been living with his partner for a significant amount of time, this party seemed to be meaningful as a night on the town with friends rather than as a means of expressing his change in status (Stiers 1999, 132). And though the majority of those whom Stiers interviewed did not have wedding showers, two women and one man were given showers by friends or coworkers. Unfortunately, Stiers does not provide detail on those events so that we might compare their similarities to the showers described by women in this study. Yet evidence suggests that some same-sex couples do register gift preferences at department stores (Ayers and Brown 1994; Lewin 1998), and certainly the wedding shower would be one channel for those gifts to be passed on to the couple. The profit-driven wedding industry has recognized and accepted same-sex couples planning commitment ceremonies or civil unions as an under-tapped market. They may soon even encourage them to have wedding showers to increase revenue, particularly given the fact that recent estimates calculate the gay marriage market could add nearly seventeen billion dollars to the already booming industry (Lagorce 2004).

Given the stigma and prejudice that same-sex couples face, particularly those who defy convention and ceremoniously celebrate their commitment, it is not surprising that Stiers noted that few had wedding showers or bachelor/bachelorette parties. As many had ceremonies that were markedly different from traditional wedding ceremonies, without bridal attendants, the responsibility for planning and execution of such events is unclear. Certainly, friends could gather together and throw a party for the couple; however, who specifically should, or even if the couple would want such parties, is ambiguous. Lacking the grounding in tradition and the established division of labor that characterize the rituals described by women in this study, it is more of a challenge to organize pre-wedding events. Also, since these couples rarely become "engaged" in the way heterosexual couples do (Stiers 1999), an unengaged member of a couple may not be viewed as meriting such attention. Similarly, there may not be the same time parameters or dramatic buildup and pre-wedding timetables furnished and encouraged by the wedding industry. Furthermore, as many same-sex couples wish to distinguish their union from that of heterosexual couples, it may be that traditional rituals like wedding showers and bachelor/bachelorette parties with their sexist and heterosexist undertones are not appealing.

Many middle- and upper-middle-class women in the United States have multiple pre-wedding celebrations, including engagement parties, bridal showers, and bachelorette parties. In other nations, rituals with similar elements are sometimes merged into one event, like the Ukrainian and Polish Canadian hall showers and the risqué Dominican American bridal shower described above. Rather than being formal events governed by proper etiquette, these parties, with the sexual teasing and sexualized gifts, include aspects of the bachelorette party as well. As it is likely that those who give these showers carry some customs from their countries of origin, it is not surprising that in other nations there are events similar to these types of showers.

Commonwealth Celebrations: Wales and Canada

In Western Europe, what little research that is available suggests that women engage in fairly similar pre-wedding events, although these are more often closer to bachelorette parties than bridal showers. In her study of weddings in Swansea, Wales, in the 1970s, Diana Leonard (1980) described ritualized teasing of brides-to-be by their coworkers and nights out at the local pub in celebration of upcoming weddings. Unlike contemporary middle- and upper-middle-class American brides, some of the brides in Leonard's study did not "get engaged," and their weddings were less grand productions than the weddings of those who went through the whole process. As becoming engaged is a way of formalizing and announcing intention to marry, those who were engaged had a starting point and encouragement to begin planning. However, even for those who were engaged, Leonard did not suggest that bridal showers were common or even practiced among the working- and middle-class women in her study. Some had engagement parties with both bride and groom and a small group of family and a few friends. And friends and family gave gifts to the couple prior to marriage; however, there was no formal ceremony or avenue in which this was accomplished. Instead, the custom of the "bottom drawer" prevailed, in which women family members such as mothers, grandmothers, or aunts saved items for the bride-to-be in a dresser drawer, sometimes starting from the time the bride-to-be was a teenager to the present. Like the hope chest popular in Colonial and Victorian America, the bottom drawer was where the family placed items collected over the years that they thought would be useful for the bride when starting her household. Linens, silverware, cleaning supplies, towels, and other items common at American bridal showers were put away and then presented to the bride-to-be sometime after her engagement and before her wedding. Friends and family also gave gifts to the bride or bride and groom before the wedding. Brides at this time did not register gift preferences, unlike the American ritual. Leonard wrote, "People do not ask what is wanted: they simply arrive with a present. There is no particular time when these are handed over" (1980, 126). The gifts given were more often perceived as being for the bride (rather than for the couple) as they were commonly associated with stereotypical or traditional women's household tasks, as was the case with the bridal showers described by women I interviewed.

Ritualized teasing was very much a part of the pre-wedding activities for the women in Leonard's study. This took two forms: joking at work and the "hen party." Joking was common among working-class women employed in factory settings or at other jobs in which large groups of women were employed; friends of the bride-to-be played little tricks on her in the days and weeks prior to the wedding. These jokes included putting confetti on the bride-to-be's clothes or hiding items that would embarrass her, such as penis-shaped carrots or toilet-paper rolls, in her coat or desk. Sometimes coworkers put signs on the bride's back that said things like "Getting Married" or slightly more suggestive slogans. Women also had "giggly sherry part[ies]" at work, "when the present was handed over, with some risqué jokes or cards, and confetti" (Leonard 1980, 146). Leonard observed that teasing at work was indicative of the close relationship between the bride-to-be and her coworker friends as well as her popularity, given the effort undertaken to execute these jokes.

The hen parties, women's complement to the stag parties practiced by men, were "riotous single-sex evenings which mark[ed] the change of status of the young . . . woman within the peer and workgroup" (Leonard 1980, 147). Similar in several ways to the bachelorette party, the hen party was an evening out at a local tavern or dance club and was characterized by excessive alcohol consumption. While occasionally there were sexualized gag gifts given at hen parties, this element did not seem to be important or even necessary. In fact, in the pages of descriptions of hen parties none of the interviewees mentioned a sexual element, nor was there any indication that brides-to-be had to complete tasks or approach men strangers. Rather, intoxication and its consequences seemed to be the details most often emphasized by hen party participants, and thus these parties bore strong similarity to the Girls' Night Out variety among the American women I interviewed. For both groups of women, social drinking and one last night out "getting trashed" with friends (Montemurro and McClure 2005) were important bonding rituals among women. Half of the women Leonard interviewed had hen parties; and also, like the women I interviewed, none had hen parties when their husbands-to-be did not have stag parties. Women who were officially engaged and those who had more lavish weddings involving church ceremonies were more likely to have hen parties than those who did not. Also, similar to bachelorette parties, hen parties often occurred on the same night as stag parties, and sometimes men and women would meet up at a local pub at the end of the evening. Times have changed since Leonard did her study, and women in the United Kingdom may be more inclined to have more elaborate and sexually suggestive hen parties, as they have now have more elaborate and lavish weddings (Boden 2003).

There is also evidence that Canadian women have "stagette" (also referred to as bachelorette) parties. Tye and Powers (1998) noted that the stagette party was a relatively new addition to the wedding activities and was increasing in popularity in Nova Scotia, where they conducted observation at parties and interviews with women attendees. Guests at these parties engaged in similar games and the party followed a format similar to the American version that I investigated. For example, the party usually began at someone's home, where guests consumed alcohol and the bride-to-be was decorated with candies in preparation for the Suck for a Buck game or dressed up in T-shirt with sexually suggestive messages. She was then presented with sexualized gifts such as "sexy lingerie," "a pacifier in the shape of male genitalia," "condoms in assorted styles and colors," and "a sperm-shaped key chain" (Tye and Powers 1998, 553). On some occasions a male stripper would come to the house and perform. The party often then moved on to a bar where they could share quality time with their friends and continued drinking in order to become intoxicated. Like the American women, the Canadian women viewed drinking to be a key part of the stagette party and felt that it allowed them to "let loose" and feel uninhibited, sexually and socially (Montemurro and McClure 2005).

There were several other notable differences among the Canadian and American parties. First, it was suggested that the stagette party was "eclipsing" the bridal shower, becoming more popular (Tye and Powers

1998, 551). Tye and Powers reported that, like American women, the women from Nova Scotia preferred the stagette party to the shower. However, the women I interviewed emphasized the shower's importance, and more would have abandoned the bachelorette party rather than the shower. The American women also had more showers than bachelorette parties, and though several did not have or did not want a bachelorette party, only one bride who eloped did not have a shower. Also, perhaps because there were no accessible clubs, the authors did not mention visits to strip clubs, scavenger hunts, or elaborate rituals of club hopping as part of the stagette party. Tye and Powers (1998, 551–552) described Nova Scotia's economy as weak at the time of the research. And though they noted that "women came from a broad range of socioeconomic backgrounds," it seems that overall the women they observed were from lower social class backgrounds than most of the women I interviewed. Their parties were less "lavish" and less detailed than the American parties. It may also be that the extravagant wedding has not become the dominant model in some parts of Canada as it has in the United States. Thus, the rituals that precede it are not seen as setting the stage for the big event and need not be as involved or elaborate. Finally, Tye and Powers described "a new premarriage custom supplanting both the stagette and stag (bachelor party): the Jack and Jill or stag and doe party including both males and females" (1998, 559). At this party men and women went out together, and such events were more subdued with less drinking and little sexual play. The authors explained that these parties might be increasing in popularity because of concerns about what might happen during the gender-segregated events. Only one woman whom I interviewed mentioned a "Jack and Jill" bachelorette party. Luanne had attended a party given for a British bride-to-be coworker and her fiancé. The party began at someone's house, where the bride was dressed up (for the home portion of the evening only) as a groom and the groom was dressed up as a bride. However, the group dissolved into separate single-sex celebrations when they went out, with men going to one club and women to another. Given women's negative reactions to the coed wedding shower (Montemurro 2005; see also chapter 3), it seems unlikely that the Jack and Jill party would become popular among women like those I interviewed. In fact, Tye and Powers curiously commented that women preferred the stagette party to the Jack and Jill party because the Jack and Jill party "represent[ed] an encroachment on recently appropriated female cultural space" (1998, 559). Yet they did not explain the contradiction between its secondary preference and its increasing popularity or its possible succession of the single-sex event. The stagette party of Atlantic Canadian women has many similarities to the American ritual and provides a useful comparison. Although there are also some significant differences, given the regionally specific nature of the Tye and Powers study, it may be that Canadian women who have more comparable socioeconomic backgrounds or who live in urban areas where night clubs are in abundance may have even more similar experiences.

SCANDINAVIAN AND SCOTTISH BACHELORETTE-LIKE PARTIES

In some nations, women and men have parallel pre-wedding celebrations. In Finland, a nation known for its gender equity and progressive politics, both brides-to-be and grooms-to-be participated in a ritual called *polttarit* or *polterabend,* and there seemed to be few distinctions in the way this ritual was performed whether men or women were involved. As Oikarinen noted, "There is no actual difference between a bachelor party and a wedding shower in Finland. There is always a lot of alcohol involved and the . . . fiancé is dressed up by his/her friends and usually has to do some embarrassing things in public. Usually the person has to peddle some object on the streets to the opposite sex and the objects can be easily connected to sex. The most common is [a] kiss for a certain amount of money which has to be paid to the fiancé" (1997b).

The words *polttarit* and *polterabend* translate from German as "noisy night" and "noise evening." Though the gendered words of *svensexa* (stag party) and *mökväll* or *möhippa* (hen party) are used in Sweden to identify a similar ritual, in Finland the more gender-neutral polterabend and polttarit are the terms of choice (Åström 1989). Of the international pre-wedding rites about which I was able to find information, polttarit seems closest to the American customs of bachelor and bachelorette parties. In this ritual, held approximately a week before the wedding, women go out with their women friends (and men with their friends) for a celebration that involves drinking, dressing the guest of honor up in costume, and teasing or embarrassing her (Sinclair 1995).

Unlike the bachelorette party, polterabend has a long history tracing back to the nineteenth century (Åström 1989). Anna-Maria Åström traced this ritual from the time of its documented origin, in approximately the 1870s, through the turn of the century, during the 1920s, 1930s, and 1940s, and then re-examined it in the 1980s, analyzing its components and changes in different generations. Evidence suggests that polttarit, like the American bachelor party, began as an upper-class men's ritual involving drinking and joking about men's status transition (Åström 1989; Oikarinen 1997b). Åström noted that the earliest documentation is of men's parties in 1871 and 1872 and that evidence suggests that these were the parties of "Helsinki's noble, academic, and bourgeois milieu" (1989, 84). Women's parties followed; and though it is unknown exactly how soon after, the earliest evidence suggests they emerged in the early 1890s. The parties were gender-segregated, and during the women's parties the bride's friends dressed in costumes, most often as men in tailcoats and top hats. They played men suitors who were trying to woo the bride-to-be or men who pursued her before she committed to marrying her fiancé (Åström 1989, 86). These parties took place at the homes of friends or at restaurants and were private affairs, attended only by the bride's or groom's closest friends. Men's parties did not involve costumes, although the theme of saying farewell to the groom's past dominated. Friends made jokes about women of the groom's past, his transition to adulthood, and his increasing responsibility. As early as the late 1800s, elite Scandinavian women acknowledged that marriage involved sacrifice for them and their lives, particularly, that their relationships with women peers would change after they married. Notably, "the male and female parties have a common feature. . . . [T]his is the choice, the selection of a partner and the rejection of unmarried life, former admirers, and lonesomeness. This choice is affirmed, even when it is done in mocking terms"(Åström 1989, 88).

Åström found a great deal of evidence regarding the practice of polterabend during the 1920s and 1930s. Photographs, interview materials, and written documentation suggested that this was a common prewedding event for both women and men in that time period. As the ritual continued to be practiced, it disseminated from elite brides- and grooms-to-be to those in the working classes. As women were more likely to be working outside of the home during this era, marriage meant a significant change in their daily lives. These parties followed a format similar to that in previous generations, with women dressing in costumes, alcohol consumption, and a program during which the bride was given advice about marriage, sexuality, and caring for home, husband, and children (Åström 1989, 90). Women guests dressed up as men and play-acted as suitors or past boyfriends of the bride-to-be. The bride was supposed to resist the temptations of these potential mates as a means of underscoring her choice of fiancé and showing that she was confident in that decision. Alcohol consumption was an important part of polterabend during this era because most women were not experienced drinkers. Drinking alcohol was associated with both masculinity and adulthood; thus, women drank to demonstrate that they were mature and equal to men (Åström 1989, 93). Brides-to-be were hazed or initiated into marriage by their peers, who joked about the wife and mother roles, teasing them about what to expect their lives to be like, similar to the contemporary American ritual. Åström noted some alterations in the polterabend ritual following the First World War; namely, it was a bit more bawdy, included direct references to sex rather than veiled inferences, and involved the consumption of greater amounts of alcohol.

In the late twentieth century, polttarit usually began with a gathering of friends at someone's home or at a restaurant. The group then proceeded from a restaurant to a public park, and sometimes strippers were hired to entertain the group in the public setting. The party continued into the night at restaurants, bars, or someone's home. The polttarit event often lasted for one (or more) full day, with bonding time for friends during the day and then the wild night out with friends in the evening (Oikarinen 1997a, 1997b). The "program" for the ritual was summarized as follows:

> [The bride- or groom-to-be is taken to someone's home and dressed in a costume.] The dressing up is usually in someone's home where drinks and some food are consumed. . . . There follows a trip downtown to the center of Helsinki or often direct to a restaurant. . . . The victim has to do various tasks, undergo tests planned in advance, such as holding a speech, selling something to a passerby, singing a song to an audience. (For boys only) there is a visit to a public sauna, where a private female bath attendant has been booked for the victim.

> Alternatively, a woman, often older, is engaged for various duties, to seduce the man or to give him advice. They visit a dance restaurant and make the victim attract attention and be asked to dance. The group then becomes an extra item on the programme for the people in the restaurant. Boys in particular undertake pub crawls, the idea being to get the bridegroom drunk, but not insensible. Girls also drink a lot. The victim is brought home, or sometimes to a friend's home, where the drinking continues into the small hours. (Åström 1989, 95)

Also, like at a bachelorette party, the Scandinavian bride-to-be was similarly costumed, most often dressed in clothing to make her appear "sexy," such as "thin tights or lace stockings, mini-skirts and low necked bathing suits, and heavy make-up with rouged cheeks" (Åström 1989, 95–96). She engaged in comparable types of flirtation with random men, as a symbolic acknowledgement of what she was giving up and also as a means of taking a last look and inviting men to take their last chance with her (Åström 1989).

In some cases the party was a surprise and the guest of honor was kidnapped by her friends and then made to put on a costume and play a role. As Sinclair (1995) noted, "the costume can be humorous, or it may be grotesque, or even sinful." The bride-to-be is teased and given tasks to complete, such as singing in public or selling a sexualized item like those common at bachelorette parties (e.g., condoms, lingerie). For example, one woman was dressed up as Eve and was then made to sell apples to men passersby in downtown Helsinki (Oikarinen 1997b). Another "trie[d] to sell carrots tied up with two radishes, leaving little to the imagination. She [wore] a nun's outfit and ask[ed] passersby to choose the arrangement to match their manhood" (Oikarinen 1997b). The party attendees wore similar clothing so they could be distinguished from non-attendees. Like the bachelorette party, friends planned and attended the party, with the maid of honor taking charge. Also, there were variations in the format of the party with some women opting for licentious drinking binges and others avoiding the public spectacle and instead going to a spa or beauty salon (Oikarinen 1997b). It seems that spending quality time with friends is as important to Finnish brides-to-be as it is to American brides-to-be. Oikarinen noted, "The meaning of polttarit is to do something funny, special, and memorable, to do something that really differs from the daily routines and to have a good time with close friends" (1997b). There are few differences between the Finnish ritual and the bachelorette party as both involve excessive alcohol consumption, public teasing and embarrassment of the bride-to-be, and task lists. With the longer history of the Finnish parties and the striking similarities, it seems quite possible that polttarit may have been an influence on the development of the bachelorette party. Interestingly enough, at the time Oikarinen completed her research (1997a) the American party was still relatively unknown, at least internationally. This was evident in the closing of her article, where she wrote, "In the United States . . . a bachelor party group rents a place, where they watch porn films and drink alcohol. They might even have a stripper there. The women have a very good-natured wedding shower, where a bride-to-be's female relatives gather in her home, bring gifts and look through her trousseau. Even this celebration might later become a little more wild" (1997a).

The Swedish rites of passage of *möhippa* for women and *svensexa* for men are similar to polterabend. During a möhippa, women dress up as men and go out for a night on the town with their close friends in celebration of their upcoming wedding (Hellspong 1988). Research suggests that these parties begin at home and then proceed to a club or restaurant where the celebration continues. Though men's parties have a longer history and can be traced to the mid-nineteenth century, the möhippa, or "hen party," is dated to the turn of the twentieth century (Hellspong 1988). It seems that the tradition originated among women students and artists as a response to men's parties. As women achieved greater levels of equality and "emancipation" in Swedish society, they began to engage in activities that had been previously restricted to men. Hellspong (1988) observed that möhippa parties tended to be more detailed and involved more advance planning than the men's parties. One unique aspect of the möhippa, similar to some polterabends, is that the party is usually a surprise. The bride-to-be is "lured to a certain address under false premises or else she is picked up without warning. She is abducted and blindfolded so the she loses her bearings" (Hellspong 1988, 114). It seems brides are viewed as initiates who must oblige the requests of their captors, as in hazing or initiation rituals characteristic of fraternities or sororities. Women are then dressed in costumes, either like men or like "little girls with ribbons in their hair, or perhaps as a sort of mock bridal procession with groom, priest, and wedding guests" (111). No sexual elements are mentioned as part of the party. Heavy drinking is normative, though women's parties are less characterized by intoxication than are men's. An interesting gender difference in these parties is that the groom is not dressed in costume during his party. Yet the bride "is constantly reminded of the forthcoming wedding" while "the drinking at the stag party rather leads the groom to forget all about the reason for the party" (Hellspong 1988, 116). Though notably more progressive in terms of gender politics, the Swedish parties ritually convey gender differentiation in attitudes toward marriage.

In Scotland, women and men also participate in pre-wedding rituals. Unlike in Finland, however, brides have parties that are like showers as well as parties like bachelorette parties. Brides are showered with gifts at parties called "sprees," attended by their friends and family (Mordecai 1999). Light refreshments are served, gifts are usually items for the household, and, following their opening, gifts are displayed in the bride-to-be's mother's house (or wherever the shower is held) with a card and the name of the giver, similar to the Victorian custom of the trousseau shower. Typically, "taking out the bride" occurs after the shower. Like at a polttarit, brides-to-be are often dressed in costume, sometimes a veil, and are paraded through public areas and made to perform embarrassing tasks. For example, "the bride and her friends sing at the top of their lungs and bang pots and pans [and] they visit villagers. Carrying a baby doll and a plastic pot containing salt for good luck and prosperity, the bride kisses villagers in exchange for money they place in the pot" (Mordecai 1999, 182). In Scotland, as in Finland, there is less gender differentiation in the ritual as compared to rituals in the United States. Scottish grooms-to-be are also dressed in costumes, sometimes made to look like pregnant women, on their "stag nights." The groom and his friends drink heavily and he is made to "endure harmless tricks and joking and at the end of the party he may be stripped of his clothing and tied up to a tree near his house" (Moredcai 1999, 182).

Although less information is available about pre-wedding rituals in other nations, anecdotal evidence from research on weddings provides some interesting insight into complementary practices around the world. For example, in Argentina both brides and grooms are given showers separately and such parties are sometimes surprises. This gender segregation is not indicative of gender convergence or equity as the bride and groom receive gendered gifts that presumably each will need in marriage (Hew 1991, 54). In contrast, an older custom in a traditional society recognized that marriage involved sacrifice for women. In Bulgaria, before the wedding day, when the bride was taken from her home to prepare for wedding, "unmarried boys and girls danced special wedding dances accompanied by musicians playing folk music. Songs of lament were sung at the girl's party, for the bride was about to leave her friends, to be separated from the unmarried" (Mordecai 1999, 170). All of these international pre-wedding rituals have some similarities to the American bachelorette party, and all share an underlying theme. Marriage involves both gain and sacrifice, and these rituals allow a forum for the conflicting emotions associated with it to be expressed and publicly acknowledged, with the bride-to-be thus demonstrating her awareness of the seriousness and magnitude of the status transition.

The traditions and rituals of nations around the world demonstrate that women's status transition from single to married has been formally recognized for quite some time. Some nations, like Finland, have a longer-standing history of this and feature less gender differentiation in pre-wedding celebrations. Women from other cultures, like Mexican Americans and Dominicans, participate in more traditional and blatant hazing of the bride-to-be as a means of preparing her for her change in status, so she may ease into her new role as subservient wife. Within the United States and Canada, pluralistic nations with blends and variations in ethnic traditions, there are different ways that wedding showers are performed depending on the social and cultural location of brides-to-be and their families. As the women interviewed for this study were similar in demographic characteristics, it is important to address these different practices as a means of understanding alternative pre-wedding practices.

Chapter 7

Conclusion

Bashful Brides and Bold Bachelorettes

Beth: How would you contrast the shower . . . with her bachelorette party?

April: Well, I mean, obviously, it's a more subdued atmosphere, more proper, calmer. Whereas her bachelorette party was a pretty wild atmosphere. . . . I guess just the shower—you're being very proper, a good little girl, and you're crossing your ankles and being very polite. Whereas the bachelorette, she would've gotten harassed if she was anything near like she was at the shower, which is what she was expected to be. You know, the two events occurred two hours from each other and she acts a certain way and then if she would have acted at either one of those events it would have been a huge deal. But here's the same person on the same day acting totally different. But it was just the circumstances and what you're expected to do.

In the introduction to her chronicle of images of women in popular media during the twentieth century, Susan Douglas wrote, "The American woman has . . . emerged as a bundle of contradictions, seeking to be simultaneously passive and active, outspoken and quiet, selfish and selfless, thrifty and profligate, daring and scared, and who had better know which persona to assume when" (1995, 18). Douglas noted the ambivalent and inconsistent messages that women have received about how they should present themselves and who they should be. This theme is not limited to media. Those who have studied women's employment and family expectations have also noted the difficulties modern women face in trying to meet conflicting demands (e.g., Gerson 1985; Hoffnung 1998). Modern middle-class women have been raised to think that they can do what men do in the worlds of work and education, but they are still encouraged to value marriage and motherhood in the same way that their mothers and grandmothers did. Though many learn that they can achieve academic and career successes, the culture, by way of media, the education system, family, and peers, places disproportionate emphasis on the importance of succeeding in love and relationships. Women are told that they should be independent and dependent, assertive and passive, sexually available and unavailable. Although these mixed messages are pervasive in many social institutions, dominant images of weddings and marriage have remained relatively unchanged and tradition bound, with the star player, the bride, as a virginal vision in white.

However, even though bride and wife are socially valued and revered roles, they have always entailed different sacrifices and inspired anxiety among women who prepare to take them on. Throughout much of American history, for most women, marriage was the primary viable option for social recognition and financial stability (Rothman 1984; Wallace 2004), yet it came with significant costs. For women in Colonial America, marriage often meant separation from one's family, hard labor, and possible death from bearing children. At the turn of the nineteenth century, the situation was not much different as wives prepared to be servants to their husbands and to relinquish their independence. Furthermore, the difficulty and expense of travel made maintenance of relationships outside of the nuclear family more difficult and resulted in greater isolation for new wives. Even into the middle to late nineteenth century, as Rothman (1984) noted, weddings were often somber affairs for similar reasons. In spite of this, women had little choice but to marry as there were few stable or profitable jobs for single women. If they did not marry, it was likely that women would be farmed out to relatives to serve in the home (Wallace 2004). Throughout history women have had many reasons to be ambivalent about marriage; marriage entailed great sacrifice but was also necessary for survival and prestige for most women. Given the costs and benefits associated with marriage, some women quietly resisted it throughout American history. However, women's lower social status meant they had fewer options, and so any type of organized or mass resistance to marriage, or to labor conditions that necessitated it, was unlikely.

Now, in the late twentieth and early twenty-first century, what women gain and sacrifice in marriage is certainly different than what they gained and lost in earlier centuries. As Wallace noted of 1990s brides, "Women came to matrimony with college degrees, jobs, history. Sometimes they came with stock portfolios. . . . They were not willing to erase themselves to assume the identity of Bride. Some found the pressure toward girlishness to be an affront. Some were embarrassed by the vestigial references to virginity implicit in the white dress. . . . American women are neither sheltered, nor self-effacing, nor helpless. Least of all are they inexperienced" (2004, 286). For modern middle- and upper-middle-class women who are marrying later, who have begun to establish or have established themselves in careers, becoming a wife also means sacrificing independence and, for many, moving closer to having to balance or forgo a career because of family responsibility. As the bridal shower reinforces, even modern working women are expected to engage in traditional wifely pursuits after they marry. Particularly, they are expected to become caregivers for others, resulting in self-sacrifice and possible dependence on their husbands. And wedding ceremonies, practices, and pre-nuptial celebrations include patriarchal traditions and rigid gender-role expectations; the sexism of their origins is glossed over (Currie 1993; Geller 2001). Most brides do not explicitly question these rites, participating in them as social custom and thus reinforcing gender differentiation and the supposed natural worlds of men and women. However, as seen through the development of the bachelorette party and an examination of women's responses to the bridal shower, resistance to these traditions is evident and, significantly, is a part of the wedding routine. Most of the women I interviewed suggested that bachelorette parties were tradition, despite their relatively short history. When women identify the bachelorette party as such, this moves the ritual closer to institutionalization and solidifies women's ritual expression of sacrifice in marriage. Though more often symbolic practice than purposeful challenge, the bachelorette party presents a different image of the modern woman. Like the man she will soon marry, this sexually experienced woman ritually laments her last days of freedom and in so doing acknowledges the sacrifices she will make when she marries. For her, marriage is not wholly about self-actualization or being rescued from the ranks of the unmarried. Instead, she is an equal (or nearly equal) partner who has considered her options and decided to wed. Yet the modern bride is lured by the wedding industry, media, and society at large to see her wedding as a reward for her success in the dating game. The wedding itself is an attractive and appealing prize for many women. It is a chance to be a celebrity and be showered with attention and material compensation, and most of the women I interviewed enjoyed the experience immensely, in spite of the effort, expense, and stress associated with executing a "perfect" wedding. Here is the bridal paradox. The bride-to-be at the shower is expected to gush gleefully about her good fortune, and most women do, in fact, feel happy about their marriage or pending wedding. But at the bachelorette party the bride-to-be is to mourn the single life, and many women lament how their relationships with friends will change.

Most of the women I interviewed were brides or bridesmaids who witnessed their friend, sister, or future sister-in-law play this two-faced role. With the exception of one woman who eloped, all of brides I interviewed had traditional, women-only wedding showers. Though several had additional showers, some coed, the traditional shower was never eliminated. And the majority of these women also had or participated in bachelorette parties that consisted of heavy drinking and a sexual theme. As April noted in the quote at the start of this chapter, the same bride shifted her self-presentation depending on the situation. When she wanted to convey the message that she was a suitable future wife in front of her family and future in-laws, she was gracious and grateful. In the evening of the same day, surrounded by her friends, she played frisky and flirtatious. She knew which image was expected when and adapted like a chameleon, indicating her understanding of the conflicting characterizations of modern women. And April's friend is not alone. Most women know that they are to be both the wild woman lamenting the end of her sexual freedom and the lucky, appreciative woman who has found the man of her dreams—modern and traditional at the same time.

Ambivalence

Ambivalence is seen as "hold[ing] opposing affective orientations toward the same person, object or symbol" (Smelser 1998, 5). Sociological ambivalence "refers to incompatible normative expectations of attitudes, beliefs, and behavior assigned to a status . . . in society. . . . Ambivalence is in the social definition of roles and statuses, not in the feeling-state of one or another type of personality" (Merton and Barber 1976, 94–95). It is a characteristic that can be seen as inherent in particular social roles rather than necessarily in certain people. Distinct from a psychological state, sociological ambivalence refers to how particular social roles are constructed with conflicting emotional expectations. For the modern woman, the role of bride and the anticipated role of wife are viewed with ambivalence. The women I interviewed were simultaneously attracted to the bride role because of its social and material rewards and repelled by the embarrassment and formal feminine self-presentation associated with it. Though it seems most saw themselves as entering into marriages that would be partnerships, where they and their husbands would be on relatively equal footing, they demonstrated ambivalence toward this by submitting to rituals and behaviors that indicated their subordinate status. In her research on women and marriage, Dalma Heyn (1997) noted that some women gave up certain aspects of themselves, transformed who they were, in order to become wives. As my focus was on pre-wedding rituals, I did not ask all of the women how their lives would be or were changed after they married; however, the ritual expression of change was obvious.

On the surface, the bridal shower as a ritual is centered on the positive aspects of marriage. Feeling rules for the bride at the shower are rigid. A good bride-to-be acts excited about her gifts, most of which reinforce the traditional wife role as caretaker and housekeeper. The bride who acts appropriately in this situation expresses eager anticipation about marriage. At the bridal shower women are expected to convey that marriage is about gaining, not sacrifice. However, interviews and observations at bridal showers suggest that beneath the surface of the performance given at the shower there are undercurrents of resentment and hostility toward this ritual. Perhaps this generation of women feels uncomfortable participating in a ritual that emphasizes a traditional role that no longer seems relevant to their lives. For women who are educated, who work in careers rather than jobs, the notion of marrying and becoming an economic dependent whose job is caring for husband and home is an affront to what they have worked to achieve throughout their lives. The women in my study complained about being bored during showers. This boredom may have come from participating in a ritual that was created by and for a different generation of women. These women enjoyed the bridal shower more on the few occasions when they transformed it by introducing a theme, creating more of a party atmosphere, or including men. When the shower lost its focus on domestication, it was an enjoyable experience. Thus, the bridal shower can clearly be seen as a ritual in which ambivalence is central. Women are expected to convey their excitement about being wives and receiving items for cooking, cleaning, and decorating. Yet at the same time, beneath the expressions given, are sentiments of animosity.

Bachelorette parties play with the idea of ambivalence as well, ambivalence about women's sexuality, marriage, and gender roles in contemporary society. This ritual is centered on the awareness and symbolic or ritualized acknowledgment of other options in the form of other men or staying single. As norms change and suggest that one should be relatively careful in selecting a spouse, someone who will provide emotional as well as physical or financial support, ambivalence becomes a more central theme. This is particularly salient for women in contemporary American society because in the past women were expected to commit to monogamy eagerly and without hesitation, whereas men were expected to approach the altar reluctantly, as if sacrificing sexual freedom was a major and regrettable loss. As women have developed identities beyond wife and mother, as they have been able to bring more to a marriage financially, they have expressed, publicly and symbolically, ambivalence about getting married. As age at first marriage has increased, women have had more time to live independently and to establish lasting bonds with other women friends. As both men and women have been increasingly focused on finding a spouse who is emotionally compatible, the stage is set for the bachelorette party. As gender norms and marital roles have changed, the idea that women have "trapped" or "caught" men becomes less appropriate as women, too, have tangible assets to bring to the relationship. In fact, when in dance clubs and strip clubs I observed brides-to-be wearing plastic balls and chains, symbolizing *women's* imprisonment in marriage. This indicates that women, in a similar way to men on bachelor parties, publicly express ambivalence toward marriage by explicitly acknowledging that they too have something to lose by committing to marriage. Though not a new sentiment, the public and ritualized declaration of it marks a significant change in gender norms.

Most bachelorette parties in my study centered on the display of sexual sacrifice and choosing monogamy. The bride-to-be was often taken to a location where men surrounded her. These men, as representatives of men in general, were a part of what she gave up upon marriage. The bride was encouraged to flirt, to kiss and to touch these men in ways that showed that she regretted giving up the opportunity to do so in the future. She was expected to ogle men strippers and to act as if she was single because after marriage she would no longer be permitted to do so. In some ways this suggests that the wife is de-sexualized and that for her sex becomes less exciting or decreases with marriage. The film industry supports this image, displaying sexual activity and passion most often among unmarried rather than married partners (Dempsey and Reichert 2000). Despite this encouragement to hyper-sexualize behavior at the bachelorette party, some women only marginally included sexual elements, and those who had hyper-sexualized events tempered sexual expression with gender-appropriate embarrassment and humor. Even though women were encouraged to act as if they had a rich sexual history and would regret no longer being able to pursue and engage men sexually, most interviewees suggested that they were self-conscious about and not aroused by interactions with exotic dancers or other strange men. Women participated in these activities because their friends encouraged them to do so and because many considered them to be fun. Thus, the bachelorette party, which on the surface represents women's regrets about getting married because they will no longer be able to date or interact sexually with other men, also allows for an expression of ambivalence toward the role of the modern woman. Rather than celebrating themselves as sexual beings with desires or as contemporary women who are comfortable with public sexual expression, who watched strippers unabashedly, most women found the sexual elements to be awkward or embarrassing.

Furthermore, during the bachelorette party itself women were often called to enact opposing identities as both sexual object and subject. If during the ritual itself women were supposed to be both aggressor and vehicle to men's sexual pleasure, it is not surprising that women may have been ambivalent about their sexuality. In contrast to contemporary media images of single women as sexually open, the women I interviewed were more conservative about their sexuality, seeing it as private and the public activities of the bachelorette party as play. Though women like the sexually voracious (and fictional) Samantha Jones on *Sex and the City* can get away with random sexual encounters, real women are aware of the real consequences associated with being perceived as too sexual (Tanenbaum 2000). The sexual behavior of women of this generation is judged by others, women and men; and, like the ungrateful bride at the shower, the overly flirtatious bride at the bachelorette party is perceived as a bad woman, one who may not be worthy of the status elevation to wife. Perhaps younger single women may replicate the sexually liberated and promiscuous image of women promoted in media, but the soon-to-be-married reject such behavior and most are only comfortable playing along with the image rather than realizing it. Research suggests that women prefer monogamous to recreational sex (Laumann et al. 1994). Thus, for women, sacrificing sexual freedom is not likely to have the same significance that it supposedly does for men. So these rituals also reflect the ambivalence that women feel toward contemporary gender roles. If society is ambivalent about single women's sexuality, it is not surprising then that women themselves are unsure about the extent to which it is acceptable to present themselves sexually in public. These were brides-to-be after all, and none of the party participants forgot that the wedding was fast approaching—that these women had made commitments to marry that included the expectation of fidelity. A bachelorette is still a bride-to-be and her adornment with veils, buttons, hats, or other objects indicating this status serves as a reminder of the contradictory position in which she is placed. Wearing the veil, a symbol of purity and innocence, the bride-to-be is simultaneously virginal and sinful as she downs shots of alcohol or has men simulate oral sex by removing pieces of strategically placed candy from her clothing. In other words, the image of the hyper-feminine bride-to-be on her wedding day is present at the bachelorette party, given the prevalence of symbols of weddings and marriage. Directly, but perhaps subconsciously, the bride-to-be at the bachelorette party personifies the ambivalence toward women's status in modern society. She is decorated in a traditionally feminine way, made up for a night on the town, but she is called to engage in acts that are less than feminine, even when they are limited to heavy drinking.

Women's ambivalence toward the bride role may also be related to frustration with the wedding experience in general. Planning a wedding is an arduous task. Brides-to-be are expected to devote serious amounts of time to planning an event that demonstrates their families' and their own class status (Boden 2003; Currie 1993). Though most of the women I interviewed looked forward to or fondly remembered their wedding days, many were overwhelmed by the constant flow of activities and tasks that dominated the engagement period. Rather than reduce the number of events by eliminating bachelorette parties or having only one shower, most followed convention and at least publicly maintained the expected level of enthusiasm during the pre-wedding rush. As Currie (1993) found, some brides reported feeling carried away by the wedding-planning process, as if they were doing things because they were supposed to rather than because they wanted to. And some of the women I interviewed expressed similar sentiments regarding the bridal shower. Women felt compelled by tradition and resentful of the cultural mandate to perform the shower in a particular manner. Although repelled by the structure of the shower, it seems that these women were attracted to the freedom associated with the bachelorette party, its lack of tradition and formality, its ethic of release, which was distinct from all other aspects of the wedding process.

It is not just the bride-to-be who expresses ambivalence during the transition from single to married. The community at large also both pushes her into and pulls her from marriage. As is the case with sociological ambivalence, it is the social structure, the role itself rather than a particular bride, that is seen as provoking conflicting sentiments. Thus, it is logical that others will view the bride-to-be role with mixed emotions as well. For her mother, for example, the transition indicates a progression and a separation. Mothers are probably happy to see their daughters marry, yet sad to see their children grow up and formally move into adulthood, sometimes physically moving out their parents' home. For her friends, who have also been socialized to value romance and see marriage as a status elevation, the transition indicates a change in relationship. Perhaps, for unmarried friends she is seen as moving away, and for married friends as entering into their sorority. In any event, friends recognize that the future wife's priorities will change to some degree, as she views her husband and their relationship as the most significant.

Philip Slater (1963) noted that courtship and engagement are characterized by "dyadic withdrawal," where the couple attempts to move away from the community. This represents a threat to society because as the couple retreats, their attachments to others weaken. Parents, for example, who provide the majority of their children's social and psychological needs during their lives, are expected to reduce their involvement in their children's lives and direct provision for their well-being when they marry. As society is dependent on connection, on integration, rather than dyadic relationships, the community is charged with making sure that the couple recognizes and affirms their attachment to others. The community prepares the initiate by presenting the bride-to-be with a glimpse of her future and time for reflection on her past in ritual form. These rituals perform a social function in that they reinforce bonds with the larger community. Women are reminded of how they need and should value other women and how important these women have been in shaping their lives. Because marriage is met with ambivalence, and because of the rising divorce rate and changes in the nature of marriage more generally, this community is an important form of social support for the bride-to-be. Furthermore, these rituals, more so bridal showers than bachelorette parties, begin a cycle of obligation and mutual interdependence. Women who attend a friend's or relative's shower (for the most part) expect the bride to reciprocate when they marry or to attend baby showers when they have children. These rituals thus reinforce social solidarity in an increasingly individualistic world. Slater noted, "The marriage ritual then becomes a series of mechanisms for pulling the dyad apart somewhat, so that its integration complements rather than replaces the various group ties of its members" (1963, 353). The families and friends of the bride and the groom become involved in the wedding planning and the pre-wedding activities, creating gender-segregated activities that call attention to the importance and support of their respective gender communities. Women particularly are expected to maintain family relations, to do the required kin work to demonstrate the appropriate level of respect and care for others as they move through the life course (di Leonardo 1987). Given women's disproportionate responsibility for showing care for other members of the community and maintaining social bonds, it is the friends, sisters, mothers, grandmothers, aunts, and cousins who are charged with showering the bride with social and material rewards for demonstrating the necessity of the community during status transition. Certainly, the community at large but particularly the gender community has mixed feelings about the passage of the initiate into her new status, simultaneously encouraging her independence from and reinforcing her dependence on them.

Gender and Social Change

As society changes, its rituals are re-examined, modified, and new rituals are invented (Hobsbawm and Ranger 1983). Tom Driver noted the connection between social rituals and the eras in which they are enacted. He wrote, "Ritual process belongs to historical process. It is not some kind of detached thing remote from the events that it influences. Agents of transformation, rituals are themselves transformed by the histories to which they belong" (Driver 1991, 184). Modifications in gender roles, in weddings, in consumer culture, and in marriage are evident in the practices of bachelorette parties and bridal showers. The bridal shower emerged in the United States during a time when consumerism was connected with middle-class status and when women who could afford not to rarely worked outside of the home. Dependence on a husband demonstrated his masculinity in the form of his ability to provide. Engaged women were celebrated for having found a man to support them, to allow them lives of leisure. Women's social position, particularly that of middle-class women, has changed significantly since that time; thus, it makes sense that the traditional bridal shower has become outdated and the bachelorette party has been created. Through close examination of these pre-wedding celebrations, we can see how women both partake in and shape change through participation in ritual. David Kertzer's (1988) idea that revolution is accomplished in ritual is relevant here. Women, through their veiled tolerance of the bridal shower and their cautious sexual expression at bachelorette parties, are creating social change. Though much of the expression of sacrifice or ambivalence toward marriage is expressed in symbolic form, the continued practice of the bachelorette party ritualizes and publicizes these sentiments. As women participate in the bachelorette party they become part of the process of social change. Kertzer (1988) identified rituals as the "life blood of revolution," as forces of modification. And Tom Driver (1991) identified transformation as one of the "gifts" of ritual. Transformation is two-fold;

rituals are both vehicles to and reflections of change in social institutions. As rituals are modified and adapted, so are the institutions that they represent and of which they are a part. Yet rituals incite change as well. As bachelorette parties are practiced and bridal showers are modified, changes in gender as a social institution also occur. And, conversely, as the gender order changes, women's pre-wedding rituals and their feelings about participating in these rituals change as well.

The bachelorette party can be perceived as an "invented tradition" (Hobsbawm and Ranger 1983). Its invention is surely based on the bachelor party, but the notion behind it, particularly in terms of women's participation in such a ritual, is novel. During times of social change rituals or traditions are created in order to add structure to or symbolize these transformations. Hobsbawm suggested that while traditions are constructed throughout history, it is during times of great social upheaval that invented traditions are most interesting (1983, 4). As he stated, "We should expect [traditions to be invented] more frequently when a rapid transformation of society weakens or destroys the social patterns for which 'old' traditions had been designed, producing new ones to which they were not applicable, or when such old traditions and their institutional carriers and promulgators no longer prove sufficiently adaptable and flexible" (4–5). The old tradition dictated that women do not need and should not go out for a last fling. This no longer makes sense in a society where women's status has transformed. Women, particularly middle- and upper-middle-class women, experience greater levels of equality in the workforce and in norms of sexual expression and leisure activities than has ever before been the case. Women's status has changed, and thus it makes sense that a ritual would develop that recognizes and celebrates this transformation.

However, this is not to say that the bachelorette party is necessarily progressive, and I certainly do not suggest that gender convergence is occurring, despite the fact that men and women are participating in some similar pre-wedding rituals. Women still have traditional showers and men still have bachelor parties. When men do participate in showers, for the most part, the shower format is altered (Montemurro 2005). Women modify the unpleasant aspects of the bridal shower when men are included, capitulating to their interests, yet suffer in silence when it is just the girls. It is women who have adapted men's rituals and not men who have adopted women's. Only one woman described a men-only shower, but as it was a masculine, tool theme, even that is not indicative of men doing what women do. Shower gifts and shower activities continue to emphasize conventional gender roles. Why have women copied men but not the reverse? It seems that, as in many previously gender-segregated activities, when women engage in men's tasks, areas of employment, or leisure pursuits, they are socially rewarded because masculine activities are valued over feminine activities (Montemurro 2005). Given the devaluing of femininity in American culture, it is no surprise that men are reluctant to express interest in wedding activities or to fully participate in feminized rituals like the bridal shower. In a climate where women are subordinate to men, men who engage in women's activities are subject to having their masculinity challenged.

Conclusion

The bachelorette party and bridal shower are events in the progression from single to married. In many ways they are pep rallies for the big day, maintaining the momentum of perpetual excitement that the bride-to-be is expected to display during her engagement. The increasing emphasis on the wedding as a lavish, once-in-a-lifetime event that necessitates and legitimates indulgence has diffused from the ceremony and the reception to the entire pre- and post-wedding period, from the time of engagement through the honeymoon. The evolution of the bachelorette party as a standard element of the wedding routine must be evaluated within its historical context. As materialism and consumerism characterized the wedding ritual at large, public expressions of women's sexuality, though still viewed with ambivalence, were seen as permissible. At the turn of the twenty-first century, societal attitudes toward marriage, the role of the bride-to-be, the role of the wife, and masculinity and femininity in general influenced the structure and format of the pre-wedding rituals of the bachelorette party and the bridal shower. In performing these rites of passage, women expressed their mixed emotions about their present and future statuses. In so doing they contributed to transformation in societal images. Ritual is a tool for social action, for social change. Though women may not have produced the bachelorette party with the intention of expressing their equality or the paradoxical images associated with women's sexuality, such messages are clearly communicated by its practice.

Perhaps as women and men continue to move into areas that have previously been gender segregated, women will gradually modify rituals, like the bridal shower, that naturalize differences between men and women. However, in order to do so, radical changes in societal perceptions of gender, care, and masculinity and femininity will need to occur. And, more significantly, women will need to want to see these changes happen. Women enjoy bachelorette parties as girls' nights and appreciate bridal showers as opportunities to demonstrate care for brides-to-be, socially and materially. Though some would like to modify the format of these events, only a couple of the women I interviewed suggested that showers should be done away with entirely. These women recognized the importance of other women in their gender communities and enjoyed playfully hazing and seriously socializing the bride-to-be as she moved from single woman to wife.

Notes

Chapter 1 Introduction

1. Although Kertzer's (1988) focus is on the political process, his discussion can be readily applied to cultural processes, such as marriage. It seems that his discussion of ritual is as relevant in talking about the ceremony and symbolic character of wedding ceremonies and pre-wedding events as it is for political ceremony and events.

Chapter 2 Origins of Bridal Showers and Bachelorette Parties

1. Research on bridal showers prior to the 1950s is limited. Thus, the types of conversation common during them are unknown. However, consistent with ideas about women's sexuality and gender roles, it seems unlikely that women would have talked openly about sexual activity at these earlier showers.

Chapter 3 Something Old

Portions of this chapter were published in the articles "Add Men, Don't Stir: Reproducing Traditional Gender Roles in Modern Wedding Showers," *Journal of Contemporary Ethnography* 34, no. 1 (2005): 6–35; and " 'You Go 'Cause You Have To': The Bridal Shower as a Ritual of Obligation," *Symbolic Interaction* 25, no. 1 (2002): 67–92.

1. Most of the gifts I received at my bridal shower were things that my husband and I had selected and were included on our registry. Registering for gifts is a gendered process. Some men do not participate in the registry at all; however, many do in what seems to be a secondary manner. While it is an empirical question as to the degree to which men are involved in selecting the gifts, I would argue that women are more involved because doing so, expressing an interest in household items, is a feminine activity. It is a way of "doing" gender. On a related note, tradition and persuasion by mothers, bridal guides or wedding planners, and store associates heavily influence what one lists on the registry. These sources guide couples toward the appropriate departments, encourage registering for the "right" things, and also communicate gendered expectations. For example, when we registered, the sales clerk handed the scanner to my husband-to-be and said something to the effect of how men like to use it because it is an electronic device. Thus, my hands were left free to pick up items and examine them and to determine what to include on the registry.

2. The socioeconomic status of these women may also be relevant. All of these women were employed and all self-identified as upper middle class. Perhaps having the resources to buy gifts made the showers more fun for them. However, a majority of respondents in the sample were middle or upper middle class, and most did not enjoy bridal showers. Examination of the demographic background of these women did not yield any noteworthy differences.
3. There were a variety of other games played that were described as "icebreaker" or party games. In the interest of brevity, I will not be discussing all bridal shower games. For example, two popular games were Bridal Shower Bingo and How Well Do You Know the Bride? In Bridal Shower Bingo, women were given a bingo card with potential wedding gifts on it, like frying pan or bath towel. When the bride opened the gift, if the guest had the item on her card, she marked that space. When a woman had a row of gifts marked, she won bingo. While there may be some gender-related themes in terms of the types of gifts listed on the card, for the most part this activity is interpreted as something designed to hold guests' interest and does not merit further discussion. In How Well Do You Know the Bride? the hostess asked guests a list of questions about the bride (or the bride and groom), such as where she went to high school, what her favorite movie was, etc. The person with the most correct answers usually won a small prize or gift, such as a candle or flower. This game could be interpreted as rewarding women for paying attention to the interests of other women, in that the woman who knew the bride the best was rewarded for being a good woman.
4. A custom at many bridal showers is to save the bows from all of the gifts and tape them onto a paper plate or attach them to a pre-made hat. When arranged together, the bows are usually given to the bride-to-be to wear as a "hat" at the shower for pictures and/or as a bouquet that is used as flowers for the wedding rehearsal.

Chapter 4 Something Borrowed and Blue

Material dealing with sexuality and the meaning of the uses of sex objects was previously published in the article "Sex Symbols: The Bachelorette Party as a Window to Change in Women's Sexual Expression," *Sexuality and Culture* 7, no. 2 (2003): 3–29.

1. Carol had an idea that there might be a stripper at her bachelorette party as, in an earlier conversation with her maid of honor, she said she wanted to see "naked men" at her party. But she was not sure whether or not this was going to happen.
2. None of the women interviewed suggested that her fiancé or husband was dressed up or decorated with sexual paraphernalia at his bachelor party. It seems that men's employment of sex symbols (i.e., strippers, pornographic films) is consistent with norms for men's sexual expression. In contrast, women played with symbols of sexuality in a comical manner, and there was little expectation for women to appear aroused by the sexual components of these parties.

References

Åström, Anna-Maria. 1989. Polterabend: Symbols and Meanings in a Popular Custom of Aristocratic and Bourgeois Origin. *Ethnologia Scandinavica.* 19: 83–106.

Ayers, Tess, and Paul Brown. 1994. *The Essential Guide to Lesbian and Gay Weddings.* San Francisco: Harper.

Bader, Jenny Lyn. 1999. The Night the Girls Went Out to Play (and the Boys Ran Away). *New York Times,* January 24, late edition (East Coast).

Bahn, A., and A. Jaquez. 1997. One Style of Dominican Bridal Shower. In *The Family Experience,* edited by Mark Hutter, 194–204. Boston: Allyn & Bacon.

Baker, M. 1977. *Wedding Customs and Folklore.* Totowa, NJ: David and Charles.

Barker, Olivia. 2003. The Blushing Bride? Try Bold Bachelorette: Friends Flock to Vegas to Misbehave and Celebrate Last Days of Being Single. *USA Today,* May 13.

Bellah, Robert Neely, Richard Madsen, William M. Sullivan, Ann Swidler, and Steven M. Tipton. 1996. *Habits of the Heart.* Berkeley: University of California Press.

Bentley, Marguerite. 1947. *Wedding Etiquette.* Philadelphia: John C. Winston.

Berardo, Felix M., and Hernan Vera. 1981. The Groomal Shower: A Variation of the American Bridal Shower. *Family Relations* 30: 395–401.

Boden, Sharon. 2003. *Consumerism, Romance, and the Wedding Experience.* New York: Palgrave.

Bordo, Susan. 1993. *Unbearable Weight: Feminism, Western Culture, and the Body.* Berkeley: University of California Press.

Boston, Beth. 2004. Girls' Night Out. *St. Louis Post Dispatch,* March 6.

Bourdieu, Pierre. 1984. *Distinction: A Social Critique of the Judgement of Taste.* Cambridge, MA: Harvard University Press.

Brace, Eric. 1999. Girls' Night Out: Driven to Party Hardy. *Washington Post,* October 22, final edition.

Bride's Wedding Planner: The Perfect Guide to the Perfect Wedding. 1997. New York: Fawcett Columbine.

Brodsky, Heidi Hookman. 2004. Toys for Soccer Moms. *Washingtonian,* May.

Brophy, Mary Beth. 2000. Planning the Bachelorette Party. Wedding Channel, February 11. http://www.weddingchannel.com/ui/buildArticle.action?assetUID=3076&s=84&t=7&p=3776639&searchorigin=1&c=3076.

Brownmiller, Susan. 1984. *Femininity.* New York: Simon & Schuster.

Bruess, Carol J. S., and Judy C. Pearson. 1998. Gendered Patterns in Family Communication. In *Shifting the Center: Understanding Contemporary Families,* edited by Susan J. Ferguson, 183–198. Mountain View, CA: Mayfield.

Cancian, Francesca M. 1986. The Feminization of Love. *Signs: Journal of Women in Culture and Society* 11: 692–709.

Caplow, Theodore. 1984. Rule Enforcement without Visible Means: Christmas Gift Giving in Middletown. *American Journal of Sociology* 89: 1306–1323.

Casparis, Johan. 1979. The Bridal Shower: An American Rite of Passage. *Indian Journal of Social Research* 20: 11–21.

Cates Moore, Kathryn. 1997. Pre-wedding Party or the Last Fling? *Lincoln Journal Star*, January 20.

Cavan, Sherri. 1966. *Liquor License: An Ethnography of Bar Behavior*. Chicago: Aldine.

Cheal, David J. 1988. Relationships in Time: Ritual, Social Structure, and the Life Course. *Studies in Symbolic Interaction* 9: 83–109.

———. 1989. Women Together: Bridal Showers and Gender Membership. In *Gender and Intimate Relationships: A Microstructural Approach*, edited by Barbara J. Risman and Pepper Schwartz, 87–93. Belmont, CA: Wadsworth.

Chic and Affordable Wedding Gowns. 2005. www.cbsnews.com, February 23.

Chodorow, Nancy. 1978. *The Reproduction of Mothering: Psychoanalysis and the Sociology of Gender*. Berkeley: University of California Press.

Clark, Beverly. 2000. *Bridal Showers*. Carpinteria, CA: Wilshire.

Clark, Rebecca. 1985. Male Strippers: Ladies' Night at the Meat Market. *Journal of Popular Culture* 19: 51–55.

Cohen, Edie. 1985. "Tootsie" Comes to the Suburbs Devoted Fans Agree: These Guys Are Dolls. *Chicago Tribune*, February 1, final edition.

Connell, R. W. 1995. *Masculinities*. Berkeley: University of California Press.

Copeland, Libby. 2000. Fun in the Naughty Aughties: To Grasp a Modern Woman's Joys, Take a Look at Her Toys. *Washington Post*, January 27, final edition.

Corrado, Marisa. 2002. Teaching Wedding Rules: How Bridal Workers Negotiate Control over their Customers. *Journal of Contemporary Ethnography* 31: 33–67.

Cott, Nancy. 2000. *Public Vows: A History of Marriage and the Nation*. Cambridge, MA: Harvard University Press.

Currie, Dawn. 1993. Here Comes the Bride: The Making of a "Modern-Traditional" Wedding. *Journal of Comparative Family Studies* 24: 403–421.

Daum, Meghan. 1998. The World According to Meghan. *Self*, October.

Deegan, Mary Jo. 1989. *American Ritual Dramas: Social Rules and Cultural Meanings*. New York: Greenwood Press.

Dempsey, J. M., and Tom Reichert. 2000. Portrayal of Married Sex in the Movies. *Sexuality & Culture* 4: 21–36.

Depoali, Michelle. 2000. Gummy Penises, Male Strippers. *Reno News and Review*, March 1.

di Leonardo, Micaela. 1987. The Female World of Cards and Holidays: Women, Families, and the Work of Kinship. *Signs: Journal of Woman in Culture and Society* 12: 440–453.

Dlugosch, Sharon E., and Florence E. Nelson. 1984. *Bridal Showers: Fifty Great Ideas for a Perfect Shower*. New York: Perigree.

Douglas, Susan. 1995. *Where the Girls Are: Growing up Female with the Mass Media*. New York: Times Books.

Dressel, Paula L., and David Petersen. 1982. Gender Roles, Sexuality, and the Male Strip Show: The Structuring of Sexual Opportunity. *Sociological Focus* 15: 151–162.

Driver, Tom. 1991. *The Magic of Ritual.* New York: Harper Collins.

Duka, John. 1981. Star-Studded Cast for Carey Wedding. *New York Times*, April 10.

Dullea, Georgia. 1990. For the Bachelorette, a Wilder Last Fling. *New York Times*, May 13.

Durkheim, Emile. 1912. *The Elementary Forms of Religious Life.* Repr., New York: Free Press, 1995.

———. 1953. *Sociology and Philosophy.* London: Cohen and West Limited.

Ehrenreich, Barbara. 1986. *Re-making Love: The Feminization of Sex.* Garden City, NY: Anchor Press/Doubleday.

Employment Policy Foundation. 2004. More Mothers in the Labor Force This Mother's Day. *Employment Policy Foundation Newsletter*, May 6.

Erikson, Kai. T. 1966. *Wayward Puritans: A Study in the Sociology of Deviance.* New York: John Wiley and Sons.

Etter, Lori. 1998. How to Throw a Bride-to-Be Blowout. *Cosmopolitan*, April.

Falk, Gerhard. 1998. *Sex, Gender, and Social Change: The Great Revolution.* Lanham, MD: University Press of America.

Fischler, Marcelle S. 2004. A Honeymoon before the Wedding, Bridegroom Not Included. *New York Times*, February 8, late edition (East Coast).

Fletcher, J. 2002. Pre-nup Party: Bachelor Party Traditions from around the Globe. *Philadelphia City Paper*, February 21.

Fox, Ellen. 2004. Hits for Misses: Send Your Girlfriend off from Singleland in Style. *Chicago Tribune*, April 14, RedEye edition.

Fox, M., M. Gibbs, and D. Auerbach. 1985. Age and Gender Dimensions of Friendship. *Psychology of Women Quarterly* 9: 489–502.

Freeman, Elizabeth. 2002. *The Wedding Complex: Forms of Belonging in Modern American Culture.* Durham, NC: Duke University Press.

Gandy, Peggy. 1983. "Bachelorette" Bash Paves Way for Wedding with Splash of Color. *Daily Oklahoman*, March 21.

Geller, Jaclyn. 2001. *Here Comes the Bride: Women, Weddings, and the Marriage Mystique.* New York: Four Walls Eight Windows.

Gerson, Kathleen. 1985. *Hard Choices: How Women Decide about Work, Career, and Motherhood.* Berkeley and Los Angeles: University of California Press.

Giddens, Anthony. 1992. *The Transformation of Intimacy: Sexuality, Love, and Eroticism in Modern Societies.* Stanford, CA: Stanford University Press.

Gilligan, Carol. 1982. *In a Different Voice: Psychological Theory and Women's Development.* Cambridge, MA: Harvard University Press.

———. 1998. Theorizing Difference: Hearing Connection. In *Contemporary Feminist Theory: A Text/Reader*, edited by Mary F. Rogers, 341–346. Boston: McGraw Hill.

Goffman, Erving. 1959. *The Presentation of Self in Everyday Life.* New York: Doubleday.

———. 1967. On Face-Work: An Analysis of Ritual Elements in Social Interaction. In *Interaction Ritual: Essays on Face-to-Face Behavior*, by Erving Goffman, 5–45. New York: Pantheon.

Haney, Germaine. 1954. *Showers for All Occasions: A Handbook of Complete Information for All Types of Showers with Detailed Suggestions for Invitations, Menus, Entertainment, Decorations, Refreshments, Etc.* Minneapolis: T. S. Denison.

Hartmann, Heidi I. 1995. The Family as the Locus of Gender, Class, and Political Struggle: The Example of Housework. In *Feminism and Philosophy: Essential Readings in Theory, Reinterpretation, and Application*, edited by Nancy Tuana and Rosemarie Tong, 104–128. Boulder, CO: Westview Press.

Heath, Dwight B. 2000. *Drinking Occasions: Comparative Perspectives on Alcohol and Culture*. Philadelphia: Brunner/Mazel.

Hellspong, Mats. 1988. Stag Parties and Hen Parties in Sweden. *Ethnologia Scandinavica* 18: 111–116.

Hew, Shirley. 1991. *The Cultures of the World, Argentina*. Singapore: Marshall Cavendish Corp.

Heyn, Dalma. 1997. *Marriage Shock: The Transformation of Women into Wives*. New York: Villard.

Hobsbawm, Eric. 1983. Introduction: Inventing Traditions. In *The Invention of Tradition*, edited by Eric Hobsbawm and Terence Ranger, 1–14. New York: Cambridge University Press.

Hobsbawm, Eric, and Terence Ranger, eds. 1983. *The Invention of Tradition*. New York: Cambridge University Press.

Hochschild, Arlie Russell. 1983. *The Managed Heart: Commercialization of Human Feeling*. Berkeley and Los Angeles: University of California Press.

———. 1989. *The Second Shift: Working Parents and the Revolution at Home*. New York: Viking Press.

———. 1994. The Commercial Spirit of Intimate Life and the Abduction of Feminism: Signs from Women's Advice Books. *Theory, Culture, and Society* 11: 1–24.

Hoffnung, Michelle. 1998. Motherhood: Contemporary Conflict for Women. In *Shifting the Center: Understanding Contemporary Families*, edited by Susan J. Ferguson, 277–291. Mountain View, CA: Mayfield.

Holland, Dorothy, and Margaret A. Eisenhart. 1990. *Educated in Romance: Women, Achievement, and College Culture*. Chicago: University of Chicago Press.

Howard, Vicki Jo. 2000. American Weddings: Gender, Consumption, and the Business of Brides. PhD diss., University of Texas, Austin.

———. 2001. At the Curve of the Exchange: Postwar Beauty Culture and Working Women. In *Beauty and Business: Commerce, Gender, and Culture in Modern America*, edited by Philip Scranton, 195–216. New York: Routledge.

———. 2003. A "Real Man's Ring": Gender and the Invention of Tradition. *Journal of Social History* 36: 837–856.

Ingraham, Chrys. 1999. *White Weddings: Romancing Heterosexuality in Popular Culture*. New York: Routledge.

Israelson, C. 1989. Family Resource Management. *Family Perspectives* 23: 311–331.

Jenkins, Jennifer. 2000. *The Everything Wedding Shower Book*. Holbrook, MA: Adams Media Corporation.

Kavet, Herbert I. 1999. *The Bachelorette Party*. Watertown, MA: Boston America Group.

Kertzer, David I. 1988. *Ritual, Politics, and Power*. New Haven: Yale University Press.

Kingsland, F. 1902. *The Book of Weddings*. New York: Doubleday, Page, and Co.

Kulish, Nicholas. 2002. Turning the Tables: Bachelorette Parties Are Getting Risqué. *Wall Street Journal*, September 3.

Lagorce, Aude. 2004. The Gay Marriage–Windfall: $16.8 Billion. www.forbes.com, April 5.

LaPeter, Leonora. 2003. Skipping the Raunch: What Gives? These Days Any Grooms Opt for Low-Key Bachelor Parties, sans Stripper, minus the Mayhem. *St. Petersburg Times*, June 16.

Laumann, Edward O., J. H. Gagnon, R. T. Michael, and S. Michaels. 1994. *The Social Organization of Sexuality: Sexual Practices in the United States*. Chicago: University of Chicago Press.

LeMasters, E. E. 1957. *Modern Courtship and Marriage*. New York: Macmillan.

Leonard, Diana. 1980. *Sex and Generation: A Study of Courtship and Weddings*. London: Tavistock.

Lerche Davis, Jeanie. 2003. Bachelorette Party: Sexual Expression? WebMD, August 29. http://content.health.msn.com/content/article/73/81990.htm.

Levine, Lisbeth. 1996. Wedded to a Bonding Adventure. *Chicago Tribune*, September 29.

Lewin, Ellen. 1998. *Recognizing Ourselves: Ceremonies of Lesbian and Gay Commitment*. New York: Columbia University Press.

Leyser, Ophra. 2003. Doing Masculinity in a Mental Hospital. *Journal of Contemporary Ethnography* 32: 336–359.

Litwicki, Ellen M. 1998. Showering the Bride: A Ritual of Gender and Consumption. Paper presented at the Conference on Holidays, Ritual, Festival, Celebration, and Public Display, Bowling Green University, Bowling Green, Ohio.

Liveris, Gwen, and Nancy Johnson. 1998. *How to Host a Hilariously Fun Bachelorette Party*. Dundee, IL: Bacheloretti's Inc.

Lofland, John, 1969. *Deviance and Identity*. Englewood Cliffs, NJ: Prentice Hall.

Long, Becky. 2000. *The Best Bachelorette Party Book: A Complete Guide for Party Planners*. Minnetonka, MN: Meadowbrook Press.

Lorber, Judith. 1998. *Gender Inequality: Feminist Theories and Politics*. Los Angeles: Roxbury.

Lucal, Betsy. 2004. What It Means to Be Gendered Me. In *The Kaleidoscope of Gender: Prisms, Patterns, and Possibilities*, edited by Joan Z. Spade and Catherine G. Valentine, 52–63. Belmont, CA: Wadsworth.

Martin, Deirdre. 1995. Girls' Night Out. *Brides and Your New Home*, August/September.

Matza, David. 1969. *Becoming Deviant*. Englewood Cliffs, NJ: Prentice Hall.

McCaughey, M., and C. French. 2001. Women's Sex Toy Parties: Technology, Orgasm, and Commodification. *Sexuality & Culture* 5: 77–96.

McCutcheon, Lauren. 2003. How to Throw a Really Good Bachelorette Party. *Philadelphia Daily News*, September 24. http://www.philly.com/mld/dailynews/living/6846151.htm.

McLaren, Angus. 1999. *Twentieth Century Sexuality: A History*. Malden, MA: Blackwell.

Merton, Robert, and Elinor Barber. 1976. In, *Sociological Ambivalence and Other Essays*, edited by Robert Merton, 3-31. New York: Free Press.

Montemurro, Beth. 2001. Strippers and Screamers: The Emergence of Social Control in a Non-Institutionalized Setting. *Journal of Contemporary Ethnography* 30: 275–304.

———. 2002. "You Go 'Cause You Have To": The Bridal Shower as a Ritual of Obligation. *Symbolic Interaction* 25: 67–92.

———. 2005. Add Men, Don't Stir: Reproducing Traditional Gender Roles in Modern Wedding Showers. *Journal of Contemporary Ethnography* 34, no. 1: 6–35.

Montemurro, Beth, Colleen Bloom, and Kelly Madell. 2003. Ladies' Night Out: A Typology of Patrons of a Male Strip Club. *Deviant Behavior* 24: 333–352.

Montemurro, Beth, and Bridget McClure. 2005. Changing Gender Norms for Alcohol Consumption: Social Drinking and Lowered Inhibitions at Bachelorette Parties. *Sex Roles: A Journal of Research* 52: 279–288.

Moose, Debbie. 1992. A Tame Version of Sowing Wild Oats. *News and Observer*, February 9.

Mordecai, Carolyn. 1999. *Weddings: Dating and Love Customs of Cultures Worldwide*. Phoenix: Nittany Publishers.

Musante, Glenna B. 1997. Hope Has a Last Fling. *The News and Observer*, January 21.

Navratil, Wendy. 1998. Unbridled Fun Retro Club Draws Bachelorettes by the Bushel. *Chicago Tribune*. October 5, North Sports final edition.

Oikarinen, Anna-Kasia. 1997a. From "a Bride Sauna" to "a Polttarit." University of Tampere, Tampere, Finland. http://www.uta.fi/ote97/clash/ak/Polt2.htm.

———. 1997b. Too Green to Get Married. University of Tampere, Tampere, Finland. http://www.uta.fi/ote97/clash/ak/index.htm.

Oliker, Stacey J. 2001. Gender and Friendship. In *Gender Mosaics: Social Perspectives*, edited by Dana Vannoy, 194–204. Los Angeles: Roxbury.

Oliviero, Helena. 2003. Wild Night before Wearing White: More Parties for Brides-to-Be Are Taking on a Bawdy Tone. *Atlanta Journal Constitution*, July 25.

Ordway, Edith. 1920. *The Etiquette of Today*. New York: George Sully.

Otnes, Cele C., and Elizabeth H. Pleck. 2003. *Cinderella Dreams: The Allure of the Lavish Wedding*. Berkeley: University of California Press.

Owens, Darryl E. 2004. Brides Are Increasingly Exercising Their Equal Right to Lusty Female Versions of the Bachelor Party—Call Them Bridal Bacchanals. *Orlando Sentinel*, December 3, final edition.

Padavic, Irene, and Barbara Reskin. 2002. *Men and Women at Work*. Thousand Oaks, CA: Pine Forge.

Palmer, Kimberly Shearer. 2003. Planning the Perfect Bachelorette Party. *Washington Post*, March 10, final edition.

Pleck, Elizabeth. 2000. *Celebrating the Family: Ethnicity, Consumer Culture, and Family Rituals*. Cambridge, MA: Harvard University Press.

Rieff, Philip. 1966. *Triumph of the Therapeutic: Uses of Faith after Freud*. New York: Harper and Row.

Roeper, Richard. 1988. Hey—Bachelorettes Can Act Sleazy, Too. *Chicago Sun Times*, August 21.

Rogers, Jennifer. 1992. *Tried and Trousseau: The Bride Guide*. New York: Fireside.

Rothman, Ellen. 1984. *Hands and Hearts: A History of Courtship in America*. New York: Basic Books.

Rouvalis, Cristina. 2002. Naughty Wares Spice up These House Parties. *Pittsburgh Post Gazette*, September 28. http://www.post-gazette.com.

Rubin, Lillian. 1994. *Families on the Fault Line: America's Working Class Speaks about the Family, the Economy, Race, and Ethnicity*. New York: Harper Perennial.

Saulny, Susan. 1998. How to Make a Bride Blush: Prenuptial Parties Aren't Just for the Guys Anymore. *Washington Post*, July 21.

Scanzoni, John, Karen Polonko, Jay Teachman, and Linda Thompson. 1989. *The Sexual Bond: Rethinking Families and Close Relationships*. Newbury Park, CA: Sage.

Schultz, Jason. 1995. Getting off on Feminism. In *To Be Real: Telling the Truth and Changing the Face of Feminism*, edited by Rebecca Walker, 107–126. New York: Anchor Books.

Schwartz, Barry. 1967. The Social Psychology of the Gift. *American Journal of Sociology* 73: 1–11.

Schwartz, Pepper. 1994. *Peer Marriage: How Love between Equals Really Works*. New York: Free Press.

Shils, Edward. 1975. *Center and Periphery: Essays in Macrosociology*. Chicago: University of Chicago Press.

Sinclair, Stephanie. 1995. Polttarit: The Finnish Pre-marriage Ritual. *Life and Education in Finland*. February.

Slater, Philip. 1963. On Social Regression. *American Sociological Review* 28: 339–364.

Smelser, Neil J. 1998. The Rational and the Ambivalent in Social Sciences. *American Sociological Review* 63: 1–16.

Spade, Joan Z., and Catherine G. Valentine. 2004. Tracing Gender's Mark on Bodies, Sexualities, and Emotions. In *The Kaleidoscope of Gender: Prisms, Patterns, and Possibilities*, edited by Joan Z. Spade and Catherine G. Valentine, 279–285. Belmont, CA: Wadsworth.

Stein, Catherine H. 1992. Ties That Bind: Three Studies of Obligation in Adult Relationships with Family. *Journal of Social and Personal Relationships* 9: 525–547.

Stein, Sarah, and Lucy Talbot. 1997. *The Bridesmaid's Guerilla Handbook*. New York: Berkley Books.

Stewart, Arlene Hamilton. 1995. *A Bride's Book of Wedding Traditions*. New York: William Morrow.

Stiers, Gretchen. 1999. *From This Day Forward: Commitment, Marriage, and Family in Lesbian and Gay Relationships*. New York: St. Martin's Press.

Stinson, Kandi M. 2001. *Women and Dieting Culture: Inside a Commercial Weight Loss Group*. New Brunswick, NJ: Rutgers University Press.

Sykes, Gresham, and David Matza. 1957. Techniques of Neutralization: A Theory of Delinquency. *American Sociological Review* 22: 664–670.

Tanenbaum, Leora. 2000. *Slut! Growing up Female with a Bad Reputation*. New York: Harper Collins.

Tong, Rosemarie Putnam. 1998. *Feminist Thought: A More Comprehensive Introduction*. 2nd ed. Boulder, CO: Westview.

Tonnies, Ferdinand. 1887. *Community and Society (Gemeinschaft und Gesellschaft)*. Translated and edited by Charles P. Loomis. Repr., East Lansing: Michigan State University Press, 1957.

Tresniowski, Alex, Cynthia Wang, and Ulrica Wihlborg. 2003. Lights! Camera! Love! *People*, December 22.

Trice, Harrison. 1966. *Alcoholism in America.* New York: McGraw Hill.

Turner, Victor. 1967. *Forest of Symbols: Aspects of Ndembu Ritual.* Ithaca, NY: Cornell University Press.

———. 1969. *The Ritual Process: Structure and Anti-structure.* Repr., New York: Aldine de Gruyter, 1995.

———. 1974. *Dramas, Fields, and Metaphors: Symbolic Action in Human Society.* Ithaca, NY: Cornell University Press.

Tye, Diane, and Ann Marie Powers. 1998. Gender, Resistance, and Play: Bachelorette Parties in Atlantic Canada. *Women's Studies International Forum* 21: 551–561.

U.S. Department of Commerce. 2004. Income Stable, Poverty Up, Numbers of Americans with and without Health Insurance Rise, Census Bureau Reports. http://www.census.gov/PressRelease/www/releases/archives/income_wealth/002484.html.

van Gennep, Arnold. 1908. *The Rites of Passage.* Repr., Chicago: University of Chicago Press, 1960.

Veblen, Thorstein. 1899. *The Theory of the Leisure Class.* Repr., New York: Penguin, 1994.

Walker, Reagen. 2003. I Do . . . Want a New Power Drill. His-and-Hers. Wedding Registries Let Grooms Walk down the Gift Aisle, Too. *Atlanta Journal Constitution*, June 5.

Wallace, Carol McD. 2004. *All Dressed in White: The Irresistible Rise of the American Wedding.* New York: Penguin.

Warner, Diane. 1998. *Complete Book of Wedding Showers.* Franklin Lakes, NJ: Career Press.

West, Candace, and Don Zimmerman. 1987. Doing Gender. *Gender and Society* 1: 125–151.

West, John O. 1988. *Mexican-American Folklore: Legends, Songs, Festivals, Protests, Crafts, Tales of Saints, of Revolutions, and More.* Little Rock: August House.

Williams, L. Susan. 2002. Trying on Gender, Gender Regimes, and the Process of Becoming Women. *Gender & Society* 16: 29–52.

Wood, Elizabeth Anne. 2000. Working in the Fantasy Factory: The Attention Hypothesis and the Enacting of Masculine Power in Strip Clubs. *Journal of Contemporary Ethnography* 29: 5–31.

Wood, Julia T. 1994. *Who Cares? Women, Care, and Culture.* Carbondale, IL: Southern Illinois University Press.

Wuthnow, Robert. 1989. *Meaning and Moral Order: Explorations in Cultural Analysis.* Berkeley: University of California Press.

Index

About the Author

Beth Montemurro is assistant professor of sociology at Pennsylvania State University, Abington. Her research and teaching interests include gender, culture, qualitative methods, and popular media.